A Word from the Author

This book deals with Techno-Fundamental strategies in investing in common stocks, which, as the term indicates, is a combination of the technical and the fundamental approaches. The description of these approaches is simple enough. The technical approach deals with stock-price movements. The fundamental approach involves all those factors which determine corporate earnings. These investment approaches, used separately, often give inadequate investment results, but in combination the strengths of each offset the weaknesses of the other. Together they can help the investor produce investment performance superior to that achieved by using either system alone.

This book, and its discussion of Techno-Fundamental strategies, will help you accomplish the following:

- Develop an investment strategy that will enable you to put your investment funds to work efficiently.

- Improve your timing in buying and selling, enable you to recognize dangerous markets and markets of opportunity, and allow you to understand the stock market cycle and its stages.

- Learn to fight your instincts, which are often wrong in common stock investing, and to make the emotions of the marketplace work for you.

- Use technical tools, charts, market indicators, and computerized technical analysis of the market to catch the major moves of stocks.

- Make money in declining markets as well as rising markets.

- Select stocks with exceptional capital gains potential.

- Determine the intrinsic value of stocks.

- Learn the importance of patience and when to stay out of the stock market through an understanding of stock market and economic forecasting.

- Avoid many of the common mistakes investors have made in the past.

- Substantially increase—the goal is to triple it—your money over a reasonable period of time through the proper use of Techno-Fundamental strategies.

The technical approach is used to gauge the supply and demand for stocks and it is the only approach that will reflect psychology and confidence, which are such a very important part of stock prices. Its proper employment is in timing the buying and selling of stocks, in confirming the fundamentals, and in telling the investor when the market is starting to recognize the fundamentals. Its value is primarily short term rather than long term.

The technical approach is based primarily on the thesis that a trend once set in motion tends to continue. It cannot determine the potential of a stock with any reliability. The technical approach tells it as it really is. How the market reacts to news and how stocks participate in strong and weak markets are very revealing of investors' attitudes at the moment. The basic decision to buy or sell should be left to fundamental analysis.

Fundamental analysis is primarily concerned with earning power and the valuation placed on the earning power. The potential increase in earnings (leverage factors that can cause earnings breakouts), the compound annual earnings growth rate, the confidence investors have in the earnings trend (sustainability of earnings), and whether earnings are accelerating or decelerating are the most important considerations.

Price-earnings ratios (price of the stock divided by earnings-per-share) are also important, although generally of less significance than earnings growth rates and the popularity of the group or industry. Theoretically, price-earnings ratios should be related to the earnings growth rates, but they are often influenced by "stories" which can fire investors' imaginations. It usually takes some type of story or concept to focus investors' attention on a stock since there are many stocks competing for the same funds. Thus, price-earnings ratios are to a large extent the result of fads and fashions over the short run. Price-earnings ratios are, perhaps, best used as an indication of risk if they are above average, and as an indication of potential if they are below average.

Stocks can be placed in three broad groups: quality growth, cyclical, and undervalued. The quality growth stocks have crossed over to the buy lists of institutions. They are in a very special category. Usually they can command premium price-earnings because of their superior earnings growth rates and earnings visibility. They often outperform the general market during periods of market strength and hold up better than secondary issues in general market weakness because of the institutional support they receive. Cyclical stocks require a very good sense of timing, but can be very rewarding to investors. Undervalued situations may obtain their undervalued status for various reasons and they, too, can provide substantial appreciation possibilities.

Many major stock moves result from some new development which results in a sharp gain in earnings. Investors that recognize such developments often can of capital gains since actual case studies have been used to illustrate the principles of our techno-fundamental strategies.

I hope you will, however, carry away from this book more than just the strategies that have worked for investors, enabling many of them to triple their investment funds. Several chapters are designed to give you a broad understanding of the valuation of common stocks and of the underlying importance of the economy's impact on stock prices. Helpful hints are given in economic forecasting, which is an essential part of stock market forecasting. In addition, the money supply and interest rates, two related factors which importantly influence the stock market, are discussed in several chapters.

Many examples and illustrations of actual investment situations are discussed throughout this book. These exact conditions will never turn up again, but the same investment principles will recurr over and over again in different guises. One of the main problems facing the investor is recognizing the type of situation he is dealing with when he sees it. It is hoped that these examples will help the investor recognize the essential ingredients of buying and selling opportunities. The use of actual stocks in illustrating various investment points in this book is not meant either as a buy or sell recommendation, but only as an aid to the reader in helping him to learn how to handle a similar situation.

In short, I believe you will find this book to be exceptional in the manner in which it gives you practical directions in how to multiply your money in the stock market, and also provides you with a broad understanding of the actual operation of the stock market and the functioning of the economy.

Gene P. Brady

ACKNOWLEDGEMENTS

The contributions of the following people in supplying the actual investment examples used in this book are gratefully acknowledged:

Ben Ames, Richard Asbury, John Bleakie, Richard Bogacki, Robert Buchsbaum, David Dewey, Tallantyre Fletcher, Earnest Keusch, Jack Krabill, Richard Logan, Antony Mason, Sanford Roggenberg, Peter Thompson, and Joseph West.

List of Illustrations

Contents

The Stock Market Cycle Is an Important Part of the Techno-Fundamental Strategies (18) ● How the Stock Market Cycle Can Help You Improve Your Investment Performance (19) ● Understanding the Techno-Fundamental Basis for the Stock Market Cycle (21) ● You Can Benefit from a Knowledge of How Human Behavior Affects the Economy (23) ● The Techno-Fundamental Market Trend Is One of the Most Important Investment Considerations (26) ● Knowing the Four Stages of the Market Cycle Can Aid Your Perspective (28) ● How to Recognize the First Stage (29) ● The Characteristics of the Second Stage (31) ● Knowing When You Are in the Third Stage (31) ● Do Not Be Fooled by the Fourth Stage (32) ● How to Use the Market Indicators (33)

Market Indicators Can Tell You When You Are in a Top Area (35) ● Market Indicators Which Indicate Speculative Excess (38) ● Market Indicators Which Reveal a Loss of Momentum (40) ● Market Indicators Which Tell You the Supply of Common Stock Is Increasing (41) ● Market Indicators Which Point to Diminishing Demand for Common Stocks (42) ● Be on Your Guard When the Stage Is Set for Profit-Taking (45) ● A Market Top Can Be Recognized (48) ● On the Downside of the Market (49) ● In a Bottom Area Investors Are Wrung-out Emotionally (50) ● Knowing When You Have Seen the Bottom of the Market (52) ● Market Indicators That Signal When the Stage Is Being Set for New Buying (54) ● Being Aware of Emotional Excesses is Half the Battle (55)

**6. How to Use Techno-Fundamental Methods to Make
Money During the Second Stage of the Market Cycle** *(Cont.)*

Stocks Which Give You Two Chances for Profit (147) ● Issues Which May Give
You the Most Trouble (150) ● Situations Which May Be Disappointing in the
Second Stage (153) ● Signs of a Second Stage Top (155) ● Mistakes You Can
Avoid in the Second Stage (158)

Signs of the Beginning of the Third Stage (161) ● Investment Strategy for the
Third Stage (162) ● Emerging Industries and Concepts Can Be Particularly Pro-
fitable (163) ● This Investor Capitalized on His Fine Sense of Timing (164) ● The
Importance of Low-Priced Speculations in the Third Stage (166) ● The Impor-
tance of Over-the-Counter Issues (171) ● New Issues Play an Important Role in
Stock Market Profits (174) ● How to Use Conservative Issues in the Latter Part of
the Third Stage (175) ● Helping You Recognize the Signs of the End of the Third
Stage (176) ● Mistakes You Can Avoid in the Third Stage (177)

The Signs of the Beginning of the Fourth Stage (180) ● A Strategy to Make
Money in the Fourth Stage (182) ● This Normally Risky Strategy May Be the
Most Conservative Way to Make Money in the Fourth Stage (183) ● What You
Can Expect of Cyclical Stocks (188) ● What You Should Know About Over-
the-Counter Stocks in the Fourth Stage (188) ● How to Deal in Speculative Stocks
(191) ● Developing a Profitable Attitude Toward Conservative Stocks (193) ●
Quality Growth Stocks in the Fourth Stage (195) ● Knowing These Signs of the
Bottom of the Fourth Stage Could Be Very Profitable for You (197) ● Serious
Mistakes You Can Avoid in the Fourth Stage (201)

These Market Timing Tools Can Mean the Difference Between Success and
Failure (204) ● One of the Most Important Factors in Successful Investing (205) ●
Fundamental and Technical Indicators of Major Trend Turns (207) ● How You
Can Avoid Buying When You Should Be Selling, and Vice Versa (210) ● How a
Stock Can Tell You What It Will Do (212) ● How to Take A Broad View of the
Market (213) ● Taking Advantage of the Institutional Mind (214) ● Knowing the
Proper Use of Charts and Computerized Market Programs (215)

1

Using the Techno-Fundamental Method to Develop an Approach to Stock Market Investing

Some investors always seem to be making money in the stock market under all kinds of market conditions. It almost appears that these investors have some special insight or analytical powers which enable them to be on the right side of the market and in the most active stocks most of the time. Some investors may indeed have a broad knowledge of industries, individual corporations, economics, and psychology which enable them to achieve superior investment results. Other investors, however, may owe their investment success to using Techno-Fundamental strategies in common stock investing. These strategies are relatively simple in concept, although their application is somewhat more difficult. Proper use of these strategies will tend to keep you invested in the highest potential stocks at the most profitable times and assist you in maximizing the annual return on your capital investments.

Since both investor psychology and corporate earnings are so important to stock prices, it follows that you have the greatest opportunity for profit when both the technical and fundamental factors are favorable. Certainly, when the investing public is already favorably disposed toward a stock as revealed by the technical approach, half the investment battle is won. Once you have determined that investment funds are moving into a stock, fundamental analysis can indicate how sustainable the interest might be and how much potential there might be in the situation. Combining the technical and fundamental strategies can help you avoid stagnant situations and catch the major moves in stocks.

Successful investors have to continually fight their instincts. The normal impulse is for the average investor to avoid stocks which have had a good rise, thinking they are overpriced, and to buy stocks which have had a substantial decline, thinking they are undervalued. Usually the opposite procedure is the more profitable one: buying into strength rather than into weakness. Buying popular issues and groups is one of the secrets to successful investing. However, the courage of one's convictions, provided they are well-placed, can be very valuable. A willingness to go against the crowd when bearishness is rampant or when bullishness is almost overwhelming is one of the most helpful traits. Patience in waiting for buying and selling opportunities is another helpful virtue. Since highly successful investing is an art, the investors who use all the available tools, both technical and fundamental, have the best chance for achieving their goal.

Those investors, on the other hand, who continually follow the crowd and buy stocks that have had major moves and about which practically all the favorable news is out, or wait until investors are universally bearish before selling, can expect to turn in below-average performances. Practitioners of fundamental analysis frequently wait for concrete evidence before buying or selling. Often, however, stocks start moving before analysts are aware of any changes. In these situations, technical analysis may give the first indication that a stock should be bought or sold.

The Stock Market Cycle Is an Important Part of the Techno-Fundamental Strategies

The average investor may not be aware of how great an influence the market cycle has on individual stock movements, but the major market trend as measured by the popular stock market indices is responsible for a large portion of the price movement of individual stocks. Investors tend to assume that the economic and market forces that are working on the popular averages will also have an affect on stocks not in the averages. Major market trends also involve changes in investors' attitudes. Once a change in trend takes place, the market develops its own momentum in the new direction and investors begin to think of stocks moving only in that direction. If the trend has turned up, investors tend to look for buying opportunities rather than selling opportunities, and if the trend has turned down, they tend to think of selling rather than buying. In a major uptrend investors tend to ignore risks and consider only the potential of individual stocks; in a downtrend they tend to ignore potential and to consider only the risks. Major trends can change abruptly at tops and bottoms, but trends usually take some time for the buying or selling to run its course and to exhaust itself before a reversal takes place.

Pessimism usually is associated with market declines and optimism with market advances. Pessimism and optimism appear to ebb and flow periodically in the stock market cycle. It has been said that the market makes the mood, and there does seem to be much truth in the statement. News often seems to be interpreted in light of the major market trend at the time. This pessimism or optimism can change suddenly with a reversal of the market trend. Investors, thus, have to be wary of becoming too pessimistic when investors are generally bearish and of becoming too optimistic when investors are wildly optimistic. Temporary rallies in a market decline can take place if too much pessimism develops and temporary reactions in an uptrend can occur when optimism becomes too great.

The market cycle can also be considered a function of profit-taking. Investors who bought at the bottom of the cycle when the economic news was the worst and pessimism was rampant tend to take their profits when the economic news becomes favorable and optimism is widespread. Sophisticated investors do not wait for favorable economic news at the bottom of a market decline before buying, nor do they wait for unfavorable economic news at the top of a market before selling. Investors who buy and sell on such a precautionary basis will usually find themselves in step with the market and the achievement of substantial profits relatively easy. However, when the investor is out-of-step with the market he will find making money extremely difficult.

The economic cycle broadly shapes the market cycle, but the market cycle, like the economic cycle, is not well-defined and may involve several separate cycles. It can move in broad sweeps covering decades in response to sociological, political, and economic change (particularly involving periods of abnormal inflation or deflation), or it can run in shorter patterns, reflecting emotional excesses and shorter economic cycles. The broad secular stock market movements are of concern to the average investor only infrequently, however. What is more often of importance is the shorter term cycle. Among these cycles, an approximate ten-year cycle appears to recur frequently, as shown in Figure 1.

It can be seen in Figure 1 that buying opportunities occurred in 1932, 1942, 1952, 1962, and 1970. The eight-year period ending in 1970 is a reminder that too much precision cannot be expected from the stock market.

Taking advantage of the stock market cycle can be almost as important as catching the major moves of individual stocks. You cannot rely on the market cycle alone to enable you to triple your investment, but proper use of the market cycle along with a judicious selection of stocks can give you a good start toward your investment goal.

How the Stock Market Cycle Can Help You Improve Your Investment Performance

Some investment advisers advocate that investors ride out the market cycle on the premise that it is too difficult to predict market cycles. Certainly, it is not

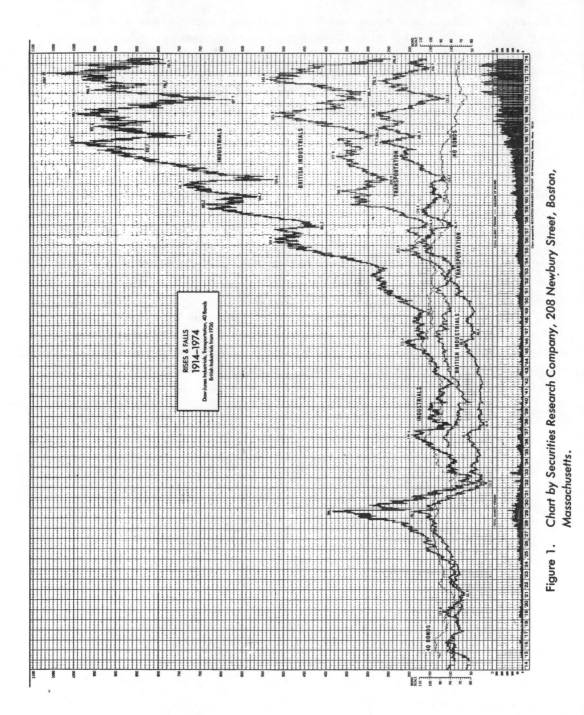

Figure 1.   Chart by Securities Research Company, 208 Newbury Street, Boston, Massachusetts.

easy to forecast market cycles. A generous portion of good judgment, objectivity, discipline, and patience is needed to be able to take advantage of the market cycle. The rewards that can accrue to you when you successfully utilize the market cycle are well worth the effort, however.

In Figure 2 you can see how much more profitable it would have been for an investor if he had bought at the bottom of the cycles and sold at the tops during a ten-year period from 1962 through 1972, rather than buying in 1962 and holding the investment position through 1972.

The total return on an investment in Cincinnati Milacron in 1962 would have been 705 percent using a strategy of taking advantage of the market cycle, compared with a 259 percent gain using a buy and hold approach. In computing the gains as a result of buying and selling during the market cycle, it was assumed that the investor sold 10 percent below the peaks and bought 10 percent above the lows. In actual practice, it is admittedly not easy for investors to buy near the bottoms of cycles and to sell near the tops. In Chapter 2, however, techniques are discussed which can help the investor recognize possible tops and bottoms of market cycles. The results of the 1962-1972 market cycle, it should be pointed out, are not necessarily representative of what might be experienced by investors in future market cycles. Nevertheless, Figure 2 shows that it is possible to triple your investment in a reasonable time, and tripling your money should be your goal.

Understanding the Techno-Fundamental Basis for the Stock Market Cycle

There is no specific reason for a ten-year cycle in the stock market, but such a market cycle can undoubtedly be related to patterns of human behavior. These behavior patterns exert their influence internally in the stock market and also on the economy. In the stock market, human behavior is manifested in emotional buying and selling and in profit-taking and bargain hunting. Emotional excesses in the market, whether speculative buying or the dumping of stocks, usually bring corrections in the opposite direction. There is no way of predicting when emotional excesses will reach their peaks. Speculative buying can become more speculative and rise to a crescendo to the point that investors think there is no top to the market. Rampant pessimism can become even more extreme until investors think there is no bottom to the market. Often some event, economic, international, monetary, etc., which cannot be anticipated, will trigger a reversal of the trend. One thing can be sure, the reversal will be unexpected by most investors.

The 1962 market decline was an example of a market falling because of excess speculation. In 1961 investors began to believe that there was no limit to

Cyclical Stocks	Adjusted % Gain 1962-1966	Adjusted % Gain 1966-1967	Adjusted % Gain 1967-1969	Adjusted % Gain 1970-1972	Total of Absolute Gains 1962-1972	% Return on Initial Investment	Total Absolute Gain Buy and Hold 1962-1972	Buy and Hold Return on Investment
Cincinnati Milacron	177%	113%	60%	52%	$ 95.26	705%	$ 35.00	259%
General Motors	130	11	9	25	89.32	201	46.62	105
Phelps Dodge	68	21	52	28	49.33	221	25.75	116
Union Carbide	64	6	2	60	50.23	121	10.50	25
U. S. Steel	33	17	5	16	26.50	70	- 1.88	- 5
Growth Stocks								
Avon Products	324	76	31	115	151.81	1600	128.25	1350
Intl. Business Machines	116	88	73	77	556.76	710	348.50	445
Johnson and Johnson	210	70	170	227	151.81	2340	126.50	1950
Polaroid	687	92	54	167	263.23	2632	139.50	1395
Xerox	1240	105	43	139	253.97	4210	165.87	2760

NOTE: Stocks are adjusted for splits and stock dividends.

Figure 2.

how high stocks could go. At the beginning of 1962 the Dow Jones Industrial Average (an index composed of 30 New York Stock Exchange stocks) soared to a level where it was selling at 23 times earnings. At the time, I believed the market was dangerous selling at such a high price-earnings ratio (the price of the stock divided by earnings per share) and I wrote a memo, noting that stock prices had outrun corporate earnings and that stock yields in relation to bond yields were at their lowest point in 50 years. Shortly afterward the DJIA began its decline. The stock market is a leading economic indicator (specifically, the Standard and Poor's composite index of 500 stocks) and investors assumed it was forecasting a recession. However, in this instance a recession did not develop and the stock market recovered.

The stock market decline in 1969 and 1970 was essentially a decline for fundamental reasons. (See Figure 3.) Toward the end of 1969 the inventory buildup was running at an unsustainable rate. The rate of growth of the money supply also was unsustainable. I commented in one of my firm's publications that the growth of the money supply would have to slow and that it would have an adverse affect on the stock market since the supply of money available to purchase common stocks is an important stock market consideration. I must admit, however, I was not conscious of how bad inflation was becoming and I did not anticipate the sharp drop in the stock market as a result of the government measures taken to slow inflation. The Federal Reserve Board severely reduced the growth in the money supply, increasing interest rates and slowing the economy.

You Can Benefit from a Knowledge of How Human Behavior Affects the Economy

Human behavior in the economy can be seen in consumer buying which borrows from the future, or in consumers' reluctance to buy and to save instead. Changes in consumer installment debt extensions and the level of savings as a percentage of personal disposable income can indicate consumers' future spending patterns.

Businesses can also spend excessively for plant and equipment, or they can cut back their expenditures. Both consumers and businessmen can be emotional in their spending. During periods of euphoria and of general confidence in the economy, spending can become excessive and borrow from the future, just as demand can drop to levels below long term trends and produce pent-up demand if consumers and businessmen become pessimistic about the future.

Federal government deficits or surpluses, also, have a major impact on the economy. Government spending is done by government officials who are subject to emotional pressures as well as anyone else. Congress, in particular, is subject

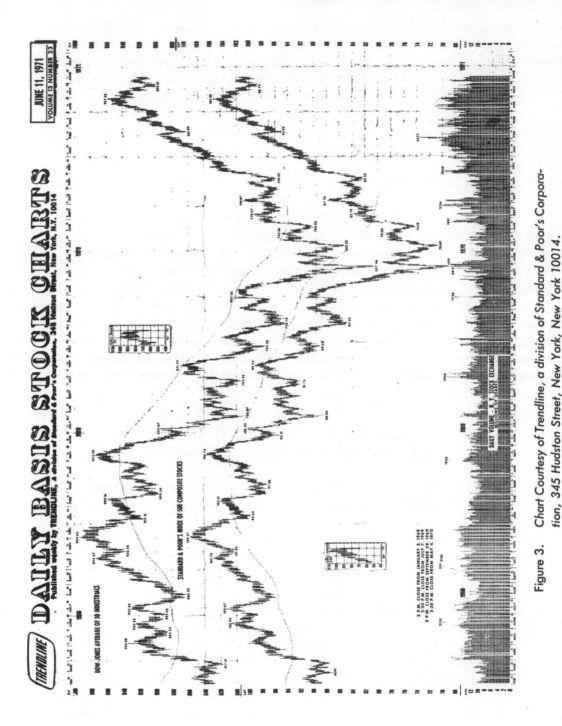

Figure 3.   Chart Courtesy of Trendline, a division of Standard & Poor's Corporation, 345 Hudston Street, New York, New York 10014.

to political pressures and finds it difficult to resist authorizing spending for social projects and public works. During periods when private demand is impinging heavily on the economy, sharply increased demand from the public sector on the limited excess resources in the economy can lead to inflationary pressures unless governmental action is taken to reduce private spending through increased taxes or some type of consumer spending controls. Wars, of course, can produce severe distortions in the economy, particularly if the economic demands of the war are superimposed on consumer demands, as occurred during the Vietnam War. The lesson that you have to learn as an investor is that growth rates above or below long term trends have to be temporary. When the entire economy is running above or below normal rates, eventually the difference will be made up by the economy in the future. In general, with regard to individual industries and companies, shortages lead to surpluses after corrective action is taken and surpluses tend to lead to shortages. The temporary nature of variances from the norm is a fact of investment life and you have to not only recognize this fact, but be willing to act on your knowledge of it, i.e., you have to be willing to sell stocks when the economic news appears to be the brightest and to buy when the news looks the worst. Certainly, it is extremely difficult to sell stocks when investors are bullish and economic activity is running at a high level. Conversely, it is not easy to have the courage to step in and buy stocks when investors are bearish and the economy is doing poorly. In the first instance, the investor believes stocks are going higher and he believes he can sell at a higher price. In the latter situation, he believes stocks are going lower and he can buy at a lower price. Thus, because it is so difficult for the investor to act against his instincts and emotions, many do not do well in the stock market. They tend to be buying when they should be selling and vice versa.

You can take advantage of the emotional mistakes of other investors once you understand the mechanism of the economy and have conviction in your knowledge of the relationship of the stock market and the economy. The stock market can often be expected to anticipate the peak of the economic cycle by as much as 18 months. Economic recoveries are also anticipated by the stock market, although the lead time is generally not as long as for economic peaks. Market indicators, which are discussed in Chapter 2, can be very helpful in suggesting when the stock market is in the process of changing direction. Nevertheless, you can do a very good job of selling near market tops and buying near market bottoms even without a knowledge of market indicators if you sell when the economic activity is running at such a high level that the surge in corporate profits has just about taken place, and buy when the economic news may be the worst expected, whether in terms of inflation, high interest rates, unemployment, or a decline in the Federal Reserve Board index of production. Your willingness to fight your instincts and sell when the economy is running at a high level of activity, industry is operating at a high percentage of capacity, and inflationary pressures are building up, and to buy when economic activity is at a low level, ample production capacity is available, and inflationary pressures have abated in one of the most important factors in your program to triple your money in the stock market. Simply stated, you should be buying when the economy is operating below par and investors are bearish, and selling when the economy has had a long rise and investors are bullish. You may have to have a good deal of patience and discipline to wait for your buying and selling opportunities, but the patience can be well-rewarded. This approach is one of the best methods of making money in the stock market.

This "contrary opinion" approach to investing can also be applied to individual industries. During periods of stable economic growth that involve no excesses, the economy may still be undergoing a rolling readjustment in which individual industries may be reaching peaks or bottoms in their cycles. Rotating from industry to industry in such an economic environment can also help you enhance your profits.

The Techno-Fundamental Market Trend Is One of the Most Important Investment Considerations

It can be said that there are two major market trends, a bull market trend and a bear market trend. In between these two major trends there are intermediate trends and a trendless or trading market. The bulk of the bull market trend usually can be expected to take place within two years. Bear market trends normally can be expected to be completed in a year. It would be difficult to argue against an investment strategy of investing in the stock market at the bottom of a bear market, selling after about two years and then waiting for the next bear market. I do believe, however, such a strategy would be very difficult psychologically for most investors to follow and, in addition, many fine investment opportunities would be missed during the long waiting periods.

Perhaps the most realistic approach in taking advantage of market trends is to ride the major bull market trend until it appears to be nearly exhausted and then to sell the bulk of the issues on a precautionary basis. After the subsequent market reaction runs it course, and enough evidence is available to indicate a bottom of the decline has been seen, you can then reinvest your funds in issues which look promising for capital appreciation (likely stocks for capital gains at this point will be discussed in Chapter 3). Performance investors can follow certain procedures for profits while the decline is taking place. These steps will be discussed later, in Chapter 10.

Perhaps one of the main reasons many investors do not maximize their profits in the stock market is that they are continually fighting the market trend. At the bottom of the bear markets they are very slow in recognizing a change in trend because no favorable economic news can be seen. After the upward trend has been underway for some time, the investor is then reluctant to believe it can change in direction again because no unfavorable economic news is evident. Trends, whether major bull market or bear market trends or intermediate trends, are not easily reversed once they have gained momentum and investor attitudes have hardened. Investor confidence is an important ingredient in market trends and it takes time for investors to regain confidence once they have lost it and to lose it once confidence is widespread. Market trends are usually characterized by two or more reactions in the opposite direction before the trend runs its course. Side issues often tend to cloud the main market consideration, which is usually economic activity and corporate profits, but usually they just temporarily interrupt the major trend. You have to have a certain amount of discipline not to allow day-to-day fluctuations to deter you from staying with the major trend. Usually there is ample time for the investor to sell at the top of an uptrend before a substantial decline sets in, and to buy at the bottom of a decline before a significant rally takes place. In the case of major trends, a change in trend should also be expected to be accompanied by some possibilities of a change in the complexion of the economy, even though hard evidence is not yet available.

In addition to not fighting the major market trend, you will find it more profitable not fighting the major trends of individual stocks and groups. Too many investors, for reasons of pride or stubbornness, often will continue to hold on to situations which are weaker than the general market and appear to be in downtrends. Certainly, the ability to cut losses is a most valuable attribute in a successful stock market program. Not all stocks and groups participate in market uptrends, and some more than others, and you will usually find it most profitable to buy those stocks or groups which are stronger than the general market and in definite uptrends. Buying popularity is usually more profitable than buying unpopular issues. At times it may be difficult for investors to buy certain stocks which are acting well because of relatively high price-earnings ratios. The subject of price-earnings ratios will be discussed in more detail in later chapters, but over the short run they are usually only a very rough indicator of a stock's performance. One qualification is that high price-earning ratios indicate investor confidence and in strong market advances will usually do better than stocks with low price-earning ratios. By and large, however, growth rates and whether they are accelerating or decelerating, and the potential for attaining sharply higher earnings levels are the primary determinants of a stock's performance.

In discussing the "market" I should define my terms more accurately. There are at least two major markets, one in which the stocks are supported by institutional buying and one in which the stocks are bought primarily by the public. Each has its own characteristics. These two markets are discussed in Chapter 3. When we talk of the general market, we are referring to the market measured by the popular stock market indices, primarily the Dow Jones Industrial Averages, and the Standard and Poor's composite index of 500 stocks. The DJIA represents stocks that are of institutional quality. The S&P composite is a much broader index, but it, too, is composed of the larger companies. Generally, the major movements of the DJIA and the S&P composite are similar. It must be recognized that many individual stocks, particularly those classified as secondary issues which are found on the American Stock Exchange and in the over-the-counter market, may not move with the popular averages. Thus, although we should be very conscious of the trends of the popular averages, we should also be very much aware of the market action of the different classes of stocks.

Knowing the Four Stages of the Market Cycle Can Aid Your Perspective

Investors who rely on price-earning ratios alone on which to base their investment decisions are often mystified by the action of stocks at different times in the stock market. Investor psychology and confidence can change radically with different stages of the stock market cycle. These changes can explain much of the varying demand for certain groups of stock at different stages of the stock market cycle. Occasionally you should stand back and take a broad look at the stock market cycle and its stages in order to understand what groups of stocks may do best. For example, American Stock Exchange and over-the-counter stocks may be in little demand during the bear market phase of the cycle (in fact, they may be artificially depressed by a lack of bids), but may be in exceptional investment demand during the speculative phase prior to a bear market.

Stocks also react differently to news according to the stage of the market of the market cycle. One of the common complaints of investors is that sometimes stocks go down on good news instead of rising, and sometimes the same stocks may advance on unfavorable news instead of declining. Although there may be something in the individual situation to account for the apparently strange behavior, such as a stock may have already anticipated and discounted the news, the phase of the stock market cycle could be the reason why certain stocks act as they do in response to news. Near the bottom of a bear market sophisticated investors tend to assume that unfavorable news is only temporary and that better news will be coming. Near the top of a bull market they tend to believe that favorable news will be short-lived and that pessimistic news will soon be seen. Technical signals should also be read in the context of the stage the market is in. A six-month high for a stock in the second stage (described in the following paragraphs) may be the last gasp, example, whereas in the fourth stage it may indicate coming out of a bear market and the start of a major rally.

The stock market cycle can be divided into four stages based on the economic cycle, profit-taking, and the time it takes for speculative fever to develop. The first stage takes place from the bottom of a bear market. The rally is usually initiated by short covering on some economic news or stock market signal, followed by traders moving into the market and then longer term investors. Investors usually have to have the feeling that the worst of the economic problems have been seen before they are convinced it is time to invest.

At the end of the first stage the market may run into profit-taking after its sharp rise, or it may merge with the second stage with very little in the way of a reaction between stages. In the second stage the market tends to rise until it has discounted the corporate earnings of the economic recovery under way. The peak of this stage can be expected to precede the top of the economic recovery by many months. The third stage is a stage in which stocks, particularly cyclical issues, tend to go into a trading range. They sell off, then have to become undervalued in terms of price-earnings ratios or yields on the reactions before investor interest develops again.

The fourth stage is usually a bear market stage in which stocks are liquidated and values produced for the beginning of the first stage, the bull market phase. There is no law that says the fourth stage has to be a bear market, however. If the economy does not deteriorate, inflation remains under control, there are no international monetary crises, no wars, and market speculation does not get out of hand, the stock market could well move into a new bull market from the third stage. Nevertheless, in order to have a vigorous bull market, a good shakeout is probably needed to raise investors' cash reserves, build up a high short interest, and to create stock values.

How to Recognize the First Stage

Prior to the beginning of the first stage, the market is characterized by universal despair. The popular market averages have been declining for some months and, more than likely, economic news has been unfavorable. The market probably has had two or more false rallies and investors are now thoroughly disheartened. Interest rates probably have been rising and the rate of growth of the money supply decreasing. The dollar may have weakened on the international front and inflation may have been increasing. The growth rate of the gross national product probably has been slowing, as well as the Federal Reserve Board index of production. It is also possible there is some liquidation of manufacturers and trade inventories, and factory new orders may be declining. Leading economic indicators can be declining, also. Retail sales, especially durable good sales, including autos, may be showing unfavorable comparisons. All of these signs may be present at the beginning of the first stage or only a few of them may be seen.

No two first stages are identical, but the beginning of all are marked by investor pessimism. Favorable economic news has not been seen yet. The only hint of a possible bottom is that both the market and economic news has been unfavorable for so long that the odds suggest some improvement before too long. Depleted inventories need to be built up, pent-up demand has developed in the durable goods sector, and it is likely the Federal Reserve is ready to expand credit and the nation's money supply.

It takes courage and conviction to step into the stock market at the beginning of the first stage. You are on your own; you do not have the reassuring feeling of being part of the crowd. Nevertheless, if you are to maximize your gain in the stock market this is when you have to make your decision to move into the market. How far and how fast the market will move will depend, of course, on the possibilities of a surge in corporate earnings, or a drop in interest rates.

Volatile stocks and growth stocks with high short interests normally do the best coming off the bottom of a bear market as traders holding short positions panic and cover their shorts. Traders, quick to take advantage of the discomfiture of the short-sellers, move in. Astute investors, noting the activity of the stock market and the likelihood of a turn in the economy, add their buying to the growing demand for funds.

Practically all stocks do well in the beginning of the first stage, including some situations that may be fundamentally unsound. The general market expansion can mask the basic weakness of these issues. It may be advisable to sell such stocks toward the end of the first stage since they may well return to their bear market levels some time in the future.

Sound stocks which become undervalued in the depths of despair of a bear market when investors tend to ignore the price-earning ratios and turn to yields for security, return to reasonable valuations of earnings in the first stage, after which they may spend some time consolidating. As investors gain confidence, in general they become more willing to pay for the earning power of stocks expected to be seen with the economy recovers to a high level of activity. Investors become less concerned with yields for downside protection and are willing to buy on the basis of improving earnings.

Cyclical stocks also participate in the first stage rally, and, in some cases, may even see their market cycle peaks in the first stage.Usually, however, the cyclical stocks do not reflect their earning power in a full employment economy until the second stage.

The Characteristics of the Second Stage

The line of demarcation between the first and second stages is often not very clear. Sometimes the two stages combine to form a bull market leg. This leg is characterized by higher highs and higher lows and there may be two or three sharp declines before the top is seen. The second stage of the market cycle is the one in which the cyclical stocks fully reflect their potential. This stage may mark the top of the trading range of the popular averages for some time, possibly several years. The DJIA, which is made up primarily of conservative and cyclical stocks, usually just about exhausts its potential once industry is operating at 90 percent or more of capacity. The stocks themselves often anticipate a higher level of economic activity by many months. Investors usually become complacent toward the end of the second stage and start thinking that stocks will soar skyward—just before the downturn. Growth stocks can be expected to become amply priced early in the second stage, but they are in such strong hands (widely held by institutions) that as long as the major market trend remains upward these stocks resist selling off and can go higher.

Knowing When You Are in the Third Stage

The third stage starts out with a reaction from the rally in the second stage. The decline often confuses and confounds investors because it is so unexpected. At first investors assume it is just a technical reaction, but as the decline wears on and more and more stocks participate, investors start assuming a recession or credit crunch, or both, is imminent. A recession, or financial crisis, is always possible and there is really no way of being sure whether one will occur or not. However, it is more likely that just a slowing of the economy will take place and that once this becomes apparent the market is apt to bottom out.

Early in the third stage the secondary stocks and the over-the-counter and American Stock Exchange stocks may become friendless. The public, which undoubtedly was badly burned in the previous bear market, in all probability used the first and second stages to sell and break even, and they may be very reluctant to return to the market until they are convinced money will be made and not lost.

Later in the third stage, once a bottom appears to have been well-established, the public may return to the market. In this event, the over-the-counter market and American Stock Exchange may become active again. Investment popularity can also be expected to rotate from industry to industry and from group to group as investors shift from exploited issues to relatively unexploited issues in search of profits. Following popularity and market strength can be one of the most rewarding ways of making money in this stage. Fads and fashions abound in this stage, and if you overstay the market you can lose much of your profit. If you wish to continue your quest to triple your investment you have to be flexible and willing to move out of issues that are topping out and into issues bottoming out. As the fads and fashions run their course you have to abandon them. This is not easily done. Investors tend to fall in love with stocks, or they think that the trend can never change. It is also easy to sell too soon and miss substantial profits, or to switch into issues which may not be ready to move or may even decline. The techno-fundamental approach can be a big help in accomplishing the switching maneuver successfully.

Toward the end of the third stage speculation can be expected to increase in intensity as investors are caught up in the excitement of making money. If you lower your quality standards in the latter part of the third stage you can often do better than if you insist on value and conservative stocks. At the end of the third stage speculation often reaches a peak and conditions become ripe for the fourth stage.

Do Not Be Fooled by the Fourth Stage

The fourth stage is not necessarily a bear market. It is conceivable that the third stage could linger long enough to lay the groundwork for a new bull market. The probabilities, however, are that a bear market will ensue because of excesses in either the stock market or the economy. Government management of the economy has helped moderate the economic cycle, but it has exacted a price in inflationary pressures on the economy, increasing the longer term risk. Thus, the control of inflation may have replaced the control of the economic cycle as the major economic problem. At present, it seems that there are three major weapons against runaway inflation: a reduction in the growth rate of the money supply, lower federal spending, and wage and price controls. The employment of monetary policy to restrict economic growth is particularly unfavorable for the stock market. Wage and price controls also have their long-range adverse effects in the distortions they create in the economy, and consequently in the stock market. In an inflationary environment, policies which bring capacity and demand into better balance are more favorable for the stock market than policies which increase inflationary pressures.

Although the reasons for a bear market are rooted either in the economy or in the market itself, bear markets tend to feed on themselves and to pick up a momentum of their own. A bear market then becomes more of an attitude of investors, rather than a reflection of actuality. It becomes a fashion to sell in a bear market just as it is a fashion to buy in a bull market. Fear of the unknown and the examples of others lead investors to start dumping stocks indiscriminately. The stocks thrown into the marketplace at any price may be the same ones investors will be chasing in the next bull market. The very trend of the market has set investors' moods and the selling of stocks tends to continue until values become obvious. Bear markets are characterized by lower lows and lower highs. Current yields become more important among secondary stocks than price-earnings ratios, many of which become extremely low historically until yields become reasonable.

Bear markets are usually marked by two or more false rallies when investors fear they will miss a buying opportunity and traders who are short stocks panic and cover their short positions. These are all technical rallies without any economic basis. After a prolonged period of decline and a substantial percentage drop in the popular market averages, the stage is being set for the next bull market. When there is enough bearishness around so that most stockholders who are not true long term holders have sold their shares, and the market has been exposed to a great deal of unfavorable economic news, the conditions are ripe for a turnaround in the market. When it happens, it can happen with such suddenness that even experienced market technicians may be surprised. It requires a tremendous amount of discipline not to succumb to the general bearishness and pessimism found at the bottom of a bear market and to sell stocks at rediculously low prices. At the bottom of a bear market stocks sell at artificially low prices just because of a lack of bids and there is little relationship between stock prices and stock values.

At the bottom of a bear market investors should welcome the buying opportunities rather than worry about depressed prices. At some point when pessimism is widespread enough investors should be less concerned with the movement of the popular averages and start looking for individual values in stocks. It is not possible to indicate statistically at just what point a bear market should terminate. No two bear markets are the same and market indicators do not display exactly the same behavior patterns each time. The length and depth of bear markets are basically determined by the economy and any problems that may be besetting it. The important thing you should remember when you are ready to abandon hope is that you probably should be buying stocks, not selling them. It is quite possible, of course, that the problems besetting the economy may not be easily solved and it could take some time to bring them under control. If substantial risks also overhang the economy, the best investment strategy may be one of caution until the risks are reduced.

How to Use the Market Indicators

The stock market indicators, which number over 50, essentially indicate the degree of any excesses which may exist in the market. Certain ones are also very useful in revealing just how the various sectors of the market are performing (cyclical stocks, quality growth stocks, secondary stocks, new issues, etc.), what the current supply-demand situation is, and what funds may be available to buy stocks. They can also suggest the state of investor confidence, which we have noted before is a most important factor in the stock market.

Investors should not place too much emphasis on any one indicator or group of indicators alone, however. They are more properly used in the context of the economic and market cycle. In fact, their interpretation can depend a lot on just which stage the stock market is in. By and large, they should be used to help read the signals being given by the economy, and to indicate how much the economic cycle is being anticipated by the stock market. How the stock market reacts to economic news, together with some notion of what additional news to expect, is still one of the best approaches to stock market forecasting. Thus, it can be seen that you have to have some idea of what the economy is likely to do in order to properly interpret the market indicators. A good sense of economic trends and excesses can be very helpful in keeping you from being carried away by the action of stock market indicators. They will tend to look bullish at tops of markets and they tend to look the worst at stock market bottoms. Realizing that the economic cycle may be near a peak or a bottom can help you interpret the action of the indicators. Of course, you may end up questioning your economic assumptions if the market indicators persist in behaving in a certain manner opposite to what you would normally expect.

The specific level attained by individual stock market indicators can vary considerably, depending on the degree of bullishness or bearishness. What is more important than the absolute levels reached is how rapidly changes take place and the amount of the changes.

Market indicators which can be most helpful are those which suggest whether the stock market is in a basic uptrend or downtrend. The indicators alone cannot tell which stage the market cycle is in. Some knowledge of the economic cycle is needed, in addition, to arrive at a determination of the stage of the economic cycle. Certain indicators are used by traders as a means of timing buying and selling. On a short term basis, the market can move in relation to indicators which reveal technical overbought and oversold conditions, independent of economic developments. The indicators are most helpful in allowing you to recognize dangerous markets and top areas, and markets of opportunities, and bottom areas. They usually do not pinpoint tops and bottoms unless obvious excesses are taking place (discussed in Chapter 2), but they can indicate when a top or bottom has been seen once it has occurred.

2

Using the Techno-Fundamental Approach
in Putting Your Market Strategy
to Work

Chapter 1 showed how you can benefit from taking advantage of the stock market cycle and the four stages into which it can be divided. This chapter will describe the market indicators that are characteristic of market tops and bottoms. These market indicators will rarely tell you the exact day the popular stock market averages will see their tops or bottoms since often relatively unpredictable events trigger rallies and declines. They will suggest, however, when the market is becoming dangerous or when buying opportunities exist. It should be noted that there are different types of tops and bottoms. When dramatic events precipitate the advance or decline, the market may make an inverted " V"-type top of a " V" bottom. If no particular developments mark the tops or bottoms, a rounding-type of pattern may be traced by the popular averages at both the tops and the bottoms. You should, also, be aware from the outset that all stocks and groups do not bottom out or top out at the same time. Some stocks and industries may lead the market averages by a year or more. It may well be, in fact, that the bulk of the stocks in the market, particularly the secondary issues, could lead the popular average by many months. Thus, you can see that you have to be careful not to let the popular averages mask what is happening to individual stocks and stock groups.

Market Indicators Can Tell You
When You Are in a Top Area

Professionals in the investment world often have an objective of trying to catch the exact tops and bottoms of markets, assuming they are better qualified to accomplish this feat than the average investor. However, these professionals, to their dismay, frequently find they have outsmarted themselves. Getting in at the very tops of markets and out at the bottoms is more luck than anything, even for professionals. More often than not they overstay the tops of markets and get back in too early in declines. What is more feasible, though, is to recognize top and bottom areas in the stock market cycle. Even though you do not buy at the bottoms or sell at the tops, you can still accomplish your goal of tripling your investments if you can recognize bottom areas and top areas.

The top area of the stock market cycle is defined as that area in which stocks can still go higher, but eventually will go substantially lower. Most stocks should be sold rather than bought, or bought only on a trading basis, in top areas. The bottom area is defined as the area in which stocks may still go lower but will eventually end up substantially higher. Stocks with sound prospects can be accumulated in this area, even though they may go lower near term. It is not too difficult to recognize top and bottom areas. Investors' emotions are usually running to excess at both extremes, and even without market indicators the average investor should be able to recognize dangerous markets and markets of opportunity once he knows the symptoms.

It should be realized, however, that it takes quite a bit of discipline for you to act on your knowledge. Stock markets may take months to form a top or bottom, and if you sell at the beginning of a distribution pattern the urge to get back in the market too soon is almost irresistible, and if you buy at the beginning of a consolidation pattern it is very easy to panic and sell before an upward move begins. Figure 4 shows a consolidation pattern from July, 1971 through February, 1972, and a distribution pattern from December, 1972 through January, 1973. (See Figure 4).

The market indicators of a top area are grouped according to: 1) those which are a gauge of speculative excesses in the market; 2) those which indicate a loss of momentum; 3) those which indicate a shift in the supply-demand equation toward supply; and 4) those that indicate a diminution of demand. A bottom area is characterized by 1) emotional excesses, 2) a slowing of downside momentum, and 3) improving conditions for increased demand and new buying.

There are two schools of thought on whether the investor should buy when he believes he is in a bottom area and sell when he thinks he is in a top area, or whether he should wait until the indicators suggest he is past the bottom before buying and past the top before selling. The risk in anticipating tops and bottoms is that you may sell or buy too early. On the other hand, if you wait for solid evidence of a bottom or top you could miss many good buying opportunities, particularly if the bottom turns out to be a rounding-bottom type, and lose substantial profits if you wait too long before selling.

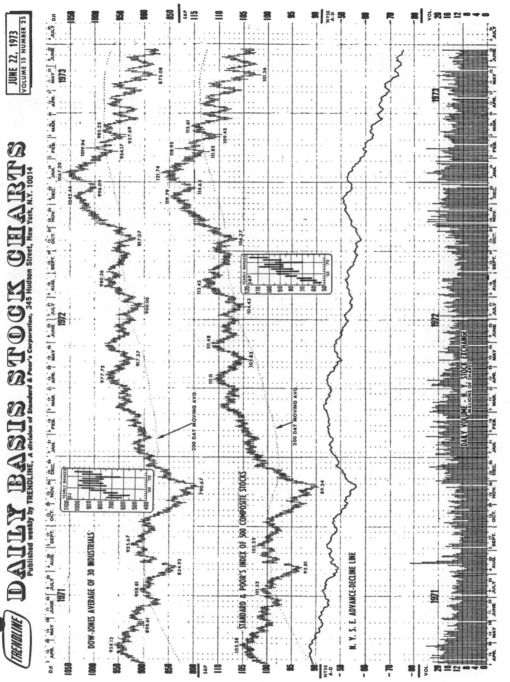

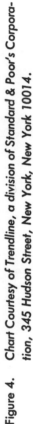

Figure 4.   Chart Courtesy of Trendline, a division of Standard & Poor's Corporation, 345 Hudson Street, New York, New York 10014.

Market Indicators Which Indicate
Speculative Excess

If there is any one sure indication of a top area, it is the presence of specula-tive excesses. These excesses can take many forms and an investor often will not recognize that he is witnessing such excesses. The DJIA, for example, may be selling at a reasonable historical price-earning ratio, and there may be just pockets of speculative excesses. At the top of the 1961 bull market the DJIA itself rose to an untenable level. The bull market which terminated in the latter part of 1968 was characterized by excesses in new groups and industries with which the in-vestment community fell in love. Such love affairs in which stocks go practically straight up usually run their course before too long. Under the pressure of compe-tition, excess capacity, and saturation of markets, new industries usually run into price cutting and narrower profit margins. The fashion to buy then turns into a fashion to sell, and the stocks come down as fast, if not faster, than they went up.

You really do not need any indicators to tell you excesses are present once you are aware of what to look for. Basically, when you get that feeling that the market is going to run away from you if you do not rush in and buy, you are in a speculative atmosphere. This speculative atmosphere, however, can last for months and can get more speculative. The market indicators help you gauge the extent of the speculation. The strength of the speculation can vary from bull market to bull market. You can get an idea of how great the excesses might be relative to other periods by comparing the current economic conditions with previous conditions. The momentum of the market may also be a clue to how far it will go

In addition to speculative excesses, other market indicators of a top area include:

1. Sharp rises in over-the-counter stocks, American Stock Exchange stocks, and new issues. Coming off a bottom of a bear market investors are usually so beaten-down that they normally tend to confine their purchases to well-known companies. (You notice how carefully we choose our words. It would be rash to say that investors always do anything consistently since investing philosophies can change from one market cycle to another.) It is only after investors have built up their confidence from watching the market climb for some months that enthusiasm spills over into the secondary and more speculative stocks. The rotation of investor interest from the better-known stocks of larger companies to the lower-priced stocks of small-er companies generally found in the over-the-counter market and on the American Stock Exchange usually take place after other sectors of the mar-ket have been fully exploited. New issues, of course, are the least seasoned

and the most speculative. They are particularly in demand when investor confidence in the economy and the market are near a peak.

2. The volume of the American Stock Exchange increases sharply as a percentage of the New York Stock Exchange volume. The gains in volume on the ASE occur concurrently with the rise in interest in these stocks (statistics on the weekly volume of the NYSE and ASE are carried in the stock market statistics in Barron's). The NYSE volume also can be expected to be running at a relatively high level. Stocks are being distributed by knowledgeable investors at the top and the high volume tends to lure the unwary into the market so the distribution can take place.

3. A relative lack of historically low stock values. It follows that after the stock market has had a substantial rise the price-earnings ratios of stocks are selling near the upper end of their price-earnings ratio ranges. As noted before, all stocks may not be historically richly priced. The sharp increase in price-earnings ratios may take place in only a relatively few sectors. At such a time new theories to explain why stocks are selling so high may be advanced. In 1968, the theory was offered that emerging technological companies would be good buys at any price because of the possibilities of earnings breakthroughs. One would think that investors would become more cautious as stocks became more richly priced. However, in the real world of common stocks, the get-rich-quick atmosphere of the stock market becomes contagious and investors find themselves chasing stocks. The "bigger fool" theory becomes operative. Investors will pay almost any price for stocks because they assume they will go higher and they can sell them to someone else. This theory works—until stocks stop going up.

4. The current yield of the DJIA is relatively low compared with bond yields. The yield from cash dividends investors are willing to accept appears to vary with the degree of investor confidence. When confidence is high investors do not worry too much about any lack of dividends. They are more enamored with earnings growth. When confidence is low investors tend to become more concerned about yield protection, particularly with regard to cyclical and speculative issues, and price-earnings ratios tend to be ignored regardless of how low they become until there is a reasonable yield. At a minimum, the total return on stocks (current yield plus capital appreciation potential, discussed in Chapter 3), should equal the yield to maturity of bonds (the yield to maturity is the current return adjusted for the discount or premium gained or lost at maturity). In bull markets investors tend to be willing to be optimistic about the capital gains portion of the total return, but in bear markets, they are pessimistic about the capital gains potential and desire greater current yield.

Market Indicators Which Reveal
a Loss of Momentum

The loss-of-momentum indicators are similar to the speculation indicators in the sense that they do not instantaneously reveal when the market is topping out. This topping-out action can take place over many months. Different types of stocks will top out at various points in the top area. It is quite conceivable that you may be watching the DJIA or quality growth stocks for clues as to the market's direction, and secondary-type stocks which you may own could be on their way down while the DJIA and the growth stocks are forging ahead. In fact, the 1973 bear market as measured by the DJIA was preceded by a decline in indices which measured the entire market performance. The DJIA held well above the previous bottom of the bear market of 1970, but the Value Line index, which is not distorted by the prices of the stocks in the index or by the companies' capitalizations, and the advance-decline line, which is an accumulation of the net advances or declines on the NYSE, penetrated their 1970 lows. Individual stocks, in many instances, declined much more than the averages. You can see that it behooves you not to get too wrapped up in any one index and fail to watch various sectors of the market.

The market indicators of a loss of momentum include:

1. A divergence between the advance-decline line and the DJIA. When the advance-decline line does not make a new high with the DJIA, a danger signal is flashed. The divergence can be expected to last for some months before the DJIA may turn down. During this period many stocks will move higher, but many will stagnate and others will decline. What the market is telling us with the divergence is that investors are losing confidence in the secondary stocks and are taking profits. Investors tend to be more apprehensive with regard to the smaller, less strongly financed companies than with the seasoned, leading corporations when they suspect the market or economy may be vulnerable.

2. Many stocks start falling out of their ascending channels. This technical indication should be read in the context of how long and how far the stocks have risen. The longer the time period and the greater the percentage price appreciation, the more likely it is that the stocks are in a top area. Stocks will often have two or more selloffs before a major decline sets in. Computerized programs of the market can also indicate when momentum is slowing. The percentage of the stocks that are long-term buys (have broken out of major bases) start to decrease and the percentage of stocks that are long-term sells (have broken below major distribution patterns) begin to increase. You have to be careful in using such "over bought-over sold"

indicators, however, since when they look the best the market is near a top and when they look the worst the market is near a bottom.

3. A divergence between cyclical stocks in various industries and glamour stocks takes place. What makes it difficult to use this indicator is that the divergence occurs so gradually that you may not be aware of it. Auto stocks topped out in 1971, foreshadowing the 1973 decline. At the time it was difficult to believe the stocks were topping out. Sales were running at very high levels and prospects were bright for even higher sales. The stocks also looked very reasonably priced on expected earnings. It seems that the likelihood of auto industry pollution control restrictions and controls on corporate dividends and prices made investors less enthusiastic about the auto stocks than they would have been otherwise.

4. Bellwether stocks, such as General Motors, are topping out. The logic behind GM as a bellwether stock, other than it as a cyclical issue, is that it reflects conditions in the economy to a great degree and its fortunes affects a great many supplier industries. Bellwether stocks can change. In every market period there are issues which tend to provide general market and group leadership, but GM has proven to be very reliable for many years. New highs or lows suggest that the particular market trend is still intact.

Market Indicators Which Tell You
the Supply of Common Stock Is Increasing

In every market rally there is a confluence of forces that finally bring the rally to a halt. The tapering off of the demand factors for stock are the most obvious, but factors on the supply side can be very effective, although in a more subtle way, in slowing a market rise. The influence of increasing supply cannot be expected to work its results abruptly. Rather, the influence is likely to be spread over a period of months. The market is not a laboratory, however, and demand and supply factors cannot be isolated in order to determine which is the most effective. It also is sometimes difficult to pinpoint what is the cause and what is the effect. Is the market rally slowing because the supply of stock is increasing, or is the supply of stock increasing because the market has rallied so far? Fortunately, for investment purposes it is not important whether the market is topping out because of demand factors or because of supply factors. The fact that the market is topping out is all you need to know, and the market indicators we are discussing in this chapter should give you ample warning.

Supply factors which can be expected to help take the steam out of a rally include:

1. A sharp increase in the offerings of common stock. Rising stock

prices clearly encourage corporations to bring out new issues to take advantage of the high stock prices. In addition, the enthusiasm of investors for new issues after the market has had a long advance makes it easy to sell new offerings.

2. Secondary offerings of stocks increase. Not only is an increase volume of secondary offerings draining off funds from the general market, but secondary offerings often are made when insiders believe their companies' stocks are amply priced and, thus, can be an indication of a top area.

3. A sharp increase in the dollar volume of convertible debentures. Convertible debentures represent a potential increase in outstanding common stock, but their purchase (as well as that of straight bonds) can also tap funds that could otherwise be used to buy common stocks.

Market Indicators Which Point to
Diminishing Demand for Common Stocks

When speculative excesses are occurring, market momentum is slowing, and the supply of common stock is increasing, the stage is set for the onset of forces which will result in diminishing demand. The factors that add up to demand for common stock are many and varied. Stocks do not go up by themselves just because they are undervalued. First of all, investors' attention have to be drawn to these values. In addition, the atmosphere has to be sufficiently charged with confidence before investors are willing to act. If a crisis of confidence exists, whether it is a fear of uncontrolled inflation, distrust of paper money and securities as a store of value, worry about the prospects for corporate profits, concern about competition from fixed income securities, or even apprehension about the future course of the nation, investors are reluctant to commit funds to the stock market. Investors have to feel confident that earnings will progress far into the future before they will be willing to forgo current consumption in favor of channeling savings into equities, especially if they are non-dividend paying stocks. Once a mood sets in for investors, it takes time for it to run its course. Bull markets can be said to stem from a fashion that has developed among investors to buy stocks, and similarly, bear markets to a large extent are a result of a fashion on the part of investors to sell stocks. Basically, investors buy stocks because they think they are going higher and sell them because they believe they will decline further.

It is almost unbelievable how low some secondary issues can go when there is no investor interest in buying them. (Conversely, stocks can go to unbelievable heights if there is a great deal of investor interest in buying stocks.) In the bear market of 1973, not one but several confidence-shaking factors were present and some stocks sold off until they were selling at five times earnings or less. Inflation was not being restrained in spite of a wage and price freeze and wage and price controls. Interest rates were soaring, although the prime rate lagged behind general rates because of government restraints. Apparently, the rapid growth of the money supply was offsetting the restraining factors of wage and price controls and special factors, such as adverse weather conditions and the large sale of wheat to Russia, had led to a sharp increase in food prices. Concurrently, and probably partially as the result of the domestic inflationary pressures, the price of gold soared on the free market overseas and the dollar weakened substantially. The forces that affect the dollar internationally are very complex, but it does seem that the billions of dollars overseas were a constant source of instability. Europeans were reluctant to accept more dollars and not adverse to selling them. At the same time, the United States restricted the export of certain foodstuffs. This move may have been interpreted by Europeans as indicating that not only was the dollar no longer convertible into gold, but that the restriction on exports was making it less convertible into goods.

A chain reaction often is set off in the money market once the initial event takes place. Even though the decline of the dollar against the floating European currencies made many economists believe that the dollar was undervalued, rumors started that the West German mark would be revalued upward and accelerated the speculative selling of the dollar. Eventually the mark was revalued. Concurrent with these problems, the U.S. economy appears to be overheating and there was talk of the possibility of a recession. Economists noted that an overheated economy had never been slowed without at least a brief recession. Interest rates also continued to rise and there was not only a fear of a money crunch, but concern that the measures the Federal Reserve might be forced to take to slow down the economic growth rate might aggravate a business slowdown. As if the foregoing were not enough, the Watergate affair distracted and disturbed investors. It may be noted that when the stock market stopped reacting to the news of these unfavorable factors an important signal was being given that the market was groping for a bottom. When the market stopped selling off on an increase in the banks' prime rate, the signal was particularly significant. Characteristic of a market bottom area, investors were ignoring price-earnings ratios and continued to sell secondary stocks until they provided a satisfactory yield.

Even though confidence-building factors are present in the stock market, money is still needed to move the market, or various sectors of it. The entire market, of course, does not necessarily move at the same time. Various sectors of the market can get out of line, and the laggard sector can make up for lost time while the rest of the market remains relatively stable. Most of the indicators of diminishing demand are concerned with monetary factors. The indicators of a reduced potential for demand include the following:

1. A slowdown in the rate of growth of the money supply (currency in

the hands of the public plus commercial bank demand deposits). The level of stock prices has to be influenced by the amount of money available to buy stocks. The increase in the rate of growth of the money supply is bullish for stock prices; conversely, a decrease is bearish. The lead time between changes in the rate of growth of the money supply and the stock market can vary considerably. Changes can be anticipated to a large extent. For example, when the money supply is growing at an excessive rate and inflationary pressures are increasing, some slowing of the growth of the money supply can be expected. This condition was present at the end of 1968 before the sharp market decline of 1969-70. Signals of a slowing of the growth of the money supply may be seen in moves by the Federal Reserve to increase the cost of money, and to reduce speculation in the stock market. Increases in the Federal Reserve discount rate and increases in margin requirements are such straws in the winds. The 1973 market decline was foreshadowed by both an increase in the Federal Reserve discount rate and a rise in margin requirements. Frequently, the Federal Reserve discount rate will follow the commercial banks' prime rate, as it did in 1973. Higher interest rates, in fact, were used as an instrument of policy to help moderate the economic boom. The stock market seldom rises when interest rates are rising. In 1973, investors became so conditioned to respond to higher interest rates and inflation that spot news of higher food prices, sharp jumps in commodity futures, weaknesses in the dollar abroad, increases in the free market price of gold, and deficits in merchandise trade and in the country's balance of payments would send the market lower.

2. The cash reserves of institutions are relatively low. More than half of the volume on the New York Stock Exchange can be attributed to institutions. The buying of the institutions such as pension funds, commercial banks, and insurance companies, however, tends to be concentrated in stocks of the larger, better-known companies. Mutual funds are more flexible in their investment policies, depending on the type of mutual fund, but by and large they also require large capitalization and liquidity to enable them to buy and sell large blocks of stocks without disturbing the market too much. Institutions also like the larger companies because their earnings are more predictable and growth trends are more likely to be sustainable if they have dominant positions in growth industries. The cash reserves of institutions tend to be relatively low after a long market rise since the excess reserves accumulated after major market declines are dissipated after months of buying.

3. Overseas demand for domestic common stocks has been at a high level for some time. Overseas investors have the entire free world in which

to choose in placing their investment funds. They tend to avoid these countries which are having economic problems and to favor countries whose economies are doing well. Countries whose currencies are weak and could be devalued are also usually avoided. In 1973 foreign investors shunned U.S. common stocks because of U.S. balance of payments deficits, a recent devaluation, and the fear that another dollar devaluation would occur.

4. Investors' credit balances are relatively low. Credit balances are as much a reflection of the market cycle as they are one of the contributing causes. As the stock market rises, investors use up their credit balances buying stocks and at some point they have relatively little in the way of credit balances to make new stock purchases. All stock groups are not affected equally, however. The public is the major buyer of secondary stocks, and once the public stops buying, this group is hurt the most.

5. Margin debt is relatively high. As the market climbs, investors become more and more enthusiastic and expand their buying on credit. At some point, however, investors are reluctant to assume more debt and the impetus to higher stock prices from this source is lost.

6. The short interest ratio (the ratio of the short interest to the average daily volume) is relatively low. The short interest's impact on the market is determined to a large extent by the amount of the average daily volume. After a long market rise, investors are no longer confident that stocks are going to decline and are less eager to sell short (by this time many short-sellers have been badly burned, also). A low short interest ratio means there is less reserve buying power relative to the volume in the form of potential covering of short positions.

Be on Your Guard When the Stage
Is Set for Profit-Taking

The final stage in the top area is the one in which investors are ready to nail down their profits. You have to keep in mind, when you are dealing with the stock market, that many investors do not buy to hold indefinitely. Many, if not most, investors fully intend to realize their profits at some point in the future. Investors who follow the investment strategy of buying undervalued stocks and selling them when they are fully valued (the strategy recommended by this book) are especially apt to sell their stocks when the opportunity appears ripe even though nothing seems to be going wrong with the individual company. Popularity of so many stocks rests on fads which have a way of running their course. In other cases, stocks may benefit from a major earnings development, but once that is behind them unless there is something else new, investors tend to lose interest and sell. These stocks then sink because of neglect and disinterest. It also can be said that stock market cycles are functions of profit-taking. The mere presence of large profits in the market will invite profit-taking, which, in turn, can precipitate serious market declines. Investors tend to be sheep-like and sell when others sell.

Some investors, and particularly institutions, who buy the so-called "one-decision" growth stocks (stocks of companies whose earnings are expected to continue to grow even during recessions) may have a longer time horizon, but even they may sell if the risk becomes too great relative to the potential. Who holds the stocks determines to a large extent how stocks will react to unfavorable news. Traders are apt to quickly dump stocks they hold if something goes wrong. Institutions, which are large holders of quality growth stocks, do not sell so quickly if they are convinced problems are temporary. The problems that frequently trigger selling in stocks, however, are often relatively unpredictable. Also, of course, the seriousness of problems cannot always be discerned immediately.

The setting for profit-taking is indicated as follows:

1. A substantial rise has taken place in the DJIA over an extended period of time. After such a prolonged rise in the DJIA, the odds against the investor have increased considerably. At such a time stocks may still look deceptively cheap based on predicted earnings, and there are often no clouds seen on the horizon. Nevertheless, the investor has to be wary of being beguiled by the bullish day-to-day action of stocks. Even though broad stock indices may take months to top out, and quality growth stocks may continue to rise, many individual stocks could turn down sharply. If you get trapped into buying at the top it is awfully hard to get back in step with the market. Anyone who bought, for example, during the four-month period from December, 1972 through February, 1973 when investors were very bullish would have had a difficult time making any money for some months. (See Figure 4.) Conversely, the best way to be in step with the market, and to get off to a good start in tripling your funds, is to buy when the market has had a good decline and investors are generally bearish. Those who bought during the market pessimism from October through November, 1971 were in a position to realize good profits once investors became bullish later in the stock market cycle. You can see the hint of a suggestion here that interpreting the general market atmosphere properly is an important path to stock market profits.

2. The economy is operating at a high percentage of capacity. Not only is there a danger that the next major move of the economy will be down, but when the economy is operating near capacity the surge in profits is likely to

be behind the economy at this point. Also, at high operating rates corporations often find earnings hurt by production bottlenecks, lack of skilled labor, shortage of materials, and overtime.

3. Several industries are running at or near peak rates. This economic indicator is very similar to the one just discussed. The point being made here is that individual industries may reach their peak operating rates at different times, and the stocks of companies in these industries may anticipate these peaks at varied times. If the economy becomes less cyclical under increased government management, it may be characterized more by a rolling readjustment among industries than by changes in the overall economic level.

4. Interest rates are at a relatively low level. The Federal Reserve is becoming more and more an instrument for controlling the economy and inflationary pressures. The bottom of the market in 1966 was marked by a reversal of the Federal Reserve from a tight money policy to an expansionary policy. The top of the market at the end of 1968 occurred concurrently with a sharp slowing in the growth rate of the money supply. The bottom of the decline in 1970 coincided with a bottoming out of interest rates. The 1973 decline was largely attributed to expectations of tighter money and to higher interest rates as a result of inflationary expectations and an expansion of the economy. Interest rates, indeed, climbed to historic heights. It does appear that the interest rate cycle is now having a very important influence on the stock market cycle since monetary policy has become so important in controlling inflation.

5. Practically all the foreseeable good news is out. How the stock market reacts to news is telling it as it is. There is no guessing. The market is showing how much the market has (or has not) already anticipated the news in real time. When stocks do not respond to excellent earnings reports, for example, the short term outlook cannot be considered bullish. The situation may be particularly bearish if the economy has had a substantial recovery and the main surge in corporate profits is behind it. Regarding individual stocks, if the stocks are believed to be essentially fads and fashions, or the major earnings development may have occurred, then failure to respond to good news is ignored at the investor's peril.

6. A majority of the investment advisory services are bullish. This indicator follows the "contrary opinion" approach that says that when the overwhelming majority are bullish, stocks may be near at least an intermediate top and when investors are mostly bearish the market may be near an intermediate bottom. Investment advisory services are considered more sophisticated than most investors, but they are subject to mistakes under emotional stress, also. Probably the most important reason, however, is that

after a long period of bullishness investors have used up most of their cash reserves and have already bought the stocks they wanted to buy. Conversely, after a long period of bearishness, most investors who are willing to sell have sold their stock. It is also a fact that investors usually expect trends to continue until they change.

A Market Top Can Be Recognized

Once the investor is convinced he is in a top area he should start looking for specific signs that the DJIA and individual stocks are topping out. You should be careful that you have seen the signs of a top area before you expect to see signs of a significant top. It is possible that you might see some topping out indications which turn out to be an intermediate reaction in a major uptrend unless the criteria of a top area are met. The most dependable sign of a top of the DJIA is the failure of the DJIA to rally on further favorable economic news, particularly good corporate earnings. The lack of market response is particularly significant if the market had been responding positively to a certain type of economic news and then failed to react to more of the same type of news. In 1971, the first indication that the automotive group had topped was noted when the auto stocks no longer rallied on increased auto sales and earnings. They rallied in 1972, but were unable to reach the peaks of 1971. The action of the auto stocks was puzzling at the time for it was hard to believe that the auto stocks could have seen their peaks while the economy appeared so strong. It later became evident that the auto stocks had anticipated the top in the DJIA by many months. Another coincident indicator is a "blowoff" of the DJIA or of individual stocks. The DJIA has a sharp rally on relatively high volume followed by a selloff, closing near the low of the day. This blowoff often marks the exact peak of the DJIA or of individual stocks.

Most of the market indicators, however, will not provide a positive indication until the top has been passed. These major indicators include the following:

1. The DJIA moves below a major ascending channel (see Figure 4). The penetration of a major trendline on the downside is not conclusive in itself, but it can be a significant piece of evidence that a top has been seen.

2. The six-month price momentum (current price compared with the price six months ago) turns negative. This signal is not infallible. Quality growth stocks may well break below their price level of six months ago during general market weakness and yet recover to new highs. Nevertheless, the market and situations which show weakness over a period of six months are definitely suspect. The six-month momentum deterioration of speculations and fads and fashions are ignored at the investor's peril.

3. The DJIA has decisively penetrated the 200-day moving average on the downside. This indicator which covers a span of approximately six months is somewhat similar to the six-month momentum indicator. What it reveals is that the short term strength has turned weaker than the six-month strength. It can give false signals and should be confirmed by fundamental considerations.

4. The "neckline" (bottom trendline) of a head and shoulder pattern is violated (see Figure 4). This is one of the most treacherous of the chart patterns and should be confirmed by fundamental considerations.

5. The market has been exposed to all the favorable economic news that can be foreseen. The market should have had a look at the potential earning power of the economy at full employment. The economy should also be operating at a high level of capacity. If shortages of materials and skilled labor start showing up, the scenario is even more convincing that the economy has pretty much exhausted its upside potential.

On the Downside of the Market

You will find it very difficult to accept the fact when the stock market has finally passed its peak. Economic conditions are usually very good and there is little in the way of concrete economic evidence to cause you to believe the market is ready to turn down even with the aforementioned market indicators calling for caution. Unfortunately, market indicators are not only infallible, but are subject to misinterpretation. The perceiving observer might note that the economy is running at such a high growth rate or level of capacity that there is not much potential for further earnings gains. He may even note that some sectors, such as inventories, autos, capital spending, consumer durable spending, or consumer installment debt, may be running at abnormally high rates, or the money supply may be increasing at an unsustainable rate, inflation may be increasing and interest rates rising. These signs do not always mean a recession, and no one can be sure they will produce more than just a business slowdown. However, in conjunction with the technical indicators such signs would call for caution. Peculiarly enough, market analysts who suggest that the market may be turning down are subject to much hostility. Investors tend to feel that the very mention of a downturn might bring one on and reduce the value of their holdings, rather than being thankful for an opportunity to get out of the market and to cut short any losses.

The usual reaction to the initial stage of a decline, as was indicated, is disbelief. Investors usually believe they are seeing a buying opportunity in the reaction and are ready to buy once the selling appears to have run its course. Some investors who may have sold near the top may even think the decline is over on the first selloff and re-establish their positions. A substantial market decline can actually have several false market rallies, as you can see on any long-term chart of the popular market indices. It takes a considerable amount of discipline on your part to wait out a market decline before buying. With each rally the tendency is to believe that stocks are going to get away. Usually, when the final bottom has been made the indications are fairly clear and there is ample time to take positions before the major move is made. If you resign yourself to staying out of the market for at least six months once you are convinced that a significant decline is in progress, you can fight off the temptation to get back in the market too early. (Some investors think they can take advantages of some of the sharp rallies in a bear market for a quick profit, but usually they will be unable to get out in time before the market sells off again.) There is no rule regarding how far ahead the market anticipates an end of a recession or a peaking of interest rates. The prudent course is to wait at least until the economy has slowed down considerably or interest rates have held at or passed their peaks before buying. It is very easy to underestimate the heights to which interest rates can rise. In the 1973 market decline, it was widely believed that the prime rate would peak at 8-8½ percent, but it did not peak until considerably above that level. Investors who acted on the wrong estimate of how far interest rates would rise found it costly. It is also possible that the economy could have had a severe recession, and by getting back into the market too early the investor could have been trapped. The 1973 decline was not marked by a collapse of stocks across the board initially. Quality growth stocks held up well, but speculative, secondary, over-the-counter, and American Stock Exchange stocks experienced severe selloffs. Later, quality growth stocks also suffered sharp declines.

In a Bottom Area Investors Are Wrung-out Emotionally

A bottom area (stocks may go lower, but are expected to eventually recover to higher levels) is characterized by emotional excesses, just as a top area is characterized by speculative excesses. Characteristics which you can expect to see in a bottom area include widespread bearish sentiment, a great deal of unfavorable news in the market, all the foreseeable pessimistic news is known to investors, a majority of the financial services are bearish, and extensive deterioration in secondary stocks has occurred. During the 1973 decline the pessimism reached the point where some commentators were predicting the collapse of Western Civilization as a result of inflationary pressures and the years of easy-credit policies of Western countries. There is no doubt that modern states are built on a mountain of debt and consumer confidence is critical. A chain reaction of bank failures in Europe and the U.S. is not impossible. If all creditors and consumers panicked at the same time there is not much doubt the structure of modern society would collapse. Such a convergence of events, however, is not predictable and also highly unlikely. In the latter half of 1973 there were widespread worries of high interest rates, a credit crunch where credit would not be available at any price, runaway inflation, and an economic recession. There was no way of being sure, of course, that the possibilities investors were worried about would not be exceeded by actual events and the market would turn down sharply. At some point the investor has to assume that the U.S. will survive and that what investors and economists are worried about will not actually happen, and that the potential exceeds the risk. If the "worst case" situation does occur, there would be no place to hide in any event.

In the lower part of the bottom area there are indications of a slowing of downside momentum. The volume of the American Stock Exchange is relatively low compared with the New York Stock Exchange volume. The New York Stock Exchange volume is itself low. When investors are acutely conscious of economic problems, those who are not long-term investors have already sold what they intend to sell, and since most investors are afraid to buy, the market volume as a result of these two influences tends to remain low. Another indication of at least an intermediate bottom is given when stocks break out of descending channels. Whether this indication is a sign of the final bottom has to be judged in the context of how unfavorable the economy, interest rates, and inflation are expected to become. Normally, stocks will run into profit-taking after breaking out of a descending channel and spend some time absorbing profit-taking and building a base. During the latter part of 1973, secondary issues were breaking out of descending channels and strongly suggesting an intermediate bottoming out of the market. Profit-taking, however, set in immediately since investors were still skeptical.

To summarize, the important indicators of a bottom area would include:

1. Bearish sentiment is widespread.

2. The market has been exposed to all the unfavorable economic and other news that is expected.

3. Interest rates have had a sharp rise and appeared close to peaking out.

4. The DJIA and Standard and Poor's composite indices have declined for at least six months.

5. The volume of both the ASE and NYSE is holding at a relatively low level.

6. The DJIA and Standard and Poor's composite indices have broken out of their descending channels.

7. Individual stocks have broken out of their descending channels and have had rallies.

8. An abundance of good values are available.

9. The utility index appears to be bottoming out.

Knowing When You Have Seen the Bottom of a Market

In all honesty, there is no sure way of knowing whether a market has seen a final bottom or just an intermediate bottom, or of knowing how long it might go sideways before a new major uptrend may begin. Technical indicators are not particularly reliable beyond the short term, so the market outlook depends to a large extent on the prospects for an economic upturn and an improvement in corporate profits. Nevertheless, if you have correctly assessed the market to be in a bottom area, the length and percentage of the decline has been significant, and the market has been exposed to practically all the unfavorable economic news expected, the possibility of a final bottoming of the decline is increased. (If the economy has actually deteriorated or interest rates have topped out, there is added insurance.) An inverted head and shoulders chart pattern of the popular averages spread over a period of several months is usually characteristic of a bottom. The penetration of the 200-day moving average line on the upside is also a good indication a bottom has been seen. (See Figure 4, November-December, 1971 period.) A peaking of the odd-lot short selling, the new lows on the New York Stock Exchange, and of the volume of the declines on the NYSE, and a bottoming on the new highs and of the volume of the advances on the NYSE can be very helpful in marking the bottom of a decline. Practically the reverse of these indicators can be used in determining tops. (See Figure 5.) Note how a vertical line can be drawn through the peaks and bottoms of the indicators. The odd-lot short sales, new lows, and the net declines and volume of declines on the NYSE do not differentiate between intermediate bottoms and final bottoms, except for the amount of the volume and the degree of the oversold condition. How "oversold" a market becomes (how much and how long the selling takes place) depends on the temperament of the market. Conditions change with each major decline. A rounding-type bottom also will probably result in a less extreme oversold condition than a "V"-type bottom which may result from some dramatic news.

Summarizing, the important indicators which suggest that a market bottom has been seen include the following:

1. The indicators of a bottom area have been seen.

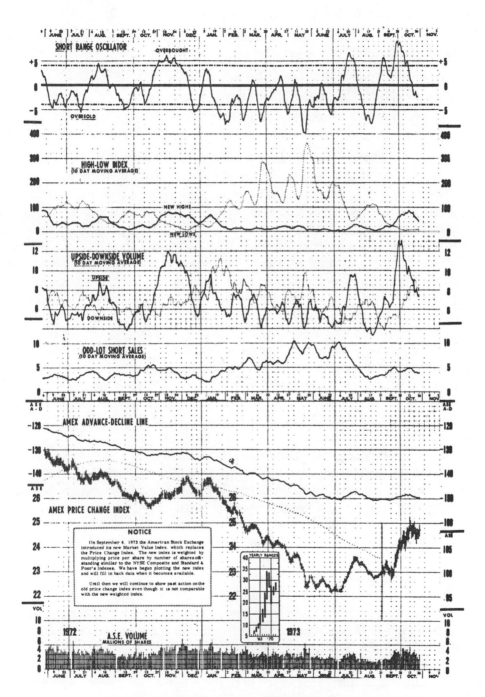

Figure 5.   Chart Courtesy of Trendline, a division of Standard & Poor's Corporation, 345 Hudson Street, New York, New York 10014.

2. Interest rates have topped out, or nearly so.

3. Inverted head and shoulder chart patterns of the popular averages and of individual stocks have formed.

4. New lows on the NYSE have peaked.

5. New highs on the NYSE have bottomed out.

6. Net declines on the NYSE have bottomed out.

Market Indicators That Signal When the Stage Is Being Set for New Buying

It may be a truism that stocks go down because they went up and go up because they went down. What I am saying is that when stocks have had a rise investors tend to take profits and when stocks have had a sharp decline investors tend to buy the bargains. Perhaps the stock market cycle is just that simple. Cash reserves of institutions are relatively high after market declines because they either sold near the top or refrained from investing inflowing funds in the market when the decline began. Many individual investors are in the same situation. Some investors, of course, are always out-of-step with the market. They did not sell when stocks were high and thus do not have funds to buy when stocks are low. There are plenty of investors, however, who did take profits when stocks had sharp rises and who are in a position to buy when stocks are cheap. Indicators of the potential for increased demand by individual investors include a relatively high level of credit balances and a relatively low level of debit balances. The short interest ratio often is relatively high, also. Usually investors get increasingly bearish the lower stocks go, rather than more bullish, which would be more logical, and the temptation to sell short is almost overwhelming. The high short interest, in fact, is what often leads market rallies off bear market bottoms.

Rounding-type bottoms are influenced primarily by high interest rates. They are usually not characterized by high short interest ratios since the gradual rise in interest rates is not dramatic enough to give traders confidence to sell short. Another indicator likely to accompany a rounding bottom is an abundance of good historical values, although the entire market may not be historically cheap. Quality growth stocks, for example, may not be historically cheap, but many secondary stocks may be selling at the lowest price-earnings ratios in decades, as was the case in 1973-1974. Another sign that the market is bottoming out is a turning up of the Dow Jones Utility Index after a long decline. A bottoming out of the utility index may be a precursor of a topping out of the interest rates. In these times of inflation and high interest rates, the interest rate cycle appears to be influencing stock prices as much as anything. The bond and stock market cycles actually appear to be coinciding, whereas in the past they were divergent.

Inverted head and shoulders-type formations are found in both rounding and "V"-type bottoms. Selectivity is more evident in rounding-type bottoms since a story or unusual value is needed to attract investors' attention. Stocks which run into problems can still experience earnings declines, however. During the time the DJIA is bottoming out many individual stocks will be breaking out of descending channels and rallying. These rallies, however, are likely to be short-lived since there are many skeptics who are anxious to sell into these rallies. The lack of convincing economic news to bring in buying and stave off further selling is what shapes the rounding bottom. Interest rates are also likely to hold at relatively high levels, rather than decline sharply. The "V"- or selling-climax-type of bottom is usually characterized by some dramatic turn of events, such as a sudden change in policy by the Federal Reserve, as occurred in 1966, and also in 1970. The 1970 bottom was precipitated by the Penn Central Transportation Company bankruptcy, of course. In the old days when stocks could be bought on thin margins, wholesale margin calls were responsible for many selling-climax bottoms.

If psychological factors that have discouraged investors from buying or provided an excuse for selling, such as the Watergate affair which figured in the 1973 decline, tend to lose their impact, and overseas investors regain their confidence in the U.S. stock market, the stage has been set for a better tone to the market. The U.S. devaluations finally started taking effect in 1973 to help improve the confidence of both domestic and overseas investors. However, the sharp increase in the price of petroleum, which is causing balance of payment problems in all the Western nations, and continued high rates of inflation in the U.S. and other industralized Free World countries are among the most serious problems that have to be overcome before investor confidence can be expected to return.

Summarizing, the important indicators that signal when the stage is being set for new buying are:

1. Cash reserves of institutions are at a relatively high level.

2. Credit balances of individuals are relatively high.

3. Margin debt is relatively low.

4. Overseas investors are developing confidence in the U.S. stock market.

Being Aware of Emotional Excesses
Is Half the Battle

Many investors are always looking for that one magic index which will infallibly tell them when to buy and when to sell—a purely mechanical device which requires no thinking or skill and will unerringly lead them to a fortune in stock market profits. There are indices that can be helpful, but they always seem to let the investor down at the critical time. Whenever I discuss market indicators I always think of the analyst who had developed an index of his own. At important market junctures, he would confide that his index made a little "wiggle." He would never say which way it would wiggle, and he was always very secretive about the components of his index. The interest in this analyst's index was most surprising to me and was something of a commentary on how investors want to get something for nothing, or at least for a minimum amount of effort. This desire seems to be at the bottom of the eternal longing for a single index to call turns in the stock market.

The performance of an index may seem just short of miraculous to an investor who has been participating in a particular market rally or market decline, and in the decline every sell recommendation may have worked out without fail, and similar results may have been achieved on the buy side during the uptrend. What the investor may not have realized is that as long as an index is consistent in its signals it will be right while the trend continues intact. The real test, however, is how well the index catches the turning points. In my opinion, there is no single index that is superior to the indicators that are discussed in the chapter, or that can replace the trained judgment of the investor.

I have listed quite a few indicators in this chapter. Most of them are associated with human behavior, economics, and supply-demand factors. An understanding of these indicators, in my opinion, will enable you to forecast dangerous markets and markets of opportunity consistently. The stock market does not move willy nilly; it is shaped by broad forces set in motion by the economy and investor-confidence factors. The indicators described in this chapter gauge these forces. You may have read about some esoteric indicators which I have not included in my list. Admittedly, there are a great many indicators in addition to the ones I have described, but it is highly improbable that these indicators will add anything to your market forecasting ability. Many market indicators duplicate one another or are influenced by the same confidence, economic and/or supply-demand factors. Thus, 50 indicators are not likely to be more helpful than the limited number of indicators in this chapter.

I will even go further than saying the indicators in this chapter are sufficient. Although I have no way of proving it, I think you can be very effective in recognizing dangerous markets and markets of opportunity in most cases just by becoming aware of emotional excesses. Top areas of a market are noted by the pervasive optimism in which the favorable market outlook becomes a general topic of public discussion, the widespread expectation that stock prices will continue to go up indefinitely, the feeling that you have to buy quickly before stocks get away, and the belief that regardless of the price paid somebody else will buy them from you at a higher price. Bottom areas are characterized by the universal pessimism regarding the stock market outlook, the general public talk conceiving the difficulties besetting the market and the economy, and the fear that you have to sell before stocks go lower. The market is full of "air pockets" in which stocks sell off sharply on any adverse news. Although some of the indicators may help you in gauging the degree of emotion in the market, they are not needed to permit you to recognize the signs of top and bottom areas just described. The emotional excesses are not a precise indicator of the exact tops and bottoms, but if you observe when the market stops responding to good news (in a market uptrend) and to unfavorable news (in the market downtrend), you can do a good job in calling tops and bottoms. If you take the effort to understand the economy, inflationary pressures, and economic excesses, and watch the additional indicators we have described in this chapter you should be able to pinpoint major tops and bottoms with a great deal of effectiveness.

3

Placing Stocks in Groups
Can Aid in Using
the Techno-Fundamental Approach

Commonly-Used Categories in Classifying Stocks

Investors, including institutions, tend to put stocks in categories or groups when making investment decisions. Not only is it easier to make investment decisions about a limited number of categories than about numerous individual stocks, but there is some logic involved in this approach. Economic and market forces tend to affect all the stocks in the category or group in the same way. Thus, if the investor has analyzed an industry thoroughly he can automatically apply his analysis to all the stocks in the industry without any additional work. Of course, there may be some stocks in a group which, for some reason, can outperform the group, or are not affected equally by the economic and market forces. Unfortunately, these stocks are usually lumped together with the others and given the same treatment. As the old Wall Street adage goes, "When the paddy wagon rolls up, they take all the girls, the good as well as the bad."

A great many different groups can be used in classifying stocks. Classification by industry is usually the first step in analyzing stocks. Most companies in an industry will be affected by the factors that affect the industry broadly. Sometimes the factors will even cut across industries. For example, an increase in the minimum wage would affect all those industries which have a large labor content in their overhead. During a period when interest rates are rising investors tend to sell the stocks of all companies which are hurt by higher interest rates. The management of a company may have anticipated the higher interest rates and taken the necessary precautions to protect the company; nevertheless, likely as not, investors will sell the stock of this company as readily as the stock of a company that was completely unprepared. As my old professor once said, "The uninformed dollar in the market is just as important as the informed dollar." The stage of the market cycle might suggest the grouping of stocks. Toward the end of a bull market, low-priced, over-the-counter, and American Stock Exchange stocks might be in vogue. On the other hand, in a bear market investors tend to shun this group as too risky. Perfectly good stocks whose earnings are continuing in an uptrend are sold indiscriminately just because they belong to a group which has become the fashion to sell.

Stocks are also classified as to whether companies derive their demand from consumer spending or capital spending. Consumer spending can be broken down into stocks benefiting from durable goods and soft-goods spending and spending for services. In times of national emergencies when funds may flow from the private sector to the public sector, investors are concerned with classifying stocks according to these two categories. The multinational corporations can be considered a separate group. International trade agreements and regulations governing the operations of multinational companies can have an impact on all multinational companies. At this writing there is a bill in Congress to increase the taxes of multinational companies. At present, corporations do not pay taxes on foreign earnings which are not remitted. Among other things, the bill would impose taxes on these earnings even if they are not remitted.

Five Main Categories of Stocks
for Market Strategy

Categorizing stocks can be of considerable assistance to you in organizing your investment strategy. Certainly, knowing which groups are popular or unpopular and being able to recognize which group or groups stocks are associated within investors' minds is one of the major keys to successful investing. It is usually a futile exercise to keep fighting the market and buying unpopular issues (even if they appear cheap), unless there is a good reason to believe a change for the better is coming. It is usually far better to buy stocks which have been moving upward than to buy stocks which have been declining.

In addition to the groups already discussed, stocks can be grouped according to the nature of the company and their rating as investments. Such groups cut across industries, and various other categories, and can be especially useful in developing your investment strategy. The five groups I have selected are: 1) quality growth stocks, 2) cyclical stocks, 3) undervalued stocks, 4) speculative stocks, and 5) secondary growth stocks. Each group has its own investment characteristics, its own following in the investment community, and its own peculiar behavior in the various stages of the stock market cycle. An understanding of these characteristics will improve your understanding of the stocks that fall into these groups. Institutions are the major purchasers of quality growth stocks. Some institutions have a long-term time horizon and are willing to buy richly-priced growth stocks if the earnings have a high "visibility," and are believed to be sustainable. In view of the substantial investment information these institutions have access to, they do not panic easily if a temporary setback occurs as long as the basics still remain intact. Institutions tend to have a constant inflow of funds and can provide continual support. Quality growth stocks may be favored in periods of uncertainty over stocks whose earnings are closely tied in the economy. The favorable earnings record of quality growth stocks is well-known, of course, and the price-earnings ratios have already reflected their prospects to a large extent. Capital appreciation may not increase any more rapidly than earnings growth, and it could grow less if the price-earnings ratio tends to contract. The fact that institutions have such long holdings of quality growth stocks imparts risk to the group. If institutions should become disenchanted with a stock, their selling could put considerable pressure on it. By and large, the best time to purchase quality growth stocks is during periods of general market weakness.

Cyclical stocks present their own peculiar problems to investors. Although many have a secular growth rate at least equal to the historic 4 percent growth rate of the economy, earnings can nevertheless fluctuate widely. Some cyclical stocks may be influenced by the broad economic cycle and others may have their own cycle independent of the economy. Cyclical stocks often are issues of companies that have large fixed costs. Capacity, inventory, and pricing conditions in the industry usually have the greatest impact on cyclical stock prices. Investors who wish to make money in cyclicals have to have an exceptionally good sense of timing and the discipline to follow through on their judgment. What makes it difficult for investors to make money in cyclical stocks—and also which provides an exceptional opportunity for knowledgeable investors—is that cyclical stocks tend to anticipate earnings, sometimes many months in advance, and should be bought when the news is as bad as it is likely to get and sold when earnings and economic activity may be running at peak rates for the foreseeable future.

Undervalued stocks offer some of the best capital appreciation possibilities of any group. Stocks can become undervalued for a variety of reasons. The price-earnings ratio may be low in relation to the price-earnings ratios of other stocks with similar sustainable earnings-growth rates, or the total return, the current yield plus the estimated annual capital gains (assumed to reflect the estimated earnings growth rate) may be high in comparison with the total returns of most other stocks or with the return provided by alternative investments, such as bonds. Too, stocks can be undervalued in other ways that may not be as apparent as in the foregoing examples. A stock may be undervalued in relation to the share of the market the company has the potential of commanding. It may be undervalued because of temporarily depressed earnings in relation to potential earning power. It also may be undervalued in relation to the company's assets. The book value is not a good measure of the liquidating value of an industrial company since plant and equipment and inventories could be obsolete. (There is also the possibility the liquidating value could be greater than book value because of inflation and rising replacement costs.) If the stock price is less than the net working capital per share (after the deduction of long-term debt) it would likely be considered undervalued, although the earnings growth rate is still the primary determinant of stock prices of the "going concern" concept in which it is assumed companies will remain in existence indefinitely. The undervalued approach exemplifies the time-honored method of making money in the stock market of buying undervalued situations and selling them when they become reasonably priced or overpriced.

There is a great deal of truth in the statement that uncertainty creates stock values. The theory is that when all the information about a company is known by all investors, they will have acted on the information and the price of the stock will have discounted it. In practice, the theory is not completely accurate. Investors may place different interpretations on the same information; it is not likely investors will receive the information at the same time; and investors may have varying time horizons. One investor may be trying to maximize his annual return on capital while another may be investing for the longer term. You should be aware that it is illegal to use material information gained from insiders in buying and selling stocks. Under the Securities Exchange Commission's regulations people who have special access to corporate information cannot take advantage of this information in their stock transactions. It is generally true that to achieve exceptional capital gains, above-average risks have to be taken. When uncertainty of events exist, a stock has to be considered a speculation. Speculations vary in the degree of risk involved. Outright speculations are nothing more than gambling. The company may hit it big or it could go bankrupt. You want better odds than that, or putting it in other terms, a more favorable risk-reward ratio. The ideal speculation is a stock that is reasonably priced on fundamentals, but if the events work out as hoped the stock could have substantial appreciation. You should be on your guard, however, since it is easy to be mistaken about whether a stock has already reflected the speculative potential and whether it will sell off if the event does not occur.

The strategies for buying and selling speculative stocks are peculiar to this class of stocks. Knowing the stage the stock market is in is important. There are always traders who are willing to buy exceptional speculations in any stage of the market, but usually it is best to confine purchases of speculations to the first three stages. In a bear market speculative stocks usually come under the greatest selling pressure. In bull markets, speculative stocks may be in special demand. Speculations may also be fads and fashions. Fads and fashions have a way of building up in the stock market and then fading out. Demand may taper off, styles may change, traders may have bought for a major earnings development and take profits on the news. It is not easy to recognize when fads are running out, but when you are in speculations you have to be aware of the possibility. Since the earnings of speculations, by definition, are relatively unpredictable and may have been erratic in the past, it is not a bad strategy to sell speculations when they have had a good rally and everything looks favorable on the theory that events could take a turn for the worst.

There is no sharp dividing line between the secondary growth stocks and the quality growth, undervalued and speculative stocks. The main differences between secondary growth stocks and quality growth stocks include the size of the company, dominance of their markets, and the nature of the industry. Quality growth stocks are usually stocks of companies with substantial sales and large capitalizations that have a dominant position in a recognized growth industry. Secondary growth stocks are more likely to be stocks of smaller companies that are less seasoned and without a dominant position in their industry. The industry itself may have less economic justification than those of the quality growth stocks. Undervalued stocks, in some instances, may be growth situations, although their special attraction is not their growth rates as much as the undervalued condition. Once the stocks have returned to a normal valuation, their prospects for capital gains have diminished considerably. Speculative stocks may also be growth situations, but they are mainly characterized by their dependence on relatively unpredictable events. Secondary growth stocks with equal or greater growth rates than the quality growth stocks normally will have lower price-earnings ratios. The main reason is that institutions tend to support the quality growth stocks. There is also lower visibility in the earnings of secondary growth stocks and less confidence in their sustainability. Secondary growth stocks can work out well in most markets, but they usually are best bought when investor confidence is at a low level and the public has withdrawn from the market. At such times secondary growth stocks are depressed because of lack of buying interest and a general fear of the market. Once investor confidence returns, these secondary growth stocks can show sharp gains just returning to reasonable values. Secondary stocks are best sold when you believe the signs indicate the market is in for a major decline (discussed in Chapter 2) since they, as just noted, are among the most heavily sold stocks in a market decline.

Trying to Pinpoint the Value of a Common Stock

Trying to determine the exact value of a common stock is like pursuing the will-o'-the-wisp. There is just no way to tell with any certainty what a stock is worth. The more cynical would say that a stock is worth what the market says it is worth. The scientific school would pull out their slide rules and plug in their regression formulae and announce with finality that the stock is worth such and such. In the real world of common stocks, the truth lies somewhere in between these two extremes. The market itself is very fickle, emotional, and faddish. In periods of pessimism stocks may sell far below their "intrinsic value" just because investors are afraid to buy and are easily scared into selling. In periods of optimism, stocks may sell far above their intrinsic value because investors are reluctant to sell and are anxious to buy before stocks go higher. Investor attitudes, you can see, are all important in the stock market. The scientific approach also has its drawbacks. The basic scientific approach is to determine the present value of a future stream of dividend income. Present value computation involves two major assumptions: the future dividends that will be paid by the company and the rate of discount to be applied to these dividends. The results cannot be any more accurate than the factors that go into the equation, however, and both these variables are very uncertain.

We can see that arriving at an accurate valuation of common stocks is not easy. Nevertheless, we do not have to abandon the field completely. The investor still has tools at his disposal to arrive at a valuation which is very helpful in making investment decisions. This system is discussed in the next section.

How Knowing the Theoretical Basis for Evaluating Common Stocks Can Help You

As has been discussed, there is no practical way of pinpointing the value of a common stock. This statement is particularly true for the short term when psychology and investor confidence have such a large influence. Even though there are limitations on the accuracy on the valuation of common stock, even a rough approximation of the value can be very useful. Except during periods of dire emergency when liquidating values and dividend yields take on greater importance, stocks are valued on expected earnings and potential dividends. Since stockholders own all the earnings of a company, investors tend to assume that earnings indicate potential dividends whether they receive them or not. In fact, corporations may often earn a higher return on the earnings it does not pay out than the investor could. In some instances, of course, liberal accounting practices of companies, inventory profits, or inadequate depreciation may weaken the tie between earnings and potential dividends. Investors will tend to pay less for stocks when they are uncertain of the quality of earnings. Values also do not exist in a vacuum. Alternative investment opportunities, whether bonds, real estate, or short term securities, can compete for funds and influence what investors will pay for common stocks.

Getting down to actual practical methods of evaluating stocks, the historical approach is probably the most widely used. The relationship of the price of a stock to its earnings (the last 12 months earnings) over a period of the last ten years can provide a good gauge of the range within which the price-earnings ratio might fluctuate. Thus, when the price-earnings ratio is near the bottom of the range the stock would be considered undervalued and when it is near the top of the range it is amply priced. In evaluating a stock with this method, however, you must consider how much conditions may have changed during the period under review. If the earnings growth has slowed considerably, the stock would not be expected to command the price-earnings ratios of former days. General investment conditions would make a difference, too. If interest rates and competing bond yields appear to be on a permanently higher level than before, some downward adjustment in price-earnings ratios would be expected (to be discussed in the next section). This method, also, does not lend itself to evaluating emerging growth companies or speculative stocks whose earnings may be erratic and relatively unpredictable.

Another method of evaluating stocks is to compare the price-earnings ratios with those of similar companies or other companies in the same group. Supposedly, all the companies in an industry would have much the same problems and competition, and tend to grow, at approximately the same rate as the industry. Allowance would have to be made, however, for difference in efficiency and industry position. Institutions tend to buy the dominant company and the low-cost producers in an industry since in times of economic stress they will usually do better than the less competitive, high-cost producers. The stocks of the former companies would be expected to carry highr price-earnings ratios than the stocks of the latter companies, even if their earnings growth rates were about the same in good times. The price-earnings ratios of individual stocks can also be related to popular stock market indices, such as the Dow Jones Industrial Average or the Standard and Poor's composite index. This approach automatically makes allowance for the investment environment and compares stocks to an established benchmark. Since individual stocks are more apt to move to excess in relation to a mean than is an entire index of stocks, this approach tends to indicate when stocks are overpriced or depressed. Here again, though, you have to consider whether the fundamentals of the individual stock have changed.

Perhaps the purest and most useful method of evaluating stocks is the absolute method. This approach is concerned only with the estimated earnings average annual growth rate of a company, taking into consideration such parameters as the cyclical nature, predictability, and sustainability of earnings. Given parameters which are approximately the same, stocks with equal earnings growth rates should have the same price-earnings ratios. Differences in price-earnings ratios may then be identified as stemming largely from the emotional attachment of investors or the buying of institutions.

You should readily appreciate by now how difficult it is to say what a stock is worth. Nevertheless, it is still worthwhile to have some realistic system for valuing stocks. On the emotion-tossed investment seas an anchor windward can be very helpful. Not only does a sense of value assist you in recognizing potential gains, but it can also alert you to risks involved. Stocks can still exceed the theoretical computed value both on the upside and on the downside, but if you consistently use value considerations as a guide, your chances of achieving success in investing should be improved. In cases of over-evaluation, even though earnings may be doing well, it may take a continued strong earnings performance just to maintain the current price level. In such cases, any disappointment in earnings could have a very adverse effect on the stock. (If a stock cannot advance much on good earnings reports it may be telling you something.) Thus, even though methods of evaluating common stocks leave much to be desired, they still can have a practical use in helping you triple your money in the stock market.

How to Approximate the Value of Growth Stocks

In my evaluation approach I place stocks in two separate groups: growth stocks and conservative stocks. The growth stocks include stocks whose earnings-per-share growth rates are 6 percent or more annually on the average (although many analysts will not classify stocks as growth situations unless the growth rate is 10 percent or more). Investors who buy growth stocks are buying for capital gains and not dividends, and they actually prefer earnings to be reinvested in the company to increase the growth rate rather than have them paid out as dividends. In the growth stock category, the earnings-growth rate and the price-earnings ratio are the primary considerations in determining value. With regard to conservative stocks, dividends are an important consideration and cannot be ignored in determining value. Investors who buy these stocks want dividend income not only because their investment objective requires income, but they also desire the downside protection the current yield provides for the stock.

As I have already pointed out, interest rates have a significant influence on the prices of common stocks and any system of evaluating stocks should take interest rates into consideration. In the rule-of-thumb system I have devised for evaluating stocks, interest rates play a direct role in computing the price-earnings ratios of growth stocks. Since common stocks compete directly with bonds for investment funds, it only makes sense that the price investors are willing to pay for stocks should be related to what investors are willing to pay for bonds. For example, an 8 percent coupon bond at par has a return of 8 percent and is selling at 12.5 times income. Growth stocks which pay no dividends are dependent entirely on their capital gains for their returns. Capital gains tend to stem from the growth rate of earnings when earnings have settled down to a sustainable rate. Thus, it is only one step to the conclusion that if a bond with a return of 8 percent is worth 12.5 times income, and 8 percent return on common stock from capital gains resulting from an 8 percent annual growth rate in earnings makes the stock also worth 12.5 times earnings (income). The price-earnings ratios associated with various earnings growth rates in the same interest rate environment can be extrapolated. It would follow, for example, that a 16 percent earnings-growth rate would be worth 25 times earnings. This system of evaluating common stock appears to provide a very realistic rule-of-thumb approach to growth-stock evaluation. (Admittedly, there is not a linear relationship between the payout period of a stock and its earning growth rate, but the foregoing approach is still adequate for our purposes.)

In the table in Figure 6, price-earnings ratios were computed for various growth rates under different interest rate conditions. Recognizing the lack of precision that can be attributed to the valuation of common stocks, most of the price-earnings ratios have been rounded off to the nearest multiple of 5 so they can be easier to remember and to use. We also did not include any growth rates over 30 percent since such high growth rates are not likely to be sustainable. Also, when the earnings growth rates approach 6 percent, a tradeoff between the price-earnings ratio and the dividend yield comes into play. The extrapolation process in determining price-earnings ratios does not work among the stocks with relatively low growth rates because the dividend yield (and the total return evaluation approach discussed in the next section) provides support. A bond yield below 6 percent was not included in the table since interest rates are likely to hold above 6 percent in the foreseeable future. If interest rates should fall below 6 percent, historical price-earnings ratios probably would carry more weight. You can also note that in a 7 percent interest rate environment the price-earnings ratio is twice the earnings growth rate. This relationship might well be considered normal. Conservative estimates of earnings growth rates have to be used, of course, since the interest return of quality bonds if fairly reliable. The individual, also, might

Annual Earnings Growth Rate

Annual Earnings Growth Rate	10% Bond Yield	8% Bond Yield	7% Bond Yield	6% Bond Yield
6%	6 P/E	10 P/E	12 P/E	16 P/E
8%	8 P/E	12 P/E	16 P/E	20 P/E
10%	10 P/E	15 P/E	20 P/E	25 P/E
15%	15 P/E	25 P/E	30 P/E	40 P/E
20%	20 P/E	30 P/E	40 P/E	50 P/E
25%	25 P/E	35 P/E	50 P/E	60 P/E
30%	30 P/E	45 P/E	60 P/E	75 P/E

Figure 6

want to make P/E adjustments to allow for greater risks for stocks in individual situations. The 9 percent Bond Yield column was omitted because the P/E's would not have differed significantly from the P/E's of the 10 percent Bond Yield column.

How to Spot Growth Stocks Which Are Undervalued Relative to Their Price-Earnings Ratios

The table in Figure 6 is an excellent tool for use in searching out undervalued growth situations, and also in alerting you to situations which may be overpriced. This strategy is not as simple a matter as just comparing growth rates, however. Even if you have a stock whose compound earnings-per-share growth rate over the past three or five years has been at a certain rate and according to the table in Figure 6 the price-earnings ratio should be much higher, you still cannot be sure the stock should be bought until you have considered several other investment factors. First, is the earnings-growth rate a true growth rate, or does it result from non-recurring economic conditions and cannot be considered sustainable? Many a company has put together several good years, only to run into increased competition, overcapacity, and price-cutting which have served to sharply limit growth. The problem is even more difficult when it is considered that stocks selling at modest price-earnings ratios are not yet generally recognized by investors as true growth situations. They could turn out to be fads, with only a brief time to flash across the firmament. Once you are satisfied that the stock is undervalued you still have the general market and technical aspects to consider. You do not want to step into the market, even if you are buying an undervalued situation, if the general market is dangerous and vulnerable to a sharp decline. Using the general market in timing your stock market transactions was what Chapter 2 was all about. The last part of the strategy is waiting until the technical indications are favorable. If you know the stock is cheap, but nobody else does—or cares, you can have your money tied up in a stagnant situation for some time. It would be nice to see some popularity come into the group, or to have a story that could fire investors' imaginations once it became known. At the very least, the stock should act well in the market, resisting selling off in market declines and showing some firmness when the general market is doing well. In a computerized program of the stock market, its strength should show improvement relative to other stocks and it should at least have turned positive short term. On a bar chart, it would be very helpful if the stock had built a sizeable base showing accumulation, and be on the verge of breaking out on the upside. If all the foregoing conditions were met, you would have an excellent chance of realizing substantial capital gains in line with your goal of tripling your investment. If institutions finally agree with your analysis and start buying the stock, you could do very well, indeed.

Starting with a depressed price-earnings ratio can have a substantial leverage effect on the price of a stock, and if you have successfully recognized the sustainability of a superior growth rate you could wind up with dramatic results, although as we have noted before, there is no sure way of knowing when a growth rate is sustainable. If the company has a dominant technological or marketing position in a field in which there is an economic need and has substantial room for expansion, there is a good possibility the company has a sustainable superior growth rate.

Perhaps an actual investment case history can best illustrate the capital gains possibilities of an undervalued stock that has a sustainable superior earnings rate. Mr. Fred B. was an administrator with a national charitable institution. His income was adequate, but not extravagant. Over the years he had invested small sums rather regularly and in the early 1960s at the age of 53 he had accumulated a portfolio of various odd lots worth about $40,000. Through contacts with many local businessmen in his area of employment he was exposed to a number of small companies with good growth prospects. He had decided on an investment philosophy of buying and holding emerging growth companies, which was very successful. In line with his investment policy, Mr. B. liked the prospects of International Flavors and Fragrances. It had a unique position in the production of compounds that imparted flavors and fragrances to numerous products from food to cosmetics. He purchased 50 shares on October 26, 1961 for a total cost of $1406. At the time, the stock had experienced a 22 percent compounded average annual earnings-per-share growth rate and was selling over-the-counter at approximately 27 times earnings. The interest environment at the time was on the order of 6 percent. We can see from the table that a price-earnings ratio of about 50 would be reasonable for a 20 percent growth under 6 percent interest conditions. After the purchase there were two 2 for 1 stock splits, a 3 for 2 split, and regular small annual stock dividends. On July, 1972, the date of the last communication with the customer, he owned 350 shares of International Flavors and Fragrances worth $28,000. This investor did quite a bit better than tripling his investment. It is quite possible that Mr. B. could have done even better if he had taken advantage of the stock market cycle, but he might have lost his position if he did not have the discipline to buy when despair was rampant. In any case, he did not do badly. The price movement of International Flavors and Fragrances from 1962 to 1974 can be seen in Figure 7.

As I have indicated, the table in Figure 6 can be helpful in singling out undervalued situations. It can also be useful in indicating when a stock may have exhausted its potential, the risk is approaching potential, or there is just too much risk involved for the average investor to assume. In the latter part of 1973 the growth rate of International Flavors and Fragrances had slowed to 13.5 percent (average compounded rate for the last five years) and the price-earnings ratio was 55. The economy was in an 8 percent interest environment at that point and, according to my table, a 15 percent growth rate was worth approximately 25 times

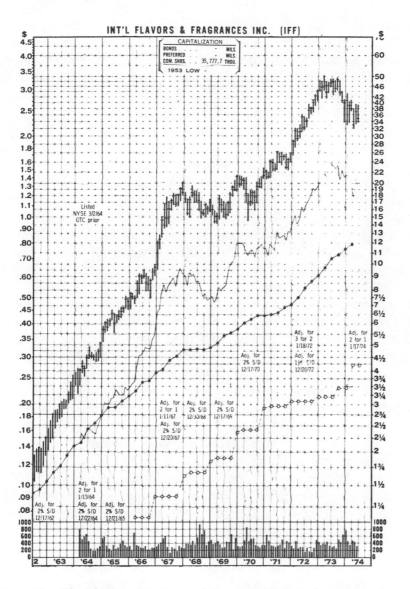

Figure 7. Chart by Securities Research Company, 208 Newbury Street, Boston, Massachusetts.

earnings. There is another consideration in using this table which I have not mentioned, and that is, if interest rate levels are considered temporary, investors may be willing to ignore current levels and fix their sight on more reasonable levels. In this instance, however, even if a 7 percent interest rate environment were used (which would assume inflationary expectations of about 3 percent annually on top of an estimated true interest rate of 4 percent), the price-earnings ratio in the table associated with a 15 percent earnings growth is only 30. International Flavors and Fragrances would have been adequate priced on this basis. Also, there is another possible consideration here: the growth rate could be temporarily depressed. Whether the growth rate could increase is something the investor has to judge for himself in determining a reasonable price-earnings ratio for a stock.

Our job is not done, however, even if we conclude that a stock is amply priced. Fully priced stocks do not necessarily turn down and play dead; they can become even more fully priced (as many an unhappy short-seller can testify). What is usually needed is some event or happening which can dramatize the fully priced nature of the stock or of similar stocks. In the case of International Flavors and Fragrances, short term weakness resulted from at least two developments. The one decision, quality growth stocks for months held up relatively well in the 1973 market decline while the bulk of the stocks on the market dropped to historically low valuations. The gap between the price-earnings ratios of the quality growth stocks and the rest of the market, a phenomenon called the "two-tier" market, became glaringly obvious to investors, including institutions. In this type of investment climate IBM found itself receiving an unfavorable decision in an antitrust suit. The resulting weakness in IBM attracted attention to other stocks which might be candidates in antitrust suits and also to other similar quality growth stocks. Stocks can often go on their merry way for years, considerably overpriced, until someone blows the whistle or investors begin questioning the reasonableness of the price level. Technically, International Flavors and Fragrances could be seen breaking down from a head-and-shoulder chart pattern as it broke support levels (see Figure 8). The technical deterioration of stocks is ignored at the investor's peril and particularly if the stocks may have seen their major earnings developments or the vogue or fashion appears to have run its course. Stocks are not necessarily condemned to oblivion once they have broken down technically. Technical indications are short term by nature, although they can have long term implications. Stocks which have good fundamentals can eventually recover. It is not likely, however, that a stock will be able to command its former price-earnings ratio, and often a base of several months is needed before it is ready for a major move. There is so much psychology in the stock market that a questioning of a company's growth prospects, coupled with the evidence of technical deterioration, usually detracts from a stock's image.

This Method of Approximating the Value of
Conservative Stocks Could Be Very Profitable for You

The procedure I discussed for evaluating growth stocks is not appropriate for evaluating more conservative stocks. In the first place, investors who buy conser-

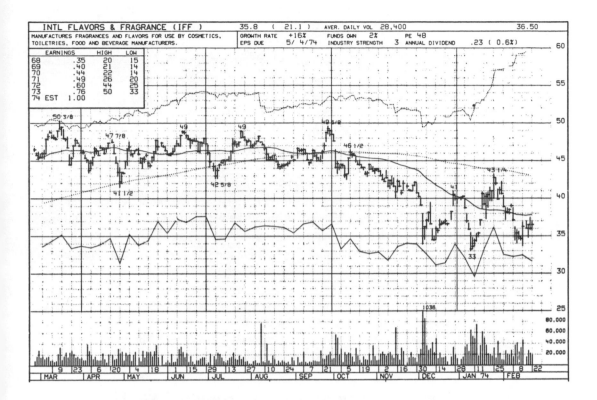

Figure 8. *Chart Courtesy of DAILY GRAPHS, P.O. Box 24933, Los Angeles, California 90024.*

vative stocks are more concerned with safety of principal and current income. In times of stress a good dividend yield can be very reassuring to investors. Speculative stocks, for example, which depend on earnings growth alone for their appeal, do not have much support if fundamentals or the fashion changes. The dividend yield tends to become more important when investors are pessimistic, and is less important when they are optimistic. Since the earnings gains of the more conservative stocks are usually not so dramatic, investors want to have the warm feeling of having income coming in while they are waiting for earnings growth. However, they also want the comfortable feeling that there is not a ceiling on their participation in the growth of the country and that their investment will be able to outpace inflation. Thus, what these investors are looking at is the total return of the common stock, the current dividend yield plus potential annual appreciation. The potential capital gains are assumed to reflect the earnings-per-share growth rate over the long run since the stock is not likely to be so overpriced that the effective gain would be less than the growth rate. This total return, rather than the dividend alone, would be what investors use in comparing the returns of common stocks with those of bonds. For slower growing stocks, the total return is more significant than the price-earnings ratio. Just what weight is given to the dividend yield or to the earnings growth rate will depend on the investment environment, as was previously noted. Buying opportunities in undervalued conservative stocks in which the total return substantially exceeds that of similar stocks or of bonds often present themselves during a sharp rise in interest rates when interest-sensitive stocks may have substantial declines. Such conservative groups as banks and utilities frequently present a buying opportunity at such a time, even though it is likely that their earnings-growth rate may have been temporarily slowed by the high interest rates. Stocks in less defensive industries may also offer a buying opportunity if for some reason earnings growth has been temporarily impeded and the dividend yield assumes a greater portion of the total return. In general, buying opportunities are presented in undervalued conservative stocks when interest rates are at abnormally high levels. Sophisticated investors in particular like the exceptional potential presented by these stocks. It is not likely that you will triple your investment in short order in undervalued conservative stocks, but they could well be part of your strategy in reaching your investment goal. Once these stocks have returned to normal valuations you could seek other capital-gains situations which might involve more risk, but also more potential. Also, once interest rates have bottomed, there is a danger of their rising and starting the cycle all over.

How Money Can Be Made in Recognizing Stocks Undervalued Relative to Total Return

It is not easy to make large profits in conservative-type stocks, but in relation to the risk involved, some substantial gains can be achieved. If you are very fortunate in locating a "sleeper," a stock which has an unimpressive record but which may have laid the groundwork for a surge in earnings, you could approach your goal of tripling your funds over a period of time. Basically, however, you should consider buying undervalued conservative stocks as just one of your investment strategies in reaching your investment goal. Once you consider the stock amply priced, the story well-known, and it seems the major earnings development has taken place, it may be time to take your profits and to look for other capital gains opportunities. The stock still could work higher, but the major move may have taken place and the stock could be becoming increasingly vulnerable to profit-taking. It is always tricky to switch from a stock doing well to one that has not proven itself yet, but that is one of the ways money is made in the stock market. The odds are in favor of you doing better in a stock in which you can see a new story developing and popularity flowing into it, than in a stock in which the story is well-known, investors have substantial profits, the major earnings development is behind it, and popularity may be flowing out of it.

How a Small Investor Made a Killing with Leverage

One thing successful investors are well-aware of is the beneficial effects of leverage on stock earnings and stock prices. Leverage comes in many different forms. The usual use of the term is with regard to large amounts of debt in a company's capitalization. If the company can earn a higher return on investment than it is paying on its long term debt, there is a net gain for the common stockholder. The greater the percentage of debt, the greater the leverage. This type of leverage is not all good, however. Too much debt can make a company vulnerable if it has any sudden reversals. Cyclical companies, in particular, have to be careful of how much debt they carry.

Another type of leverage is operational leverage in which the cost structure of the company is such that an increase in sales above break-even will result in a higher percentage gain in earnings. Companies with heavy fixed costs, especially, have high leverage. Once the fixed costs are covered, the variable costs are the only expenses left, and earnings can soar. Some companies have leverage in their ability to cut various cost factors or to spread their costs out over more units of production by increasing volume substantially. The semi-conductor companies, in particular, can realize substantial savings as the learning curve improves and the reject rate drops.

The airline industry is noteworthy for the earnings leverage it provides. Whether the airplanes fly full or only half full does not affect expenses too much. Equipment and personnel are needed to service the passengers whether the number is small or large. Thus, when load factors (revenue-passenger miles are divided by available-seat miles) rise sharply, almost all the increase in revenues flow directly to earnings. A relatively inexperienced investor, Mr. Richard M., took advantage of the leverage opportunities in the airline industry in realizing a sizable gain in his investment. In 1970 the airlines were experiencing a drop in traffic growth and the stocks were down substantially. (Just as leverage can work on the upside of the advantage to investors, it can also work on the downside to their disadvantage.) Mr. M., who was a private in the army at the time, assumed that the airlines were here to stay, and the Civil Aeronautics Board had to allow them to make a profit if they were going to remain in business. All he had to do was try and decide when the airline stocks had anticipated the worst of the traffic news. Just when the worst of the news has been discounted, of course, is the main problem in timing the purchase of cyclical stocks. He kept watching the monthly traffic comparisons and how the airlines stocks reacted to the news. Finally he noted that the stocks stopped declining on unfavorable traffic news. At this point he stepped in and bought 40 shares of TWA at 14⅝. In a little over a year, in February, 1972, the traffic news was improving and the stock had risen to 48. He knew the stock was cyclical and that cyclical stocks should be sold when the news looked the best. He sold his 40 shares, more than tripling his investment. (See Figure 9.)

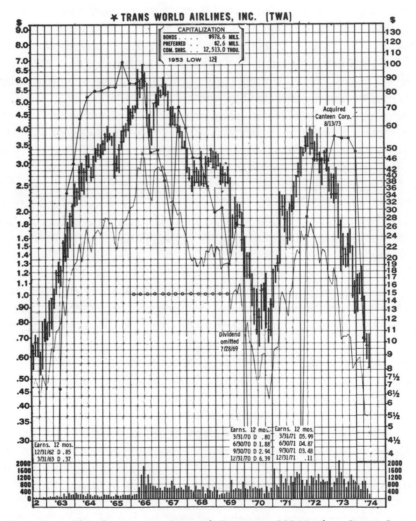

Figure 9.   *Chart by Securities Research Company, 208 Newbury Street, Boston, Massachusetts.*

4

Psychology Is an Important Ingredient of the Techno-Fundamental Approach

Fads and Fashions Should Be a Major Consideration in Your Investment Strategy

There are two schools of thought about the stock market. One school is that the investor's main concern should be the quality of management and potential of the individual company. The other is that most stocks go with the general market trend and that the investor can do very well just by buying stocks when the market is in an uptrend. In our opinion, as suggested by the title of this book, both schools of thought have much to recommend them. It certainly is true that stocks of companies with unusual potential can do well in all except the most adverse market conditions. However, it is not easy to find stocks of this caliber that have not already been recognized and bid up by investors, and thus likely to be volatile and significantly affected by general market trends. The great bulk of the stocks is very much influenced by investor confidence and general market conditions. It can be said that the general market trend itself becomes a fashion. The trend may start out based on economic and corporate-earnings considerations, but trends often run to excess, and whether the trend is up or down, the buying or selling becomes more the fashion of the moment than reflecting fundamental values. What actually happens is that the stock market itself creates the mood, and investors have a great deal of difficulty in ignoring the trend in favor of buying values. When the trend is down, investors hesitate to buy because their experience has been that stocks they have bought have gone lower. When the trend is up they are unwilling to sell because stocks they have sold before have continued higher. Anticipating changes in trend is one of the secrets to exceptional investment success. Some of the sharpest gains are made in the

75

short period following the bottoming out of a market decline. Chapter 2 was designed to help you recognize turns in the market trend. Of course, stocks offering outstanding value or potential should far outperform mediocre situations in any market uptrend. Chapter 3 should help you in the selection of stocks that have the best possibilities relative to risk. On balance, a combination of the technical and fundamental considerations, which this book is all about, should provide you with the best investment results.

How a "Story" or "Concept" Can Affect Stock Prices

Just as you can do much better if you take advantage of the major market trend, you can do even better if you go with the stronger industries or groups within the major trend. Too often, investors are continually fighting the market, ignoring the stronger groups and buying into the weaker groups. Buying the stocks with the lowest price-earnings ratios is usually not the best way to make money in the stock market. There are so many stocks competing for the investors' money that it usually takes something to focus the investor's attention on any particular industry or group. This something is a "story" or "concept" which can give an investor a reason to buy a stock. As a practical matter, it is easier for brokers to sell stocks when they have something that will give the investor a specific reason why a certain stock should be bought instead of any of the great number of other available stocks. Emotionally, it is difficult for investors to resist buying a story or concept that is popular and which helps them feel confident of the future prospects of the company. It is just as difficult for investors to buy a situation in which there is no particular story that will give them confidence in the long term outlook for the company. It is not always easy to know when an industry or group is becoming popular. Computerized market programs showing industries with improving short term or relative strength can be very helpful. Watching how individual stocks in an industry perform also is an indication of an industry's strength, of course. You should realize that it is difficult for investors to maintain a high level of interest in an industry or group for an extended period of time, and that you should be alert to any weakening of the relative strength that might indicate that the propularity had just about run its course and investors are taking profits. Some stocks, also, run up prematurely on a concept before it is ready to pay off, and then fall back until earnings develop (they may never develop in some cases). Too, we should not forget that concepts can be used as an excuse to sell stocks as well as to buy them. Many investors were mystified about the weakness in the fast food, recreational, and motel stocks in 1973 until they realized the concept for selling was that a possible gasoline shortage could hurt the business of these companies.

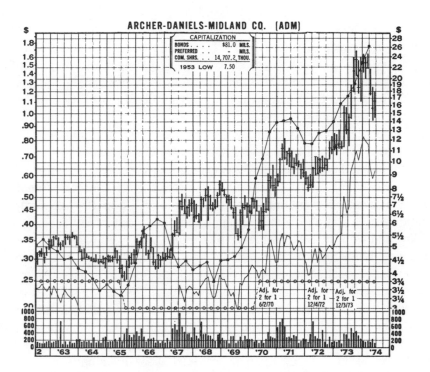

Figure 10. *Chart by Securities Research Company, 208 Newbury Street, Boston, Massachusetts.*

An example of how a stock can benefit from a currently popular concept can be seen in the action of Archer-Daniels-Midland in the 1971-1972 period (see Figure 10).

Archer-Daniels-Midland had a rather erratic earnings record over the last decade. Swings in commodity prices, particularly soybean prices, had a big impact on earnings, and the relatively unpredictable nature of these swings prevented the company from gaining a big following. Then, news of the company's breakthrough in developing a textured soybean product which could be used as a low-cost substitute for beef was mentioned in several national publications in the latter part of 1972 and in 1973. Figure 10 shows how the stock broke out of an inverted head and shoulder pattern at the end of 1972, ran up to about 26 in 1973, and consolidated. The general market was under a cloud at the time, or perhaps the stock would have done even better. However, after mid-year the country was in the grip of sharply-rising food prices, particularly beef. The rising price of beef and subsequent shortages received a great deal of publicity, and Archer-Daniels-Midland's patented process for a soybean meat substitute (which many users said could not be distinguished from beef) was a particularly good story which investors could relate to the growing long term worldwide need for a relatively cheap source of protein and substitute for beef. The stock broke away again after mid-year and at this writing was at 41. I should also point out that at the time of the rally after mid-1973 that investors were not generally expecting a sharp increase in near-term earnings. It was primarily the attraction of the story that brought in the buying.

This example demonstrates how a story can encourage investors to buy a particular stock. Earnings even do not have to be doing particularly well at the time and people will still buy. There has to be some hope held forth that earnings will spurt somewhere down the road, of course. I have another example of a company which was hurt by unfavorable psychology. From 1967 onward, Ethyl Corporation had a very satisfactory rising trend of earnings, but the stock topped out in 1967 and went into a downtrend (see Figure 11). Here was a case in which investors were ignoring favorable earnings because the stock had been associated with the expected decline in the use of antiknock compounds based on lead that were manufactured by Ethyl. At the time no one could be certain whether it would be necessary to reduce the lead in gasoline. It was thought that the catalytic converter, whose useful life is shortened by lead compounds, was the only solution to auto pollution control, but then it was discovered that it had a competitor in the Honda stratified engine. Even if the lead were eventually taken out of gasoline, Ethyl believed it could develop enough new products to offset the revenues lost as the antiknock compound was phased out.

Sometimes adverse psychology can open up buying opportunities if investors begin to realize that they have carried pessimism too far. In spite of the fears of investors, the earnings of Ethyl continued upward. With the price-earnings ratio of about five, discounting just about anything that could go wrong, investors were beginning to think that maybe they were a little too harsh on Ethyl. Whereas it had recently been the fashion to sell the stock because of the uncertain future, now it was the fashion to buy the stock because the unfavorable story had been overdone, and it was possible the worst fears might not be realized at all. It could happen, of course, that events may eventually prove that investors were originally right about the stock and that it should have been avoided. The fact that a stock is in a downtrend or an uptrend does not necessarily confirm that expectations about a company are right or wrong. The market can be wrong, but if the trend tends to confirm the fundamental opinion, it is usually best to go with it.

Secondary Growth Stocks as a Concept

I have already discussed some of the characteristics of secondary growth stocks. They have an earnings history, they are in areas that have above-average

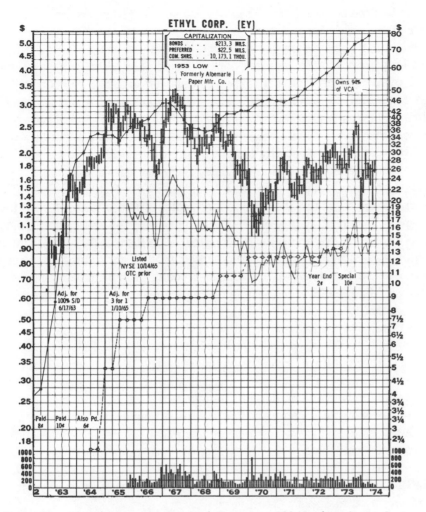

Figure 11. *Chart by Securities Research Company, 208 Newbury Street, Boston, Massachusetts.*

growth potential, the company's sales base is relatively small, and the price-earnings ratio is usually lower than that of quality growth companies with comparable earnings growth rates. Individual secondary growth stocks can become the target of concentrated buying practically any time. They have all the ingredients in place to support an investment vogue. All they need to become spectacular performers is to have some publicity or happening that will attract attention to them. There are times when investors believe that secondary growth stocks as a group offer the greatest value in the stock market and they are active in searching out all stocks that can reasonably be so classified. There are other times when attention is focused on individual secondary growth stocks because they belong to a popular group or industry.

Kendall was a secondary growth stock that was in one of the most highly regarded long term growth industries, health care. However, it was so over-shadowed by Johnson and Johnson that investors overlooked it. The potential was there under the surface, nevertheless. Betty K., a housewife, felt more comfort-able with relatively low price-earnings-ratio stocks that really had not been bid up by investors than she did with the stocks that everyone knew about and which were richly priced. She especially liked the health-care field because she had a certain empathy for the economic need here. She selected Kendall as her invest-ment vehicle to fame and fortune. She bought $3900 of stock in July, 1963. Subsequent to her purchase, the stock underwent a three for two split and a two for one split. It merged with Colgate-Palmolive share for share, and Colgate-Palmolive had a three for one split. Her original 100 shares were now 900 shares and worth $26,325, more than a six-fold appreciation of her original investment.

Another investor looked to a leader in a young growth industry for invest-ment success. Margaret M. saw the long range potential in a new communications system, community antenna television (CATV). Not only was it able to bring television to remove areas out of reach of TV broadcasting centers, but it also opened up new channels of entertainment for present television viewers. Coupled with pay TV, it might even revolutionize the industry. There were a great many CATV operators, most of which are not yet making any money since installation expenses far exceeds revenues initially, but Margaret M. thought it might make more sense investing in a company that could participate in the growth of the entire industry, rather than in just one geographical sector of it. She chose to invest in Burnup and Sims, a company that designs, constructs, and maintains facilities for the telephone, CATV, and electrical utility industries. She invested $1500 in Burnup and Sims in March, 1971. Just about two years later her invest-ment had increased to $5000. (See Figure 12.)

A Lawyer Employs a New Concept for Capital Appreciation

Sophisticated investors recognize that if they expect to have really outstand-ing success in the stock market they usually cannot buy situations which are too obvious. Once everyone knows the prospects of a company or all the uncertainty is removed, the stock price usually already reflects the prospects (unless general market conditions are so unfavorable that investors are afraid to buy even the most attractive stocks). David D., a lawyer, was impressed by the entrenched position of Xerox in the copier field and by the growth prospects of the field itself. However, since Xerox was so well-known and the price-earnings ratio of the stock had expanded so sharply over the years, he was not convinced that his money would have the greatest possible appreciation in this stock. He, neverthe-

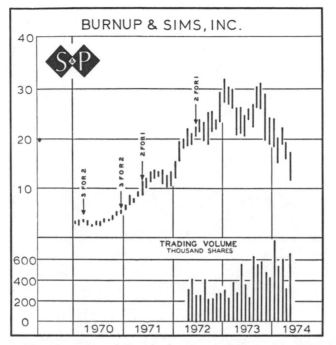

Figure 12. *Chart Courtesy of Standard & Poor's Corporation, OTC Stock Reports, 345 Hudson Street, New York, New York 10014.*

less, found a unique way to benefit from the Xerox reputation and expertise, and also to be able to realize a greater capital gains potential than that offered by Xerox itself. Xerox and Rank Organization jointly own Rank Xerox Ltd. which has exclusive rights for the manufacture and distribution of Xerox copiers in the Eastern Hemisphere, with the exception that Fuji Photo Film, which is jointly owned by Rank Xerox and Fuji Photo Film, has exclusive rights in Japan. Instead of buying Xerox, Mr. D. bought shares of Rank Organization at 5½ in December, 1969. He sold them at 16½ in November, 1972 (see Figure 13). The value of his investment tripled, while during the same period, Xerox increased less than 50 percent.

New Issues Benefit Directly from Investor Psychology

Probably nowhere in the stock market is psychology more manifest than in the new issues market. New issues have many of the ingredients that can fire the imagination of investors. A new story has a certain novelty and possibilities of unusual success that investors find hard to resist, particularly if the market atmosphere is conducive to speculation. If the new issues are in technologically advanced industries, in particular, investors can conjure up all kinds of capital gains

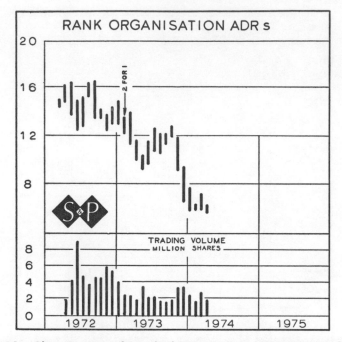

Figure 13. *Chart Courtesy of Standard & Poor's Corporation OTC Stock Reports, 345 Hudson Street, New York, New York 10014.*

possibilities (at one point in the 1968 bull market an analyst said stocks of small technological companies were bargains at any price since they had so much potential). They often are offered by companies in industries which are already popular with investors and investor reception is practically assured. Underwriting houses attempt to price new issues at reasonable values, but if the general market is in an exuberant mood some of these stocks can double or triple within a short time. The reason, of course, is that there is a limited supply of such stocks and the demand sometimes can be overwhelming. A new story and a limited earnings experience can make almost any earnings projection seem reasonable that investors are disposed to make. What has the greatest effect on investors, however, is their previous experience with the sharp appreciation of new issues when the new issues market is "hot."There is one problem, however. It is rare when the stock market makes it easy for investors to reap huge profits without incurring substantial risks. In the case of new issues, the distribution is limited and many investors are unable to buy them on the initial offering. There is often substantial appreciation left even after the new issues reach the secondary market, but the risk is now greater following the sharp rise in the stocks. At some point, perhaps months after the issuing date, investors are inclined to take profits and investors may have another opportunity to buy the stocks. One analyst of my acquaintance actually made it a practice of looking for new issues that had fallen back after their initial runups and recommending them after they had built a good base.

McDonald's, the fast food chain, made a big impression on this analyst. A new issue of the stock was made on April 21, 1965 at $1.25, after adjusting for subsequent splits (see Figure 14). The stock had a good run initially, but my friend did not chase it. He bided his time, and in the general market decline of 1966 he was able to write his report and recommend the stock at a good price. The rest is history.

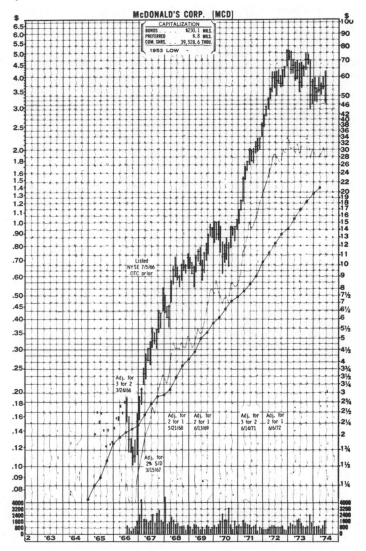

Figure 14. *Chart by Securities Research Company, 208 Newbury Street, Boston, Massachusetts.*

Franzia Brothers Winery is another good example of a successful new issue. The original offering was on April 18, 1972 at $18.50. Wine stocks had been receiving a lot of publicity. It seemed that American palates were just becoming aware of wine, and industry sales were booming. Thus, the issue was almost assured of success before it was offered. It immediately was up over 50 percent (see Figure 15). Investors who bought after the sharp rise would have been disappointed, however, at least for the near term. The stock backed and filled, and managed a small gain in June, but profit-taking came in and it declined for several months, with intermittent rallies. A rally took place in January, but it was short-lived, and the decline continued. The really first major buying opportunity was presented in August, about four months after the offering. The stock had a good rally in January, 1973, but then continued its decline. In this case, if the investor had chased the stock following the initial offering he would have had a long wait until he had a profit. A little patience, however, and he could have bought the stock at a good price.

The market action of new issues can vary considerably with individual stocks, depending on the prospects of the companies. California Computer was offered at $1.03 (adjusted for stock dividends and stock splits) on August 17, 1961. This stock was in the computer peripheral equipment group which investors

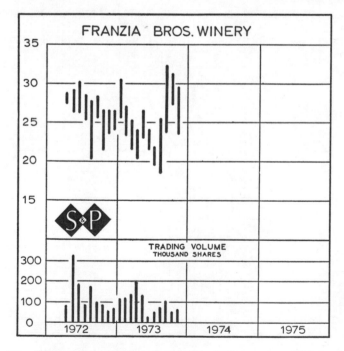

Figure 15.   *Chart Courtesy of Standard & Poor's Corporation OTC Stock Reports, 345 Hudson Street, New York, New York 10014.*

had discovered was growing faster than the computer main frame field. Peripheral equipment companies were selling equipment which, in many cases, was cheaper than similar equipment sold or leased by IBM. The market at the time was small compared to the main frame business and IBM did not seem to worry too much about the competition. California Computer made high speed plotters which presented the output of digital computers in graphic form. The stock came out near the end of a bull market and shot up very sharply. In 1962, however, a bear market was in full swing and investors again had an excellent opportunity to buy the stock. Nevertheless, even investors who bought the original offering were able to realize substantial profits. As can be seen in Figure 16, the stock climbed sharply in 1964, consolidated for about a year in 1965, and took off again in 1966.

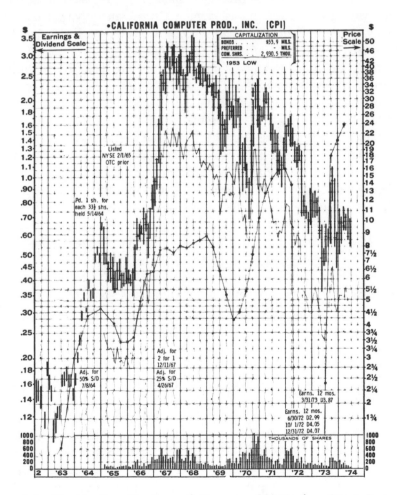

Figure 16. *Chart by Securities Research Company, 208 Newbury Street, Boston, Massachusetts.*

It ran far ahead of its earnings, and its peak was seen in 1968, even though earnings did not reach their highest level until 1971. The stock formed a distribution pattern for about two years and then started breaking down. About this time, IBM was becoming more conscious of the new competition from the peripheral equipment manufacturers and was taking a more competitive stance. The downtrend of California Computer continued, interrupted by periodic rallies. The bubble had burst, however, and each rally gave way to a fresh decline. In 1963, IBM lost an antitrust suit and was required not to use highly competitive practices to eliminate the competition. IBM is appealing the verdict at this writing and the future of many of the peripheral equipments may hinge on the outcome of the appeal.

Another new issue in which investors could have done well even if they were not in on the original offering was Damon Corp., an important factor in the rapidly growing biomedical field. The stock was offered on December 19, 1967, at \$2.17 a share (adjusted for subsequent stock splits). It had a meteoric rise to 16 before yearend, hit 35 in 1968, and without too much of a pause continued on to a peak of 71 in early 1970 (see Figure 17). Even after the price had reached its high, earnings continued to climb. Nevertheless, in 1969 the price-earnings ratio had expanded to 119 to 1, clearly a vulnerable situation in the event of any adverse news which could be recognized as a signal to take profits. The adverse news that finally came was not internal in this case, but it turned out to be a general market decline which brought in selling in 1970. The stock rallied in the market in 1971 and 1972, but much of the mystery was now out of the stock and competition had increased. It weakened again in 1973 as the general market fell again.

Major Earnings Developments Offer Some of the Greatest Profit Opportunities

What I mean by major earnings developments is some development, either internal or external, which can lift earnings to a substantially higher plateau, or can sharply increase the sustainable earnings growth rate. New products, new markets, more efficient processes, divestment of loss operations, and acquisitions which intergrate backwards or forwards or fill in product-line gaps can all result in sharp earnings gains. (I have already mentioned how airline earnings got a sharp lift when the industry converted to jet aircraft in the early 1960s.)

There are not many companies which have done as well as IBM, Xerox, and Polaroid from new product developments, but there are many examples of stocks that have, nevertheless, experienced substantial price appreciation as a result of new earnings developments. In the new product area, for example, Texas Instruments is a leader in the development of semiconductors, Great Lakes Chemical is a major factor in the development of flame retardant chemicals, and Loctite

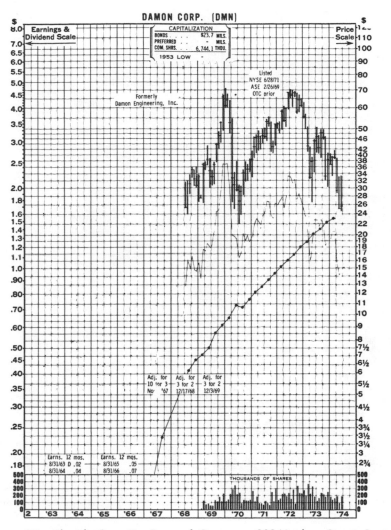

Figure 17. *Chart by Securities Research Company, 208 Newbury Street, Boston, Massachusetts.*

Corporation developed a family of anaerobic adhesives (they harden when air is excluded) for industrial use in assemblying mechanical parts. (See Figures 18, 19, and 20.)

Howmet is an example of a company that achieved a substantial increase in earning power by integrating backwards into primary aluminum production. The company had been an aluminum fabricator and bought its ingots on the open market. Then it acquired primary aluminum production facilities and the cost savings allowed earnings to increase substantially. As can be seen in Figure 21,

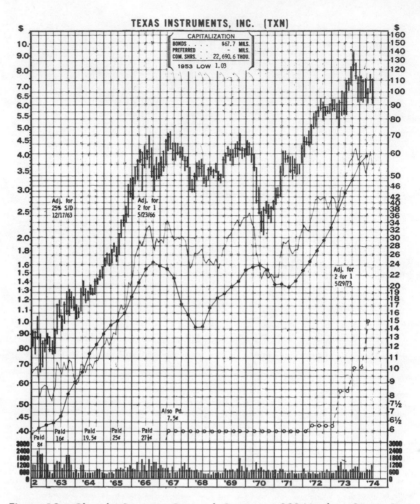

Figure 18. *Chart by Securities Research Comapny, 208 Newbury Street, Boston, Massachusetts.*

the stock climbed sharply in 1966 and 1967. The higher level of earnings, however, proved to be more of a plateau than a jumping-off point for another increase in earnings, and the stock went into a decline after it made a double top in 1968.

Sometimes the improvement in earnings does not take place in a dramatic manner, but gradually over a period of time, and the change that occurs is mainly in the mind of the investor. Preston Trucking, a trucking company operating in 17 states, mostly on the East Coast, had a consistently good earnings growth rate, but the stock remained on a plateau for several years until 1966. It seemed that then it finally dawned on investors that Preston was a well-managed company with good

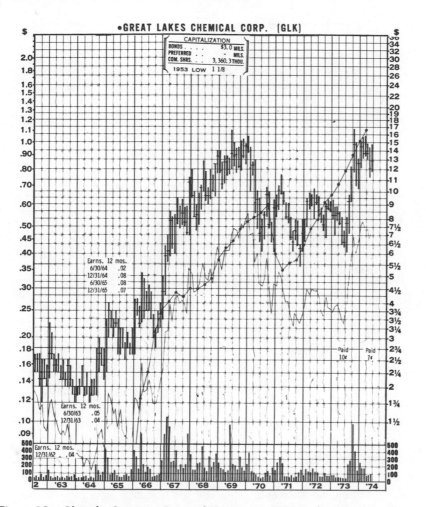

Figure 19. *Chart by Securities Research Company, 208 Newbury Street, Boston, Massachusetts.*

growth potential. One investor, John R., was quick to recognize the changing market attitude toward Preston Trucking. He was a plumber and it is possible he may have had some dealings with Preston. At any rate, he bought 100 shares of the stock at $2.66 (adjusted for stock splits) in 1967. At this writing the stock is selling at 25, and Mr. R. still holds it. (No chart is available.)

There are cases in which a combination of market factors, none of which may be particularly significant in itself, may be responsible for a sharp improvement in a company's fortunes. Skyline, a leading manufacturer of mobile homes, had shown good earnings gains for several years, but investors did not become

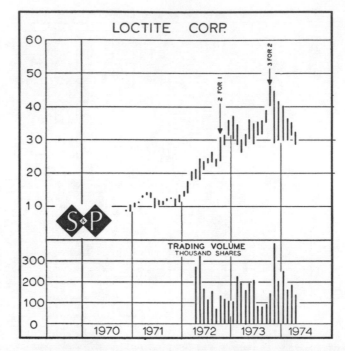

Figure 20. *Chart Courtesy of Standard & Poor's Corporation OTC Stock Reports, 345 Hudson Street, New York, New York 10014.*

enthusiastic about the stock until 1967. In that year, earnings doubled, but more important, investors were becoming aware of the growth potential of the mobile home industry. Inflation and the high cost of land were pushing the cost on conventional homes beyond the reach of the average home buyer. The mobile home was becoming the answer to the need for low-cost housing. As with many concepts, the flow of earnings is not always smooth, as capacity sometimes outruns demand or demand may slacken temporarily. The growth of the mobile home industry had been so rapid that investors began to worry that demand was being borrowed from the future. In 1972, earnings of Skyline did in fact decline, and the stock topped out about mid-year. In 1973 the general market aggravated the slide of the stock. (See Figure 22.) The question now appears to be how long it will take demand to catch up with capacity and enable earnings to resume their uptrend.

How You Can Profit by Catching Trends Early

In Chapter 2, I discussed how important it is to take advantage of the major general market trend, and how difficult it is to make money going against the

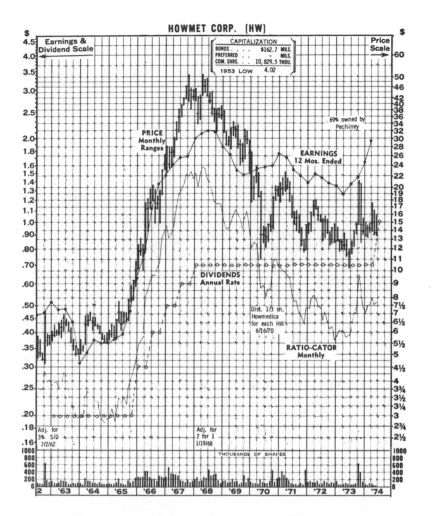

Figure 21. *Chart by Securities Research Company, 308 Newbury Street, Boston, Massachusetts.*

market trend. Within the general market trend, even if the trend is not pro-
nounced, increased investment performance may be achieved by following investors' attitudes and interests regarding individual groups and industries. By and
large, it is usually more profitably to stay with issues in which there are investor
interest and a favorable attitude rather than with issues in which there is little
interest or unfavorable investor attitudes. Whether you like an industry or group
personally is not as important as what the investing public thinks of it. Sometimes
investors miss some good profit opportunities just because they have some pre-
conceived dislike for a company or industry, even though it is clear that, at the

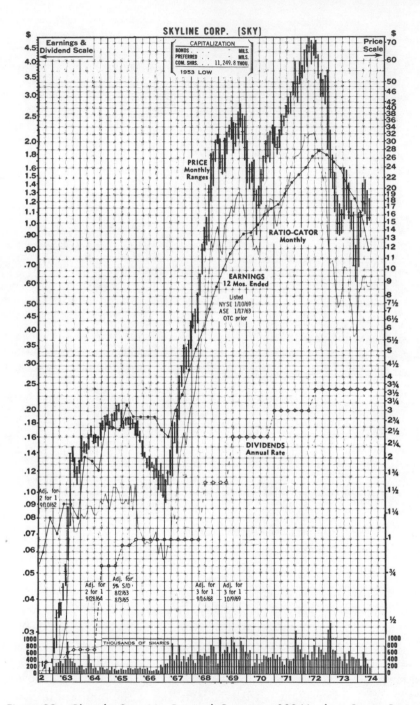

Figure 22.   *Chart by Securities Research Company, 208 Newbury Street, Boston, Massachusetts.*

moment at least, investors are favorably disposed toward it. Major upward trends of industries can last for years, as in the case of the mobile home stocks. If you can detect the beginning of a trend based on a sound concept, you can do far better, of course, than if you buy into the trend after it has been in effect for several years. When investors are well-aware of the prospects, the price-earnings ratios have already expanded sharply, and the bulk of the investors who are inclined to buy the situations have already taken their positions, much of the move has probably already taken place. There may still be buying opportunities in major uptrends during periods of profit-taking, although certainly greater profits are available when you get in on the ground floor.

The so-called quality growth stocks which receive a great deal of institutional support may act somewhat differently than the average capital-gains situation. These companies have proven themselves over the years and are usually in industries in which there is a basic economic need. They control substantial resources and often are dominant factors in their industries. Whereas many of the major trends may in fact be fads and fashions and run their course in time, the upward trend of the quality growth stocks are considered less ephemeral. These stocks also involve risks, however, primarily because of the high price-earnings ratios they carry.

An unusual case of a broker who recommended several stocks to his client based on well-thought out concepts and showing exceptional insight in anticipating the start of major trends was brought to my attention. Too frequently the investors are told about situations after they have already had extensive moves, and where fads or fashions are involved, may even be over the hill. It is not very often that a broker shows great foresight in correctly recognizing a trend after it had been underway for only a short time and advised his customers of it. The lucky customer, in this instance, Katherine K., a housewife, showed equal astuteness in being able to recognize good advice and follow it. The broker was convinced, long before the threat of gasoline rationing, that an energy shortage, particularly in the area of petroleum products, was developing in the U.S. He reasoned that the nuclear energy, which had been held back by environmental considerations, had been underway for only a short time and advised his customers of it. The lucky for the stocks that had the greatest exposure in terms of income from nuclear operations as a percentage of overall revenues, and he chose Combustion Engineering, Babcock and Wilcox, and Foster Wheeler. All make nuclear power generating equipment. Foster Wheeler, in addition, builds petroleum refineries and was expected to benefit from the acute shortage of refinery capacity and the need to build new capacity. The stocks were recommended on May 17, 1973 when Combustion Engineering was 66, Babcock and Wilcox 27 and Foster Wheeler 36 (see Figures 23, 24, and 25). What made the recommendations even more exceptional was that the general market was in a decline and investor

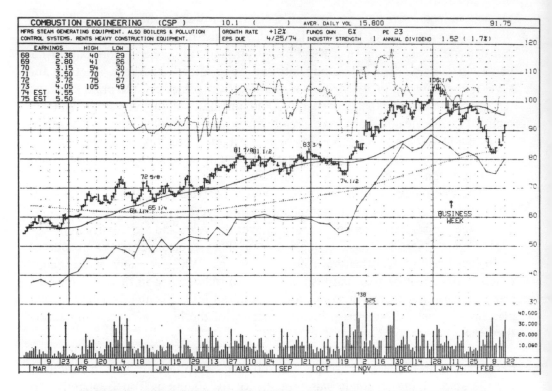

Figure 23.   *Chart Courtesy of DAILY GRAPHS, P.O. Box 24933, Los Angeles, California 90024.*

sentiment was overwhelmingly bearish at the time. Babcock and Wilcox actually continued lower after the recommendations, but rallied later. Combustion Engineering and Foster Wheeler both tended to consolidate while the general market went lower and then broke out on the upside in July.

Not content with pinpointing one of the most popular emerging concepts in the 1970s, this broker zeroed in on another concept that proved to be very profitable for his client in 1973 and also promised to give rise to one of the stronger market trends of the decade. Expanding populations and growing worldwide expectations have resulted in an unprecedented demand for agricultural products. Practically all the major industries associated with producing food, fertilizer, farm equipment, and seed companies were experiencing a strong growth in earnings. The stocks selected to participate in the growth of the agricultural sector included International Minerals and Chemical, a major fertilizer producer, and Deere and Massey-Ferguson, both leading farm equipment manufacturers. International Minerals and Chemical was recommended at 28, Deere 39, and Massey-Ferguson 18. (See Figures 26, 27, and 28.) All three stocks broke out

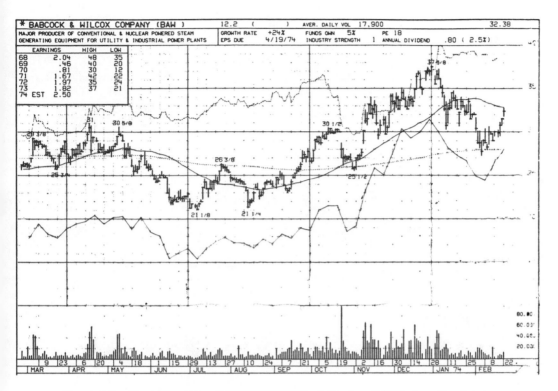

EARNINGS	HIGH	LOW
68	2.04	48	35
69	.46	40	20
70	.81	30	12
71	1.67	42	22
72	1.97	35	24
73	1.82	37	21
74 EST	2.50		

Figure 24. *Chart Courtesy of DAILY GRAPHS, P.O. Box 24933, Los Angeles, California 90024.*

and moved into ascending channels soon after the recommendations. International Minerals Broke out of a base and Deere and Massey-Ferguson broke out of short term descending channels.

A School Superintendent Cashes in on the Fast Food Trend

It was not too long ago, in the 1960s, that the fast food stocks were the hottest stocks on Wall Street. Since those days the stocks have cooled off considerably. A couple of the companies went bankrupt. The earnings of several others were found to be overstated because the companies were taking franchise fees into earnings even though the payment was to be made in installments extending for as long as ten years and in some cases franchises were unable to maintain their payments. Revelations of loose accounting practices were all the traders who had bought these stocks early needed to prompt them to take their profits. The selling "broke the back" of the stocks as the attitude of investors changed from one of buying to one of selling. Some investors protested that the stocks were still good

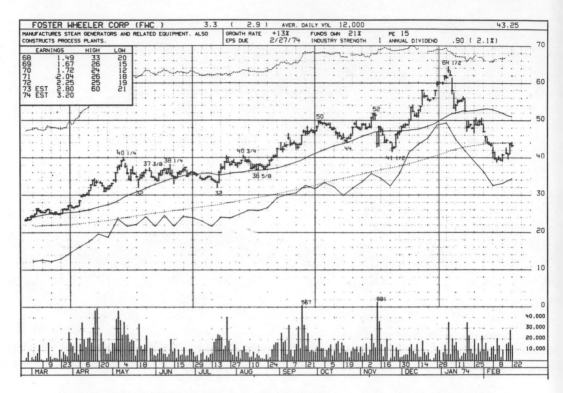

Figure 25. Chart Courtesy of DAILY GRAPHS, P.O. Box 24933, Los Angeles, California 90024.

values, but their cried were drowned out by the rush of investors to sell. Once investors have questioned the prospects of stocks which have had prolonged rises, the magic spell is usually broken and the stocks rarely recover their former popularity.

One investor, Herbert T. who was a school superintendent, played the fast food group very adroitly as far as timing his buying and selling was concerned. He purchased Kentucky Fried Chicken (now part of Heublein) in 1966 at $26.50 (after adjusting for a five-for-four split in 1967). The general market at the time had just had a substantial decline. He sold his shares at 60 in 1968 when market optimism was running high and before the severe market decline of 1969-1970. He did not triple his money, but he made a very nice profit in about two years.

A Good Way to Achieve Performance

Some investors always seem to do well in the stock market while for others it is usually a losing game. Why is this? There may not be that much difference in

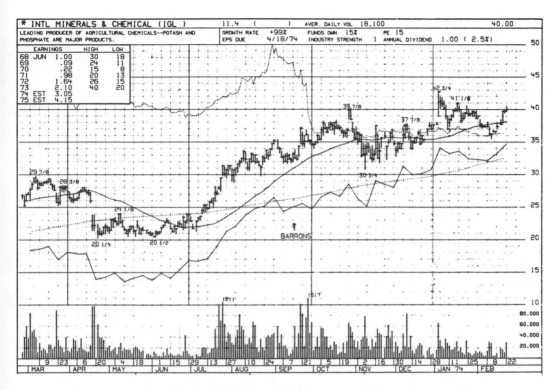

Figure 26. *Chart Courtesy of DAILY GRAPHS, P.O. Box 24933, Los Angeles, California 90024.*

the background of both groups of investors, and intelligence may not vary significantly, either. It seems to be the broad approach that is used by each of the two groups of investors that makes the difference. The group that is successful tends to be flexible. The investors in this group do not fall in love with their stocks. They are willing to go where the action is. They are well-aware that stock market popularity, to a large extent, is made up of fads and fashions and will rotate from group to group and from industry to industry. What was the fashion yesterday may be over the hill and discarded tomorrow. At one time quality growth stocks may be in fashion, at another time secondary, speculative, or cyclical stocks; natural resource issues may be in demand at another time, or technological, energy or service industry stocks at some other time, etc. Successful investors are constantly looking for emerging trends. They want to be among the first ones in, not the last. They may also have a flair for recognizing false starters. They do their best to be sure that a concept is sufficiently believable to bring in ample buying to propel the stock high enough to justify their purchase. If the stock does work out to their expectations, they are also realistic enough to assume some-

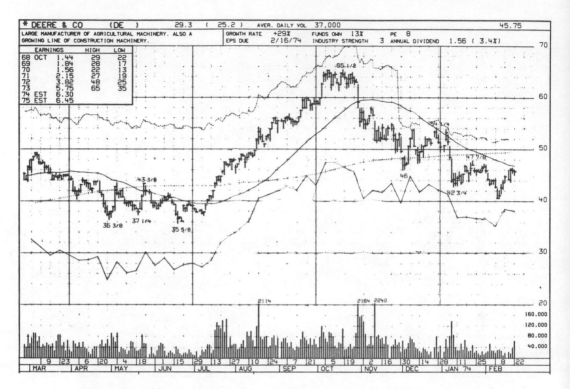

Figure 27. Chart Courtesy of DAILY GRAPHS, P.O. Box 24933, Los Angeles, California 90024.

where along the line the price will have fully reflected its potential, and they are willing to sell when there is a clamor among general investors to buy the stock. However, if the stock does not move out as expected, and after re-examining their assumptions they see a mistake has been made, they are quick to admit it and to sell their losers. In general, they do not continually fight the market. When a stock consistently acts poor technically they accept the verdict of the marketplace and sell, even though deep in their heart they think the stock is cheap. They also are not ashamed to buy a stock that has already gained followers and has had a good short term move. (One researcher found, in fact, that among the best long term gainers in the stock market have been stocks that had already seen substantial appreciation.) As important as anything, they are only on the long side of the market when the major trend is up. When the outlook is uncertain they have the patience to remain on the sidelines, unless they see unusual opportunities in stocks that can go against the trend. Summarizing, it seems that successful investors are able to blend their understanding of using fundamental concepts for determining what to buy and what to sell and applying technical tools in timing both the buying and the selling.

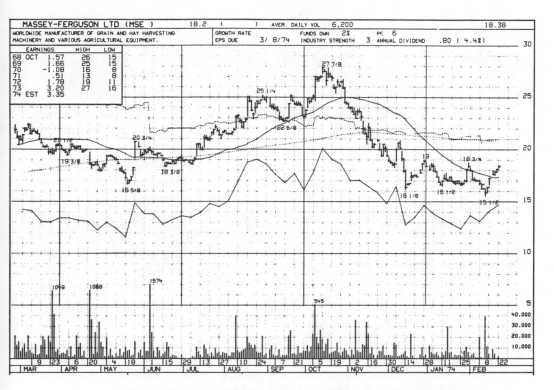

Figure 28. *Chart Courtesy of DAILY GRAPHS, P.O. Box 24933, Los Angeles, California 90024.*

We have other investors who always seem to do everything wrong. What they do seems logical, but it somehow never works out right. They think they are outsmarting the "big boys" by refusing to buy stocks that have had good rallies or that have high price-earnings ratios. They figure it too easy to buy stocks which are popular with other investors; they do not intend to fall into this trap. Instead, they will buy stocks no one else wants and which are "cheap." They are particularly happy to buy stocks of companies which have run into problems since they think they are getting a bargain, because the stocks must be bargains in view of the problems they have to overcome. They also look at the heights from which a stock has fallen and assume that if it were that high once, it can get back up there again. Occasionally, a stock they refused to chase in its early stages of growth has continued climbing for many months. They will then admit they have been wrong and consider buying it, just before the concept or fashion has run its course and everyone else is taking his (or her) profits. These investors can be stubborn, also. They will not reassess the situation if a stock turns down and the technical warning flags are flying. Instead, they are apt to try and average down the cost of their stock and try to vindicate their initial purchase. They will not cut their losses, but try to hold on to see if they can break even, regardless of whether or not there are much better situations elsewhere for making money. The explanation is often heard from these investors that "if it was a buy at a higher price, it is a better buy much lower." These investors are very hard to convince that stocks should be bought when the economy has been through a sea of troubles, the market has had a substantial decline, and investors in general are extremely bearish. However, they are willing to take a chance if the economy is running full blast, the market has had a prolonged rise, and investors are rampantly bullish. In general, it can be said that some investors make achieving success in the stock market harder than it really is. In trying to outsmart others, they outsmart themselves. They consistently avoid the popular groups and the stocks that are performing well. If they did happen to buy into a group that was doing well, they would tend to overstay the market and ride the stock back down again, rather than continually looking for signs that risk might be approaching potential or that the major earnings development was behind the company.

In the foregoing paragraphs, I hope the theme of how to achieve performance in the stock market was not obscured by the discussion of what investors have done, right or wrong. Simply stated, it is just that you should buy stocks in groups that embody a popular concept, and ones that are already recognized by the investing public as shown by the action of the stocks in the marketplace. Sometimes you can get a hint that a stock is ready to move by watching similar or related stocks attracting investor attention, but you want to see some movement somewhere. Never have I seen a clearer demonstration of the power of a concept in the stock market than during early November 1973, just after the President of the United States discussed the threatening energy crisis and the sacrifices the American people would be called upon to make to meet the challenge. The general market plunged on this news because of the uncertainty on just how the energy shortage would affect the economy and individual companies. However, many stocks that might benefit from higher prices because of the energy shortage or from increased spending in the energy area had rallies. Union Pacific Corp., a railroad holding company which had major interest in oil, gas, coal, and other natural resources, continued a rally which began in August. (See Figure 29.) Tesoro, an integrated oil and gas producer, refiner, and marketer, was a purer play. It also experienced a continuation of its rally. (See Figure 30.) Joy Manufacturing might not enjoy immediate benefits from the energy shortage since it was a manufacturer of coal mining equipment, but coal production was expected to eventually rise sharply since coal is one of the country's most abundant sources of energy. Nevertheless, it takes time to bring new mines into production and to expand capacity in existing mines. Joy at the time was in a consolidation pattern, but it, too, had an upward move. (See Figure 31.)

The reason many investors tend to shun stocks and concepts that are popular

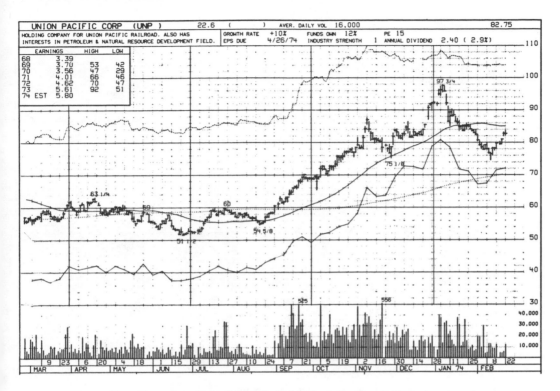

UNION PACIFIC CORP (UNP)	22.6	(	)	AVER. DAILY VOL 16,000				82.75

HOLDING COMPANY FOR UNION PACIFIC RAILROAD. ALSO HAS INTERESTS IN PETROLEUM & NATURAL RESOURCE DEVELOPMENT FIELD.

| | | | | GROWTH RATE +10%   FUNDS OWN 12%   PE 15 |
| EPS DUE 4/26/74   INDUSTRY STRENGTH 1   ANNUAL DIVIDEND 2.40 (2.9%) |

EARNINGS		HIGH	LOW
68	3.39		
69	3.70	53	42
70	3.56	47	29
71	4.01	66	46
72	4.62	70	47
73	5.61	92	51
74 EST	5.80		

Figure 29. Chart Courtesy of DAILY GRAPHS, P.O. Box 24933, Los Angeles, California 90024.

may be that it seems to easy and they want a challenge. Perhaps if a stock has gone up because investors like it, some instinctively are afraid to buy because they think it may sell off after they take a position. It certainly is possible that profit-taking may set in temporarily, but the odds are greater that a stock that is in an uptrend will eventually continue higher than that one in a downtrend will turn around and go up. Others may have had the experience of buying a stock after a prolonged rise just before the popularity had run its course, there was no new news to bring in more buying, and traders were ready to nail down their profits. Those who have made this mistake should not condemn the whole concept of buying popularity. They should, instead, be aware that stocks do not grow to the sky and that when they appear to be acting the best they may be very near their peaks. Distribution patterns can cover a period of many months, and in those patterns stocks can have substantial rallies and even make new highs. However, overall progress may be very little.

I should mention that there is another concept of buying stocks, that of "buying straw hats in January." Basically, this is not really different from buying

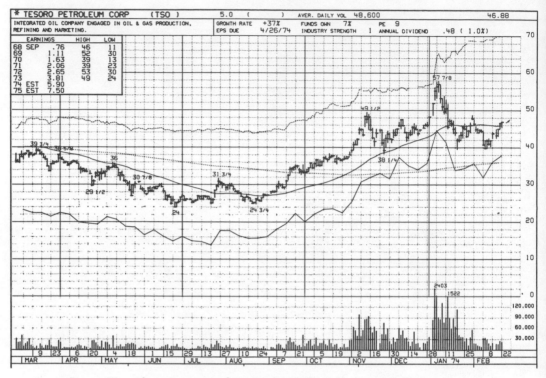

Figure 30. *Chart Courtesy of DAILY GRAPHS, P.O. Box 24933, Los Angeles, California 90024.*

popularity, although there is a difference in timing. The approach of buying stocks when they are temporarily out of vogue assumes that they will return to vogue shortly. The investor, thus, may get in on the ground floor, although he cannot be sure how long he will have to wait until the stock gets back in vogue——and he might make a mistake, and it does not become sought after. Certainly, the straw-hat approach does not recommend buying stocks that have just turned unpopular or that might remain unpopular indefinitely. My popularity approach may not catch stocks at the bottom, but it is designed to put you into stocks when investors have demonstrated an interest in them, and to keep your money working to maximize your return on capital. The name of the game is not to buy stocks at the very bottom and sell at the very top (this can rarely be done even if you make a conscious effort), but to have your money invested in stocks when they are moving and out of them when they are stagnant for an extended period. It is not easy to accomplish this goal, either, but it is far easier than catching the tops and bottoms of stocks.

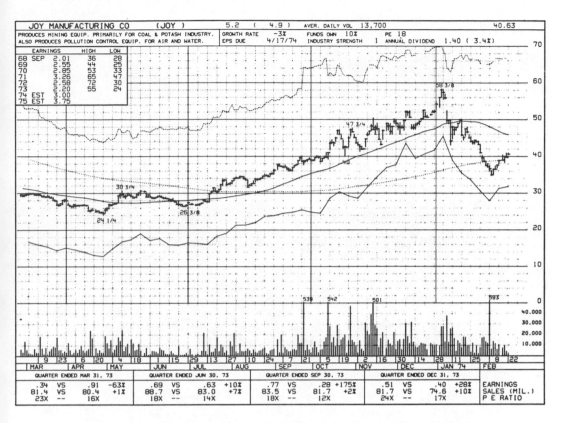

Figure 31. *Chart Courtesy of DAILY GRAPHS, P.O. Box 24933, Los Angeles, California 90024.*

5

How to Apply the Techno-Fundamental Technique to the First Stage of the Market Cycle

Recognizing the Signs of the Beginning of the First Stage Can Help You Participate Fully

The four stages I have divided the market cycle into are somewhat arbitrary classifications for purposes of recognizing the different influences on the market at various points in the stock market cycle. The shape of each stage and the length of time required varies from cycle to cycle. The boundary between the stages is usually not very sharp, and in the future may be even more blurred as government monetary policy is used increasingly to maintain stable enonomic growth. Rolling readjustments among industries, also, may characterize economies in the future more than general downturns. The first stage expansion basically is dependent on the amount of liquidation that has taken place in the fourth stage (usually a bear market). The ideal condition to start from is one in which the stock market has had a sharp decline and extensive stock selling has occurred, debt liquidation has taken place, Federal Reserve policy has turned expansionary, interest rates are still relatively higher, and a large pent-up demand for goods has developed. Rarely will all of these factors exist at any one time, however. In 1958, the economy came out of an economic downturn and pent-up demand was the primary cause of the increase in corporate profits and a rally in the stock market. Four years later, in 1962, the stock market declined largely because of speculation, and the ensuing rally resulted from the cash reserves built up from the liquidation of stocks. An abrupt change in Federal Reserve credit policy from restraint to ease was mainly responsible for the market rally in 1966. In 1970, both the prospects of an improvement in the economy and a decline in interest rates turned the market up. The market rallied in 1973 again on the outlook for a decline in interest rates, but was aborted by an oil embargo imposed by the Arab states during the Arab-Israeli War, and fears of an energy crisis in the U.S., Europe, and Japan. The prospects of an extended battle to unwind inflationary pressures which had built up over the decades was discouraging to investors, also.

Investors are generally slow to recognize a change in the downward trend in the stock market. They have seen so many false rallies that by the time the real thing takes place, investors are too numb to believe the turn has occurred. The signs of a market bottom were discussed in Chapter 2, but, in general, depending on what produced the market downturn—as discussed in the preceding paragraph—there may be a variety of signs that the first stage is about to get underway. (There are other causes of market declines, such as international monetary or credit crises, or wars, but it is difficult to anticipate these events.) Nevertheless, no matter what the cause of the downturn, the market itself usually will give pretty much the same signs of an impending upturn. Certainly, the general market indices, particularly the advance-decline line, will have had a sharp decline over a period of several months. Bearishness among the investing public is widespread, and some groups of stocks, particularly the secondary issues, have experienced sharp declines and many good values are available. If high interest rates and inflation were the primary causes of the market decline, indications that inflation may be slowing or interest rates are peaking could mark the bottom of the market. Possible signals of a peaking of inflationary pressures and interest rates include: lower rates of inflation and a decline in commodity futures; slowing bank loan demand; forecasts of federal budget surpluses; lower commercial paper rates; moves by the Federal Reserve to reduce stock market margin requirements or lower bank reserve requirements, or to reduce the Federal Reserve discount rate; a swing of open market operations toward increasing commercial banks' reserves, and a reduction in the commercial bank prime rate.

If a reduction, or expected reduction in economic activity, was responsible for the market decline the market itself might anticipate an improvement in the economy and be an indication, but it would be well to have the market well-exposed to the economic problems whose anticipation, or actual happening, caused the market to sell off in the first place. It would also be well for the market to have a decline in corporate profits already under its belt. Inventory liquidation and a decline in durable goods production, both consumer (autos, in particular) and capital equipment production, are often responsible for economic slowdowns. Such liquidations contain the seeds for their own improvement. (Energy and raw material shortages may be a factor in economic activity in future years, but at this writing the experience with shortages is too limited to forecast their impact.) One thing is very likely, however: the market will enter into the first stage before any definite signs of an economic upturn are seen. Markets usually bottom out when the news is believed to be the worst on the assumption that any future change will be for the better.

Importance of a First Stage Overall Strategy

If you look at the post war period (See Figures 1 and 4), you can note that the major uptrend in stock prices took place in about two years after a major market decline (with the exception of the 1962-1965 rally) before a significant reaction set in. In some instances, after a period of consolidation, the popular averages were able to move higher, but the major move had nevertheless taken place in about the first two years. The first stage (stocks returning to reasonable values from an undervalued condition) and the second stage (the stage which reflects the full economic recovery) were not distinct in most cases, although several rallies were followed by reactions or consolidations for a year or more and then the popular averages entered the second stage when the rally resumed and carried to a new high. You can see in Figures 4 and 32, for example, that in the 1970-72 rally the first peak was reached in April, 1972 at the DJIA 977.72. After a consolidation for about six months, the DJIA rallied to 1067.20. The move from the low of DJIA 627.46 to 977.72 actually accounted for 80 percent of the total rally to 1067.20. It can also be noted that the DJIA spent two to three months in two consolidation patterns before the major rise began. (The second consolidation appeared to be a false bearish indication.) The foregoing discussion does not mean that there are not plenty of capital gains opportunities in the stock market subsequent to the first stage. Uncertainties in the marketplace can be expected to produce undervalued situations at any point in the market cycle. Emerging new industries and new fads and fashions can develop at any time and speculation is never out of style.

There are two different strategies that can be used in attempting to take advantage of the stage 1 (and possibly stage 2) rally. You can look for signs of a selling climax and try to pick the bottom of the decline (Stage 4), or you can wait for several months while the market builds a base. The major problem of trying to identify a bottom through the emotional excesses that take place (as discussed in Chapter 2) is that you may get back in before the actual bottom is reached. For example, it looked very much as if the bottom had been seen in January, 1970 (see Figure 32), but before a base could be completed the Penn Central Transportation Company bankruptcy threw the market into another plunge. It can be said, though, that after a long decline and when the extreme emotional excesses characteristic of a major bottom are present, even if it should slide again, the market is likely to be near the bottom and any decline on unexpected news might be the last selloff. Certainly, what is very much desired before you assume the bottom has been seen is that the market should be exposed to the actual unfavorable economic news that it may have been anticipating. You can never be sure the market has fully discounted bad news until you see the event actually happening.

If you elect to wait for a base to be built, you will not get in at the bottom, but you still should be able to catch the major move in the market and also have your money invested while stocks are moving and avoid having your funds idle when the market is stalemated. You have added assurance that the bottom has been seen once the downside has been well-tested and a breakout on the upside has occurred, as during the September-November 1970 period. (See Figure 32.) There are exceptions, however, to this general rule. The 1973 decline was primarily the result of high interest rates and an expected slowing of the unsustainable economic growth rate. When investors thought that interest rates were peaking out in the summer, the market appeared to be bottoming out and a rally took place. (See Figure 33.) The rally was very convincing, although there was still not enough evidence for investors to determine how much an economic slowdown there might be in the months ahead. Actually, we will never know whether the market had made a valid bottom, since the Arab-Israeli War, the Arab oil embargo, and fear of a severe energy crisis sent the market into a steep decline.

I have been discussing taking advantage of the first-stage profit opportunities by getting in on the market rally early. A legitimate question is when should you take your profits? There is no simple answer to this question. As I have pointed out, it seems that the largest portion of the rally occurs during the first stage in about two years after a major bear market. Some stocks, particularly cyclical issues, may even get a second wind in the second stage of the market cycle. However, you have to be aware that cyclical stocks can anticipate the peak of an economic cycle by many months. The DJIA apparently anticipated the top of the economic cycle in late 1973 by several months when it peaked in January, 1973. The bulk of the market (the advance-decline line), however, topped out in April, 1971.

Stock Which Will Give You the Best Run for Your Money

You do not have to be a wizard to make money when stocks are coming off the bottom of a bear market. Practically all types of stocks—quality growth, secondary growth, cyclical, speculative, and undervalued—tend to participate in the sharp rally of the first stage. There is a special group of stocks, however, that is likely to give you the wildest ride of any group or industry. This group is the volatile, high short-interest group. When the market turns at a major bottom, investors (using the term in its broad sense) who are short volatile stocks are apt to panic and to rush to cover. Traders who are aware of this phenememon are quick to take advantage of the discomfiture of those with short positions, and their buying is added to that of the shorts. Once the rally gets underway, long term investors may join and add their buying power to that of the others.

If you want to take advantage of the capital gains potential of the volatile stocks in the first stage, you do have to play the odds very carefully. This group is

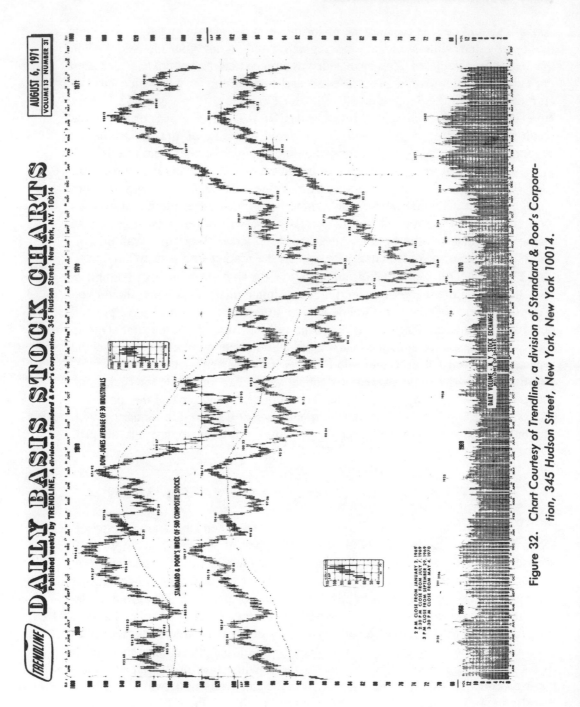

Figure 32.   Chart Courtesy of Trendline, a division of Standard & Poor's Corporation, 345 Hudson Street, New York, New York 10014.

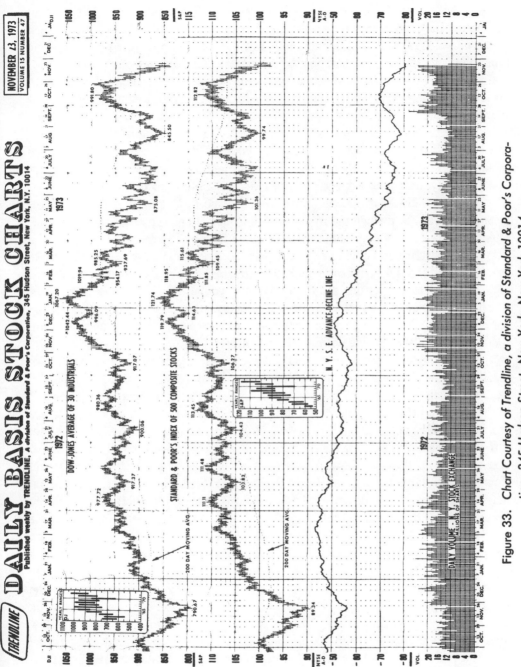

Figure 33.   *Chart Courtesy of Trendline, a division of Standard & Poor's Corpora-*
tion, 345 Hudson Street, New York, New York 10014.

usually the first to move out (unless it is a rounding-type bottom and there is no selling climax), so that if you wait for solid evidence of a rally you will miss much of the move. It takes a keen understanding of the risk and potential in determining when you should buy. There should be extreme pessimism on the part of investors and some tangible evidence of the corporate problems which the market has been anticipating. Sometimes you can even predict what type of event might turn the market around. You may not know whether it will happen or not, but when the market is extremely oversold and it seems that all the unfavorable news you can think of is in it, if this event should occur you are likely to see some very sharp advances in the volatile stocks. Of course, something else favorable may occur and you may miss your opportunity, or even get caught on the short side.

Often, stocks that appear to be the best short sales turn out to have the greatest appreciation when the market turns around. I can remember a horrendous experience in 1968 which taught me a valuable lesson. The market had suffered a very severe decline and bearishness was just about universal. Many volatile stocks had head and shoulder patterns which appeared very ominous. On top of this, the U.S. seemed to be getting more deeply involved in the South Vietnam War. Then, the unexpected happened. President Johnson announced he would not run for re-election. Several high-short-interest stocks, some of which I had sold short, were up 50 to 100 percent within a few months.

How do you know which stocks will provide the most action in a major market upturn? Past volatility is a guide. If you have "beta" tables available you can tell which stocks have a history of the highest volatility (beta is a measure of the volatility of the stock relative to the popular market indices). Such beta tables are not actually necessary if you are a close observer of the market. It is not difficult to pick out some of the more volatile stocks followed by the traders. All you have to do is watch how they act over a period of time when the market fluctuates. Volatile (high beta) stocks will tend to fluctuate more than the general market, both on the upside and downside. Knowing the latest short interest can be helpful, also, in selecting volatile stocks. *The Wall Street Journal* and *Barron's* publish a list of the stocks on the New York Stock Exchange and American Stock Exchange that have high short interests. The short interest should also be related to the number of common shares outstanding or to the float (the shares in the hands of the public or not closely held) and to the average daily volume of the stock. Obviously, the same short interest could have a bigger impact on the stock of a company with a small capitalization or in which the trading volume was low than on a large-capitalization, high-volume stock. Five stocks that exemplified how sharply volatile issues can rally after a major market bottom were Communications Satellite, Tektronix, Natomas, Control Data, and Hewlett-Packard. In the two years following the 1970 bottom, Control Data, Communications Satellite, Tektronix, and Hewlett-Packard tripled in price, and Notamas increased in price more than seven-fold. (See Figures 34, 35, 36, 37, and 38.)

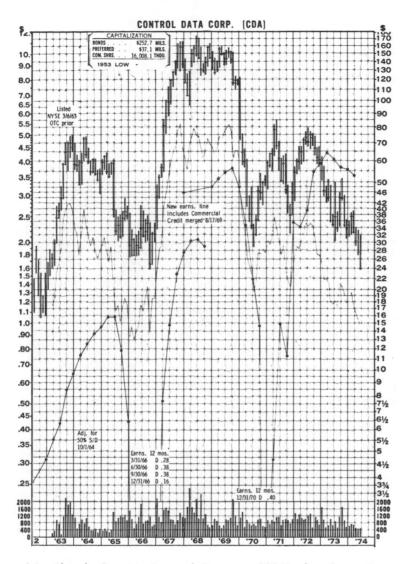

Figure 34. *Chart by Securities Research Company, 208 Newbury Street, Boston, Massachusetts.*

Other Stocks Also Can Be Very Profitable

The ability to anticipate major market rallies is an important element in your program to triple your money in the stock market, but this ability alone does not assure you of success. You also have to be aware of the type of stock you have bought and know something about its behavioral characteristics. Is it a stock in which good earnings gains can be expected to sustain the rally that began in Stage

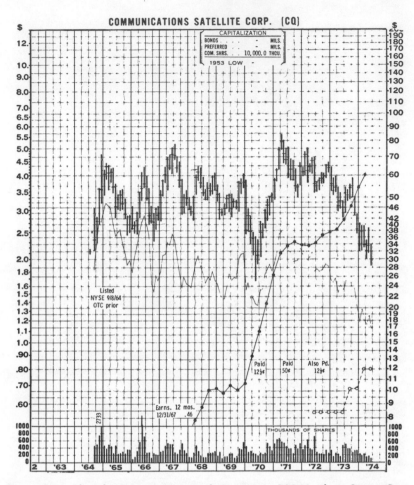

Figure 35. *Chart by Securities Research Company, 208 Newbury Street, Boston, Massachusetts.*

1, or is it a stock which just basically benefited from short covering, and once the shorts have covered there is no sustainability of earnings to encourage buying and support by the institutions or the general public? Too often the investor assumes that if a stock rallies he was correct in assuming that the company had great potential. You will later see the folly and the danger of this assumption.

Money can be made in even the most speculative stocks during Stage 1, as we have discussed earlier, but you have to use a different strategy toward stocks that do not have staying power from the strategy you use for stocks that have excellent long term prospects. Stocks that have "seen their day," that are "over the hill," or that are "fallen angels," will participate in the first stage, but the probability is that once the traders have a good profit in these stocks they will sell

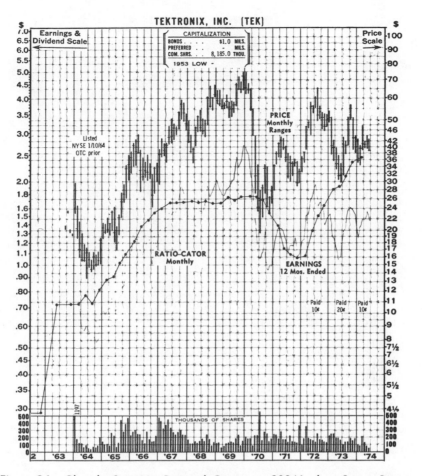

Figure 36. *Chart by Securities Research Company, 208 Newbury Street, Boston, Massachusetts.*

them and look for "greener pastures." In the first place, there are too many investors with losses in these stocks who will sell once they can break even. In addition, a concept does not have the same appeal the second time around, and, also, it often happens that conditions may have changed and the same profit opportunities no longer exist for these stocks. Usually, there is nothing new to bring in fresh buying. The concept has run its course and investors are looking for new ideas. Under these circumstances, the best thing for you to do is not to get carried away with the program. Be thankful you achieved a good gain in such stocks and take your profit. Otherwise you may find yourself riding them back down again. Occasionally, a stock which had a sharp decline may still be in a viable business. The stock probably will not be accorded the high price-earnings

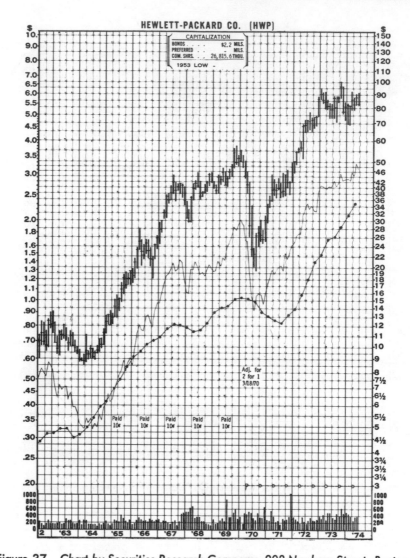

Figure 37. *Chart by Securities Research Company, 208 Newbury Street, Boston, Massachusetts.*

ratio when it was the rage of Wall Street, but if earnings continue up it could work higher in time. The burden of proof, however, is on the stock. Examples of relatively speculative situations that ran out of steam after a sharp rally off the 1970 low can be seen in Figures 39, 40, and 41. High Voltage Engineering, Farah Manufacturing, and Litton all had been eagerly sought after by investors, and following the 1969-70 market decline many investors assumed the stocks would return to their old status. They could not have been more wrong. True, the stocks rallied into 1971, but unless investors were alert to sell on the signs of substantial

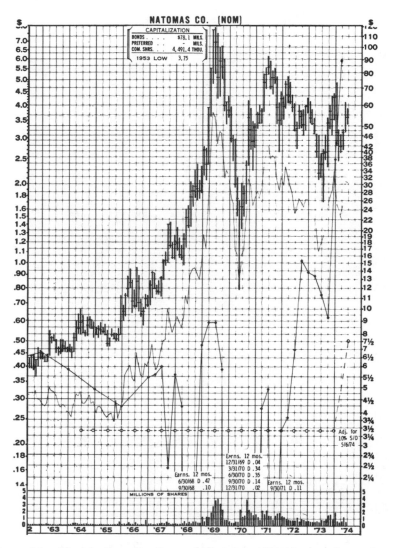

Figure 38. *Chart by Securities Research Company, 208 Newbury Street, Boston, Massachusetts.*

technical weakness, they could have seen their stocks plunge far below their lows of the 1969-1970 bear market. Earnings were too disappointing for the rallies to continue and the stocks all broke important support levels.

Profit Opportunities in Cyclical Stocks

Many investors have become discouraged with cyclical stocks because their timing has so often turned out to be very poor. Instead of buying them when the

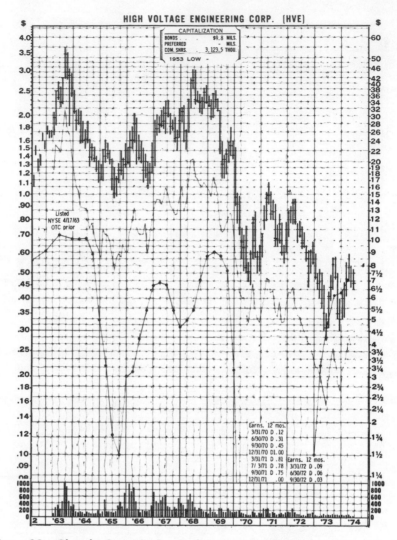

Figure 39. *Chart by Securities Research Company, 208 Newbury Street, Boston, Massachusetts.*

news was pessimistic, they bought them when the news was relatively good and the stocks were already substantially off their bottoms. When selling them, they tended to wait until they saw some unfavorable news or earnings comparisons and the stocks were then sharply down from their highs. It seemed these investors always missed out on timing, both on the buy side and the sell side.

Unfortunately, there is no sure-fire formula for timing the buying and selling of cyclical stocks. However, there are some general rules which can be very useful in helping you to make money in these stocks. Perhaps the first rule to

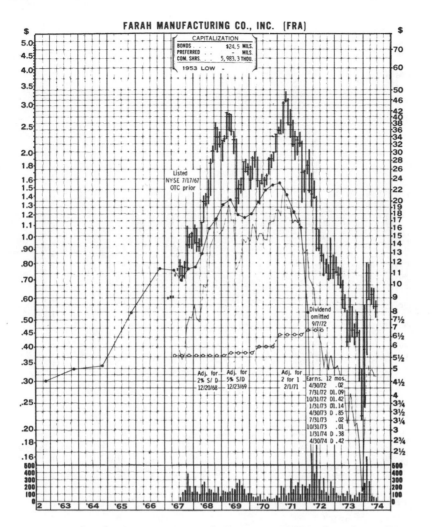

Figure 40.   *Chart by Securities Research Company, 208 Newbury Street, Boston, Massachusetts.*

observe is that you should resist the temptation to try to get in at the lows and out at the very tops. By trying to cut it too fine you can easily outsmart yourself in buying and selling cyclical stocks. This rule will be very valuable in helping you avoid buying before the decline has exhausted itself or selling too soon before the rally has run its course. Unless the markets indications that a general market bottom has been seen (discussed in Chapter 2) are very persuasive, it is usually better to wait until the general market and the individual stocks have passed their nadir and have tested their lows successfully before taking a position. In the selling climax-type of markets, most cyclical stocks will generally make their

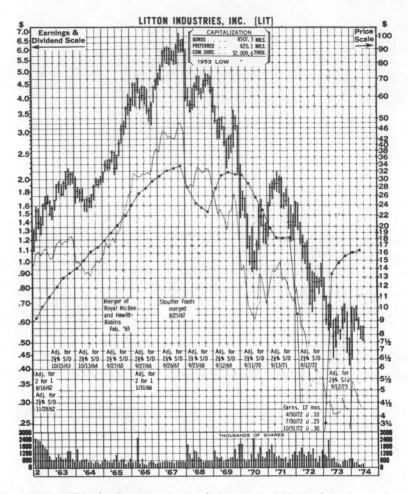

Figure 41. *Chart by Securities Research Company, 208 Newbury Street, Boston, Massachusetts.*

lows along with the general market as Chrysler did in May of 1970. (See Figure 42.) However, few cyclical stocks will hit their lows before the general market unless some unusual problem develops. Some cyclical stocks may make their lows after the general market, such as Cincinnati Milacron, Inc. (See Figure 43.) (Stocks that hold up particularly well may be among the stronger issues in the next rally.)

One of the More Comfortable Ways to Make Money in Stage 1

Too often investors play the stock market as if they were throwing dice. They pick a likely stock and say, ''Here goes,'' and their ratio of success is just about as

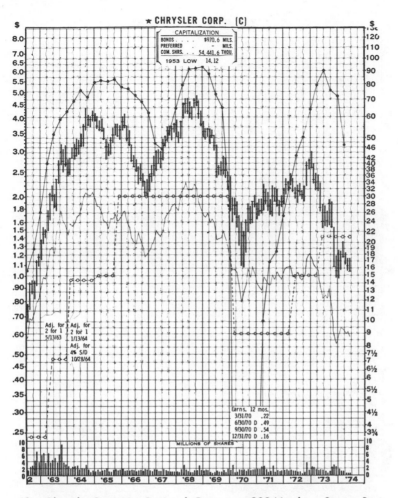

Figure 42. *Chart by Securities Research Company, 208 Newbury Street, Boston, Massachusetts.*

good as in throwing dice. The investor has far more chance to make money in the stock market than in gambling if he will just exercise the patience and discipline necessary to get the odds overwhelmingly in his side. (Of course, there is a major difference between investing and gambling. In investing, value can be added to stocks by corporate action over a period of time, whereas in gambling one man's gain has to be another man's loss.) As far as the general market goes, before you take a position you should have all the unfavorable news in the market of which you can think. Once the market has been exposed to adverse news for some months, it is likely that just about all the investors who were inclined to sell their stocks have already done so. Thus, unless you are mistaken about the worst news being behind the market, now the odds have shifted in your favor and investors

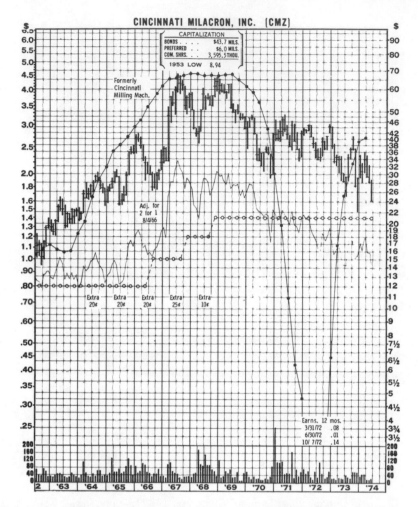

Figure 43.   *Chart by Securities Research Company, 208 Newbury Street, Boston, Massachusetts.*

are in a position to buy stocks if any favorable news develops, or if the market rally starts even for purely technical reasons. Once you have the overall market environment working for you, you can further improve your odds by selecting stocks that have everything to gain and little to lose. Such stocks are ones which have been relatively neglected by the stock market, but improvement is expected. There are not too many investors waiting to get out of these stocks, and a "new story" can bring in a fresh crop of investors. Such stocks, also, are apt to be undervalued relative to their improving prospects. If the new story can be tied to a long term trend, you may have a real winner. Stocks that fulfilled these criteria at the bottom of the 1970 stock market included Combustion Engineering, one of the

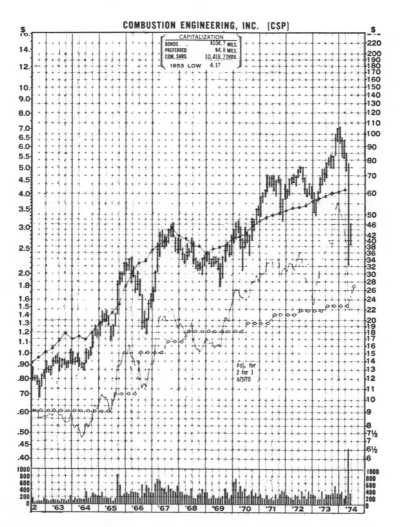

Figure 44. *Chart by Securities Research Company, 208 Newbury Street, Boston, Massachusetts.*

main beneficiaries of the need for nuclear power-generating equipment (see Figure 44), and Deere, a major factor in the manufacture of farm machinery to help satisfy the growing food requirements of the world (see Figure 45). Combustion Engineering more than doubled in two years and Deere more than tripled from its 1970 low in less than three years. The 1973 Russian purchase of wheat from the U.S. helped focus attention on the stock, but it had already seen its major move for some months by then.

Another group of stocks that did well coming off the 1970 market bottom was the relatively undervalued stocks. Many of these stocks had sunk to four or

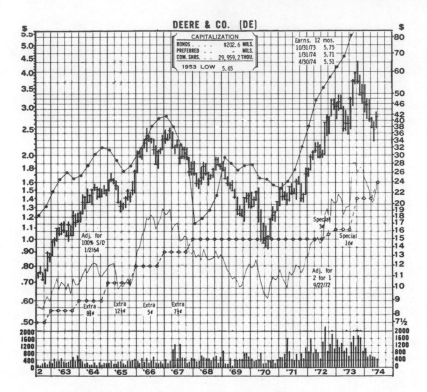

Figure 45.   *Chart by Securities Research Company, 208 Newbury Street, Boston, Massachusetts.*

five times or less earnings and had liberal yields which added to the downside protection. In the market decline, they were more the victims of the "investor panic syndrome" than of any lack of earnings performance. Earnings, in fact, often held up relatively well. The panic syndrome goes into operation when a somewhat speculative stock turns down. Investors assume something drastic is happening to the company and many sell. Then as the stock continues down and becomes cheap, other investors look at the low price-earnings ratio, assume the company is going bankrupt, and also sell. However, once the general market turns, investors tend to shake off their pessimism, become optimistic, and recognize these stock values for what they are. Three stocks that went through this process in the 1969-1970 decline and 1970 rally were U.S. Industries, Chromalloy-American, and Northwest Industries. (See Figures 46, 47, and 48.) There is a sequel to the story, however. The stocks did not hold their gains long. The popularity of these issues had faded, there was nothing new to titillate investors, and when the stocks returned to reasonable values, profit-taking came in. During the second decline investors appeared to place more importance on

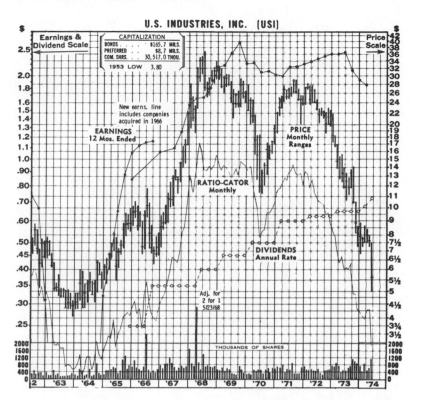

Figure 46. *Chart by Securities Research Company, 208 Newbury Street, Boston, Massachusetts.*

dividend yields than on price-earnings ratios, and the stocks had substantial declines.

One of the More Reliable Ways to Make Money

As you have seen, relatively unpopular stocks can do well in a period of stock market optimism if they are undervalued enough, but they are, nevertheless, vulnerable to profit-taking and may have difficulty maintaining their momentum very long. The downside risk initially is not too great in these stocks, especially if they have a liberal yield to support them. If your timing is off regarding the bottom of the general market, you should not be hurt too badly. Also, while you are waiting for capital appreciation you are receiving a good current return. Nevertheless, you have to be flexible in buying such stocks and willing to take your profits when you think the major move has occurred.

There is another group of stocks which can also work out very well in the

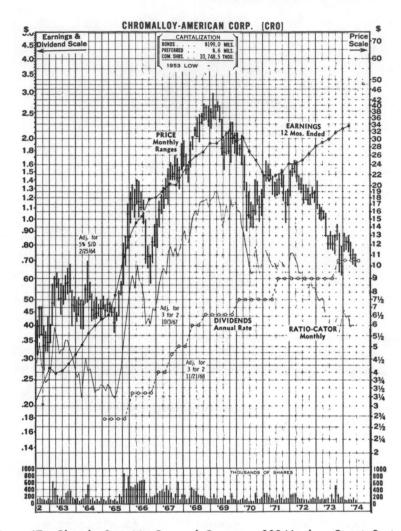

Figure 47. *Chart by Securities Research Company, 208 Newbury Street, Boston, Massachusetts.*

first stage and in which risk appears to be relatively low—the natural resource companies. In this age of inflation, natural resources can be an important inflationary hedge, and the value of the assets may provide a floor for the stock prices. It was not always true that natural resource stocks were inflation hedges. In the 1950s they often did not protect the investor too well. The problem in those days, however, was that there was an oversupply of natural resources, such as petroleum and copper, and instead of prices going up to offset inflation, prices often went down. It does seem that the era of cheap raw materials (as well as cheap energy) is behind us now, however, and that prices will trend higher with infla-

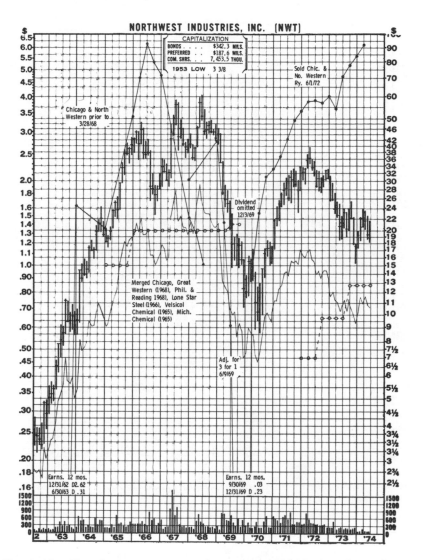

Figure 48.   *Chart by Securities Research Company, 208 Newbury Street, Boston, Massachusetts.*

tion. Moreover, most natural resources are now international commodities, and if foreign prices are significantly higher than domestic prices, the net result will be a flow of our natural resources overseas to the detriment of the U.S. economy, resulting in upward price pressure domestically. Natural resource stocks can have their setbacks, just as do any other stocks; however the assets in the ground are likely to continue to become more valuable and permit the recovery of the stocks once investor confidence returns. Three good examples of how natural resource stocks can bounce back are offered by the performances of Kerr-McGee, Phillips

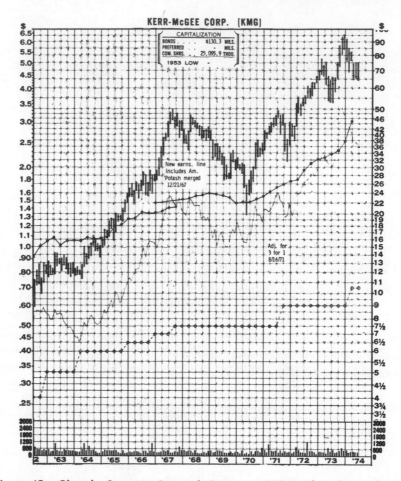

Figure 49.   *Chart by Securities Research Company, 208 Newbury Street, Boston,*
            Massachusetts.

Petroleum, and Utah International after the 1970 decline. (See Figures 49, 50, and
51.) Kerr is active in oil and gas production and is the largest producer of
uranium. Phillips Petroleum has large reserves of natural gas in the U.S. and has
an important stake in the North Sea crude reserves. Utah International derives the
largest part of its earnings from the sale of coal and also has copper, uranium, and
iron ore reserves. If we assume the first stage ended in 1971, Kerr-McGee more
than doubled in a year and both Phillips Petroleum and Utah International fell
somewhat short of doubling. However, over a three-year period, Kerr-McGee
tripled and the other two came close to tripling.

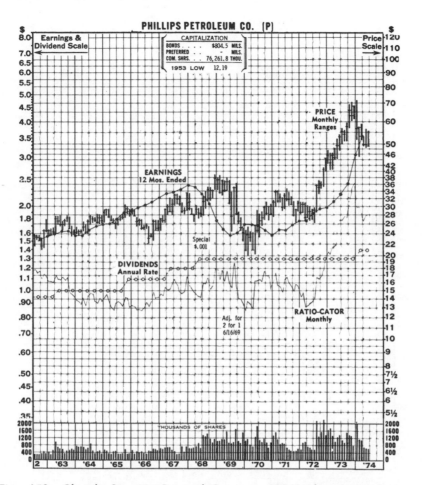

Figure 50. *Chart by Securities Research Company, 208 Newbury Street, Boston, Massachusetts.*

Having the Strength of Your Conviction
May Be Helpful at Times

I have stressed that you should confine your stock purchases to issues that are in popular areas and which are acting well, in order to avoid falling into the trap of buying stocks that appear cheap, but in which there is just no investor interest. Such advice, unfortunately, does not solve all the problems that you might encounter. For example, suppose you followed my advice and bought a stock involving a promising concept with bright prospects for sustainable long range growth. The stock had broken out of a six-month technical base, but suddenly

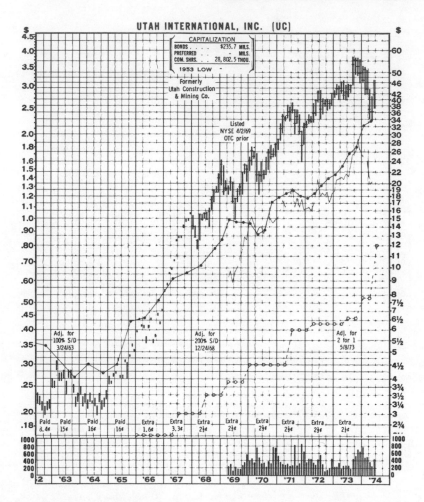

Figure 51.   *Chart by Securities Research Company, 208 Newbury Street, Boston, Massachusetts.*

turned down. What do you do? Do you quickly cut your losses, or do you try to ride it out and hope the stock turns up again? I am assuming you took the general market outlook into consideration and did not buy after the economy and the market had a long rise, investors were extremely bullish, and the market was ripe for substantial profit-taking. If you bought into such a market, it might be advisable to take your loss and wait until the market has had a decline and investors were generally bearish before re-establishing your position. If you still believe the general market trend is in your favor, then you have to consider the possibilities regarding the individual stock. It is possible that the stock is influenced by an industry or group which could be turning unpopular. It may be amply priced in relation to its industry or group, earnings may be slowing, an unfavorable earnings comparison may be in the offing, or a development which could have added to earnings potential may not be working out. You have to examine these possibilities very carefully and, of course, the only way you can do it intelligently is to know the company and its industry very well. If you think any of these possibilities is occurring you had better sell. On the other hand, it may be that it is just a technical reaction, or profit-taking, which you are seeing that will soon run its course. Decisions to hold or sell have to be made often if you are active in the stock market. If you are to withstand the doubts and fears that envelop you when a sound stock behaves adversely, you have to have great conviction that you are correct. I am not advocating "fighting the market" or "going down with the ship," but you also cannot run scared every time a stock has a contrary fluctuation. There may be a fine line between the two situations, but you should endeavor to learn the distinction. The techno-fundamental strategies I have been discussing will help you, but in the end your success will depend on your good judgment.

I might cite an example of what I have been talking about. Allied Chemical was a very promising stock. The chemical industry had changed from a surplus-industry to an industry hard pressed to keep up with demand. Allied's feedstock problems appeard to be less than those faced by the industry in general since the bulk of its chemicals were inorganic. The company also had substantial interests in petroleum acreage in the North Sea and Indonesia, a fact which was particularly significant in view of the energy shortage. It seemed that the company had everything going for it, and, in addition, the stock appeared to have built a technical base from February through July. (See Figure 52.) However, in August, for no apparent reason, the stock suddenly sold off. The stock was acting poorly and a pure technician probably would have sold it. However, an investor who knew the fundamental background of the stock might well consider the possibility that this was a false technical signal, and since he could in no way see a fundamental confirmation of technical weakness, he might well have elected to continue to hold the stock. If he had done so, he would have been right since the stock quickly turned around and had a good rally. It does often happen that stocks have a final selloff before a substantial rally takes place.

A Conservative Approach in the First Stage

Although it is likely that the most money will be made by buying volatile stocks in the first stage if you recognize the first stage for what it is, some investors may want to hedge their bets by relying on more conservative stocks just in case the bottom has not been seen. Conservative stocks by definition should be less influenced by the economic cycle than the bulk of the stocks, although they may be more susceptible to interest rate fluctuations. Thus, to insure that you are reducing your risk in buying conservative stocks, you should have good reason to

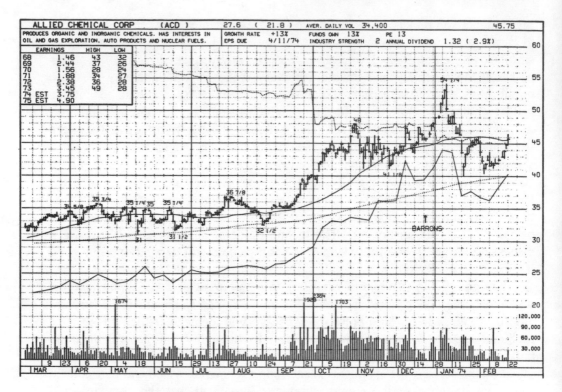

Figure 52. *Chart Courtesy of DAILY GRAPHS, P.O. Box 24933, Los Angeles, California 90024.*

believe that interest rates are peaking out. These stocks can benefit from a double leverage. Market optimism will tend to spread to most of the stocks in the list just on general principles, and any decline in interest rates should also have a direct favorable impact on interest-rate sensitive stocks. You do have to be careful with interest-rate sensitive stocks, with regard to the possibility of a relapse, however. Interest rates may turn down only temporarily and then rise, and the interest-rate sensitive stocks are apt to decline. We can see this pattern in the behavior of two stocks, Chase Manhattan Corp. and Aetna Life and Casualty. (See Figures 53 and 54.) Both had good rallies off their 1970 lows well into 1972, but rising interest rates in 1973 brought about declines. Before the decline, Chase Manhattan, nevertheless, almost doubled and Aetna Life and Casualty more than doubled.

Signs of the First Stage Top

It often seems to me that market professionals tend to claim more precision for their ability to forecast the stock market than is warranted by the history of

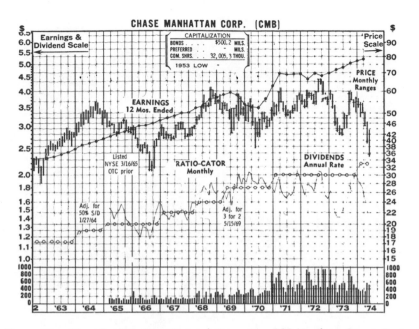

Figure 53. *Chart by Securities Research Company, 208 Newbury Street, Boston, Massachusetts.*

stock market forecasting. It also is my impression that the many stock market indicators that are trotted out by some market analysts do not contribute too much to the timing of the turns in the stock market cycle, and may even tend to be confusing. Some indicators overlap and others are going in different directions. My experience has been that the simple method of watching how the market reacts to news and attempting to forecast when all the favorable news is pretty much known (when forecasting tops) or when all the unfavorable news is known (when forecasting bottoms) is about as good as any method. Of course, the difficult part of this approach is that you should have a fairly good understanding of the economy and interest rates in order to be able to forecast how much better or worse the economy will get. We should not kid ourselves, however, that one can ever predict with any certainty what either the economy or the stock market will do. We can only arrive at a range of probabilities in predicting when the trend will change. Sometimes the trend can change suddenly (this happens at bottoms more often that at tops), but forecasting when a sudden change will occur is practically impossible since relatively unpredictable events often trigger these sudden changes. You can often sense, however, that the market is technically ready for a change if it tends to resist reacting to more of the same type of news. I keep talking about one market, but you realize, of course, that all stocks do not move in concert. Some top out before others and some bottom out before others. The

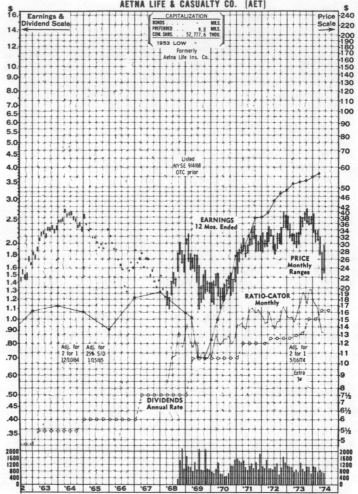

Figure 54. Chart by Securities Research Company, 208 Newbury Street, Boston, Massachusetts.

diverse action of stocks compounds the problem of using popular indices in trying to time the purchase or sale of individual stocks. It would, also, be helpful if one type of stock would behave the same way under nearly the same circumstances. What makes forecasting more difficult is that investors may place more emphasis on growth in one market atmosphere, on dividends in another market climate, and on asset values under other market conditions. This emphasis is probably mostly a reflection of investor confidence and the availability of alternative investments, such as high yielding bonds and short term paper.

As I noted earlier, the stages of the market cycle are primarily a concept for understanding the behavior of stocks. The line between the first and second stages, in particular, may not be very distinct. In those situations in which there is a distinct separation between the end of the first stage and the beginning of the second stage, the transition could be characterized by a churning on high volume, little response to favorable earnings, and technical weakness, including a peaking out of new highs, net advances on the New York Stock Exchange and the volume of the advances, a penetration of trendlines on the downside, and a breaking of support levels by the popular market indices and by individual stocks. We could say that the first stage coming off the 1970 bottom ended in February, 1971. (See Figure 55.) The further market rise to April can be attributed to the market reflecting the improving prospects of the economy and corporate profits. There is, of course, no way to say with any certainty that at a specific point in the rally investors stopped thinking in terms of undervaluation and began anticipating the earnings to be generated by the economic recovery, but the two concepts, nevertheless, are helpful in explaining the stock market action.

Avoiding Serious Mistakes in the First Stage

If one took a very detached view of the market, the behavior of investors looks almost comical at times. During a market rally investors are frantically chasing stocks before they get away, with little concern about how much they are paying for earnings or how great the current dividend return is. Literally overnight investors in a market decline will be rushing to sell the same stocks before they go any lower, extremely worried about whether the price-earnings ratio is too rich or not, and whether the current yield is adequate to support the stock. It is no overstatement to say that the trend of the market and the day-to-day action has a powerful effect on investors. This almost overwhelming influence of current market action causes investors to forget about values and risks and leads to one of the most common mistakes investors make, that of returning to the market too soon. They forget that declines may have several false rallies, and they are so anxious not to miss the beginning of the rally that they often are taking positions half down the decline. A very good policy that helps you avoid this trap is to wait until the problems that have caused the market decline, whether the economy or interest rates, have gotten about as bad as can reasonably be expected before starting to buy. I am not suggesting you wait for the solution of the problems—the market usually anticipates too far ahead for that. But watching for the unfavorable events to actually occur and for the market to stop reacting to them is, in my opinion, the best method there is to detect market bottoms. Unfortunately, the wait may require several months and few investors have the patience or discipline to wait that long. If you wait, however, when the time comes to buy, you will find that you have a very comfortable feeling that the worst is behind you and that from now on anything that happens is for the better.

If getting into the market too soon is one of the most common mistakes, not

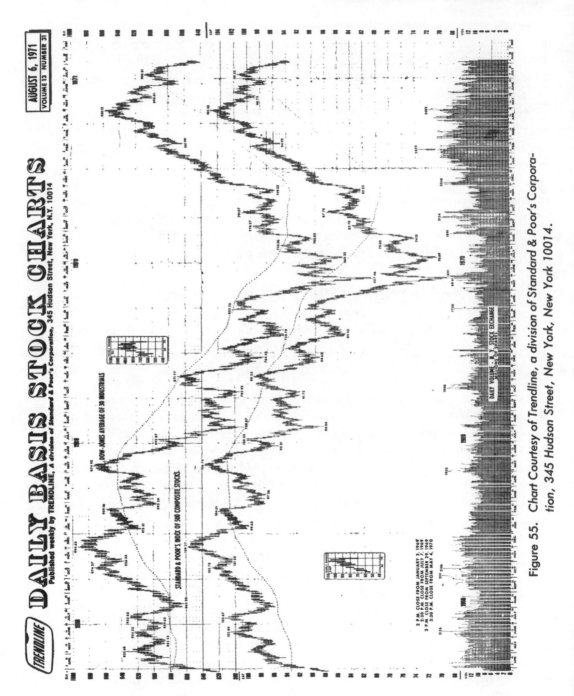

Figure 55.   Chart Courtesy of Trendline, a division of Standard & Poor's Corporation, 345 Hudson Street, New York, New York 10014.

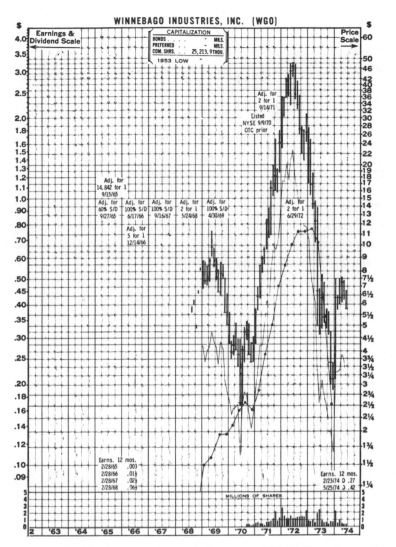

Figure 56. Chart by Securities Research Company, 208 Newbury Street, Boston, Massachusetts.

getting out soon enough is another. Once stocks are running, investors tend to believe they will never stop climbing. They do not realize that rallies become a fashion which can pass just as declines, to a large extent, represent mental attitudes that can change. Thus, when everything appears very rosy for the economy, individual industries and stocks and you no longer see any unusual bargains, start looking for signs of a top. Remember that your stocks may top out before the popular indices. Some stocks may get another wind in the second stage, but some may not. Make sure you have good evidence, such as a breakdown technically before selling, however, because there may be several false declines in the first stage before a major decline sets in.

In between the mistakes of getting in too early and getting out of the market too late, a frequent mistake is staying in speculative stocks too long. Once short covering has run its course, these stocks tend to lose much of their support. The fad or fashion that gave them the following in the first place, also, has likely played out. Often the favorable conditions for expanding profits have changed. In the case of Winnebago, overcapacity developed in the industry. (See Figure 56.) The pressure on earnings was enough to completely change sentiment toward the stock. After the first sharp selloff, many investors thought they had bargains, but as often happens, the mere fact a stock has shown a great deal of technical weakness can change investors' attitudes toward it and make it very difficult for it to come back, even if earnings hold up. However, any rally Winnebago and the motor home industry might have enjoyed was cut short by the fuel shortage. A concept working against the industry, in addition to a decline in earnings and technical weakness, is a little too much for any stock to overcome without months of base-building. At some point, Winnebago may be a buy again, but it probably is best to let the market tell you when.

6

How to Use Techno-Fundamental Methods to Make Money During the Second Stage of the Market Cycle

Signs of the Beginning of the Second Stage

As aforementioned, the second stage of the market cycle may be a noticeably separate stage, or it may be a continuation of the first stage without too much interruption. The 1958-1961 market rise showed a fairly sharp distinction between the first stage, which can be said to have ended at the close of 1959, and the second stage. (See Figure 1.) The 1962-1965 rally showed less of a separation between the first and second stages. The 1965 decline should be considered a boundary between the two stages, although it was relatively brief. Whether the separation between the stages is distinct or not, you should recognize when the stock market is no longer climbing on momentum alone. After a hectic rally from the bottom, in which many a short-seller who thought the first stage was only a technical rally undoubtedly learned a painful lesson, the market finally will at least pause as if to sense what the new direction will be. Prior to this hesitation the market may have had several profit-taking reactions. The last correction, however, will take a little longer and appear to be more significant. (The February 1971 correction could be considered such a hesitation. See Figure 55.) From this point the market will be trying to assess the outlook for the economy and corporate profits. About this time you may start reading favorable comments about the economy and maybe even see some optimistic reports on economic indicators such as the Federal Reserve Board index of industrial production, the leading economic indicators, unemployment, new car sales, or the growth rate of the money supply. You can be sure that once you are seeing a constant stream of such news that the market is well into the second stage. This is the point where you will begin to see a "separation of the men from the boys." Stocks are now coming more under the influence of the economic outlook, and investors will be looking for those areas which are likely to experience the greater profit gains. The "fallen angels," speculative stocks, and conservative issues probably have had their greatest moves in the market cycle, if they have not already topped out, and some important decisions will have to be made soon.

Your Strategy for the Second Stage

When the major market trend is up, not too many stocks go sharply against the trend unless something very obvious is wrong. Investors are in a frame of mind in which they are looking for higher prices and are reluctant to sell. However, not all stocks have the same potential in Stage 2. Some industries have better prospects than others, and, of course, speculative stocks in which earnings growth is unsustainable or which have lost their earnings momentum, or stocks in which investors have just lost interest in the concept that propelled the stock in the first place, are among the least desirable. Industries which may have been the most depressed during the prior stock market decline because of shortages, inventory liquidations, etc., or possibly because of high interest rates which stifled demand, may be in the best position for a rebound because of the pent-up demand that could have developed.

The housing industry is a perfect example of an industry that could have been expected to be among the leaders coming out of the 1970 market decline. In 1970, housing starts were running at historically low levels, primarily because of abnormally high interest rates. The housing industry, thus, was in a position to benefit from pent-up demand as well as new demand if interest rates were to decline. Masonite was one of the outstanding market performers as the scenario turned out as hoped. Interest rates did decline and housing starts were up sharply. Masonite, a manufacturer of hardboard and producer of lumber, responded dramatically to the new economic environment. It almost tripled from its 1970 low to its peak in early 1972. (See Figure 57.) A company which more tangentially benefited from the improvement in conditions for the housing industry was the Federal National Mortgage Association (Fannie Mae). This company insures mortgages, primarily those which are government guaranteed. In 1970, it happened to have a substantial amount of short term debt carrying relatively high interest rates. As this debt matured it was rolled over at lower rates and produced significant savings. In addition, the increase in housing starts generated higher mortgage commitment fees for the company. This stock almost quadrupled from its low in 1970 to its peak in 1972. (See Figure 58.)

It usually pays to buy quality stocks in the second stage, but if enough

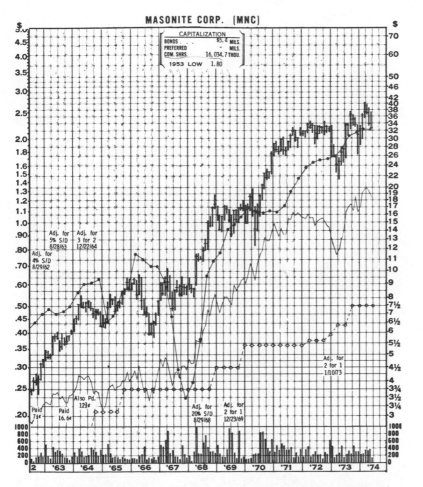

MASONITE CORP. (MNC)

Figure 57. Chart by Securities Research Company, 208 Newbury Street, Boston, Massachusetts.

glamour surrounds a second-tier company its stock can also show good gains even if it is a secondary issue. The ebullience of the second stage and the optimistic outlook for various industries tends to mask any weaknesses in associated secondary stocks. National Homes was a good example of a company that rode the wave of optimism for the housing industry. National Homes was a producer of fabricated housing and also manufactured modular homes. The hottest fad on Wall Street in 1970-71 was modular housing and any stock associated with it was immediately in demand. National Homes almost quintupled from its 1970 low to its 1972 high. (See Figure 59.) Earnings did register a good gain in 1971, but modular housing could not live up to its promise. It was not as economical as investors had expected and companies in this industry had difficulty making a

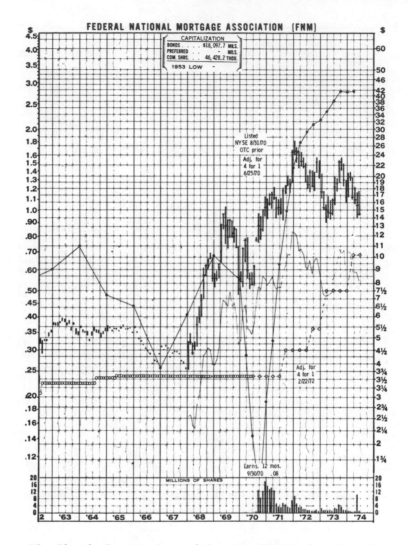

Figure 58. *Chart by Securities Research Company, 208 Newbury Street, Boston, Massachusetts.*

profit. Some, in fact, went bankrupt. Thus, modular housing had become unpopular instead of being among the most popular industries. The bubble had burst, and investors ran for cover. The fact that housing stocks had already discounted the substantial recovery in starts in 1972 and that further potential seemed limited also contributed to the selling in National Homes. The final blow was an actual decline in housing starts as rising interest rates and a shortage of mortgage money discourage home buyers.

As you can see, the second stage can be very tricky. Even while the general market trend is up, some stocks will do better than others. Many of these stocks

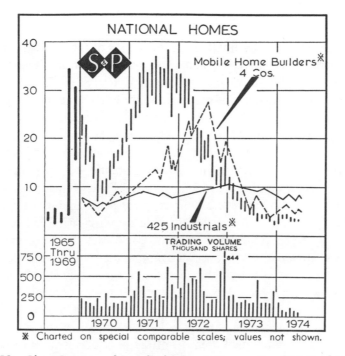

Figure 59. *Chart Courtesy of Standard & Poor's Corporation OTC Stock Reports,
345 Hudson Street, New York, New York 10014.*

should be switched out of while the news is still good. If you wait until the news turns unfavorable, such stocks may already have had a substantial decline. The "old stories" and speculative stocks which do not have a following are best avoided in this stage. Investors are mainly interested in good quality, sound stocks since they still are cheap enough to offer the possibility of capital appreciation. Quality growth stocks are likely to be in demand, but conservative issues may have seen their major move. Interest-sensitive stocks often can do well in this stage, although if inflationary pressures persist there is no assurance that interest rates will come down sharply in the second stage. Some cyclical stocks may see their peaks in this stage and should be sold. Do not expect them always to sell off immediately, however. It may take months to form a distribution pattern before they break down. There are also, as you will see in the next section, some cyclical stocks that have more left in them and could still be held.

Cyclical Stocks Which Act Somewhat Differently in the Second Stage

You cannot approach cyclical stocks as a group and expect all the individual stocks to act the same. Some cyclical companies have little in the way of long term growth prospects. Earning will slump in a recession and recover in a buoyant economy, but throughout the cycle earnings remain essentially on a plateau. The strategy for these stocks is to buy them in the depths of the recession and sell them when the economy is recovering and economic predictions become rosy. The technical indications should be watched closely during Stage 2, and if any deterioration is noted (the penetration of major trendlines or violation of support levels), the stocks should be sold. Playing the yield cycle in these stocks can be helpful, also. The yields are usually liberal when a buying opportunity is presented and are considerably less attractive when the stocks have exhausted their potential. Before buying, of course, the safety of the dividend should be considered as well as whether fundamental conditions in the industry have changed adversely. Such cyclical stocks, also, may not reach their previous peaks and investors will make a painful mistake if they wait for new highs before selling. (See Figures 60 and 61.) Chrysler actually never returned to its 1968 peak after the 1970 market bottom. Investors were apparently so concerned about the pollution control problems faced by the auto industry that they were not eager buyers of the stock even though auto sales were at record levels. Government price controls, also, no doubt, helped put a damper on the stock performance of both Chrysler and U.S. Gypsum. Cyclical companies often are able to increase prices in an economic recovery and the increased earnings help them to offset poor earnings in recession years. The government restrictions on price rises appeared to have helped cut short the rally of these stocks.

There are other groups of cyclical stocks that act entirely differently from the one I just described. Companies in this group are cyclical-growth companies, i.e., even though their earnings do fluctuate, the long term trend is up, nevertheless, and the companies are able to register new highs in earnings after each economic cycle. Another group of cyclical stocks may be emerging from a plateau as a result of new economic forces or needs. The energy crisis in the beginning of the 1970s was responsible for enhancing the outlook of a great many industries and companies. Two companies whose fortunes were thus affected were Ingersoll-Rand and Bucyrus-Erie.

Ingersoll-Rand was a leading producer of compressors used in the oil and gas industry. The stepup in oil and gas exploration, as well as the prospects of the company becoming a major supplier for the Alaska pipeline, gave the stock more the appearance of a growth company than a cyclical one. Bucyrus-Erie manufactured excavating equipment used in open pit mining operations. The need to utilize the great reserves of coal in the western United States that can be mined by surface mining made the stock particularly attractive in the minds of investors. Both of these stocks resisted declining. Ingersoll-Rand and Buycrus-Erie rallied sharply from their 1970 lows, spent some time consolidating, but ended 1972 near their highs and well above their 1970 lows. (See Figures 62 and 63.)

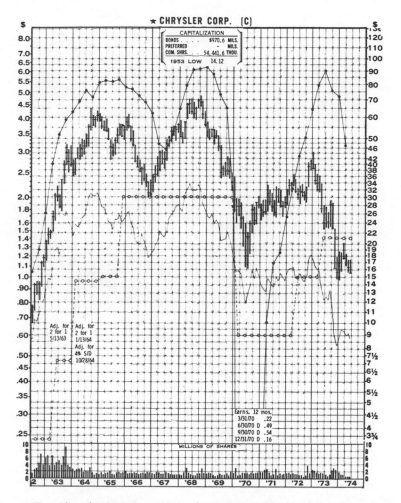

Figure 60. *Chart by Securities Research Company, 208 Newbury Street, Boston, Massachusetts.*

Stocks Which Can Still Be Profitable in the Second Stage

Stage 2 could mark the top for many stocks and, in particular, cyclical issues which are already anticipating their peak cyclical profits. Thus, you have to be careful in this stage that you do not overstay the market in stocks even though they are acting well. You should keep in mind that cyclical issues can see their peaks months before there is any hint of a slowing down in economic activity in the particular industry. Once investors believe that the price of a cyclical stock is

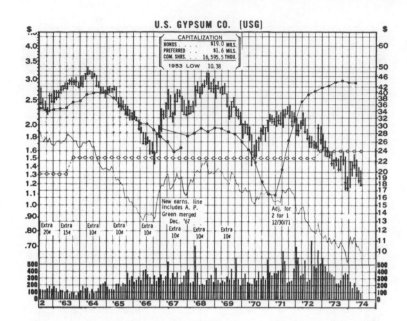

Figure 61.   *Chart by Securities Research Company, 208 Newbury Street, Boston,*
Massachusetts.

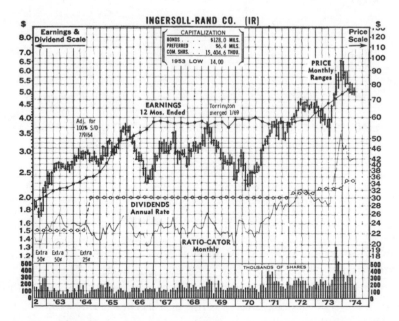

Figure 62.   *Chart by Securities Research Company, 208 Newbury Street, Boston,*
Massachusetts.

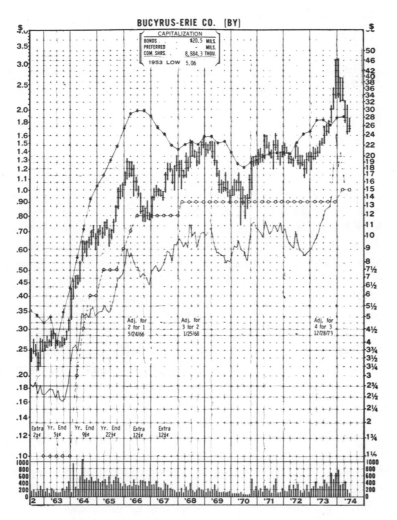

Figure 63. *Chart by Securities Research Company, 208 Newbury Street, Boston, Massachusetts.*

reasonable in relation to the peak earnings they foresee for the cycle, they are willing to sell.

There are situations in which you may want to let your profits run, however, and not try to anticipate the market reaction which usually follows the end of Stage 2. These stocks may emerge in Stage 1 or Stage 2, but it is in Stage 2 that the investor is more likely to make the mistake of selling too early. These stocks are the ones with new stories that show great promise of a strong future growth curve. I have tried to emphasize the importance the market places on new stories in other places in this book and I cannot stress the concept enough. Investors tend to lose interest in old stories; they think that because everyone knows about them further profit potential is limited. (This was not true of the quality growth stocks, however, when the institutions were supporting them, but they also joined the crowd when it became apparent that the quality growth stocks had become very richly priced in relation to other values in the stock market.) Popularity can be very ephemeral in the stock market. A new story may command a price-earnings ratio much higher than that of an old story, or of a stock without any distinct story, even though they all have been growing at about the same rate. However, once the story is well-known and there is not a new piece of news to reinforce it, investors tend to lose interest. Stocks in which the concept has become old hat actually can start drifting lower from lack of interest even though earnings are still in an uptrend. Investors often cannot understand why a stock sells off when nothing appears to be going wrong with the company. They do not realize that stocks do not always reflect their value and that if there is not enough new news to generate excitement about a stock, it can decline just from lack of buying interest. This phenomenon can happen to entire groups of stocks, particularly secondary issues, if investors get the impression that the market trend is down and that nobody wants to buy the stocks. At such a time, even good news may not bring in buying, and it is astounding how cheap stocks can become sometimes. If a stock has had a temporary interruption of its earnings-growth rate or upward trend, its decline may even be more abrupt. Later on it may well resume a strong growth pattern, but the original magic is usually gone forever. Investors have seen that it was not immune to adversity.

Cenco, a manufacturer of laboratory and scientific equipment, and a growing factor in health care, is an example of a company that maintained a good growth rate, but its steady performance did not keep investors from selling the stock off sharply when general market conditions were deteriorating. (See Figure 64.) You may protest loudly that this is not fair, but like life, the stock market is not always fair. The technical warnings were given when bottom trendlines were penetrated and support levels were violated. As you have read in this book, you should become more and more convinced that technical signals are ignored at you peril. Stocks which are able to maintain a stream of good news for the public can keep their price momentum going for some time, however. You should stay with these stocks until they are amply priced and you can see them breaking down techni-cally. Do not assume, however, that just because a high earnings-growth rate is maintained that these stocks cannot suffer serious declines eventually. Damon Corp., a producer of automated blood analyzers, was able to grow steadily over the years, but nevertheless was influenced by the general market declines in 1970 and 1971. (See Figure 65.) If investors suspect a company's years of strong growth are behind it, the effects can be devastating. H & R Block, a company providing an income tax preparation service for the public, climbed practically straight up from 1965 to 1969. (See Figure 66.) Anyone taking profits even after a

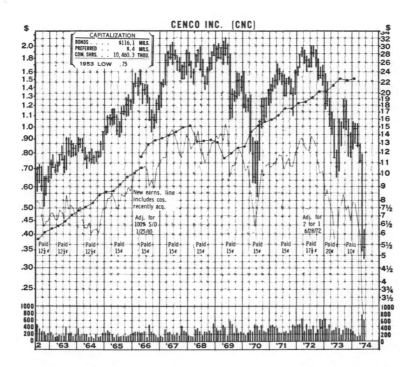

Figure 64. *Chart by Securities Research Company, 208 Newbury Street, Boston, Massachusetts.*

doubling or tripling of his investment would have missed a large part of the move. Even after the decline in 1970 the stock rallied to new highs. However, after the stock sold off in 1972 and broke the 1971 low, a clear danger signal had been given. Coupled with this unfavorable evidence were moves by the government to provide free preparation of some tax returns and the introduction of a simpler form that taxpayers could more easily do themselves. Putting the technical and fundamental evidence together strongly suggested that the stock should be avoided. What was also significant was that the stock topped out early in 1972, but the general market did not turn down until early 1973. There were investors who thought they had a wonderful buying opportunity as the stock tumbled down from its high, but unfortunately they were doomed to disappointment. It is rare that a glamour stock which collapses turns out to be a good buy in the near future. Usually there is a good reason why such heavy selling comes into the stock.

Stocks Which Give You Two Chances for Profit

Perhaps the most satisfying way to make money in the stock market is to anticipate a favorable development which the market has not recognized yet and

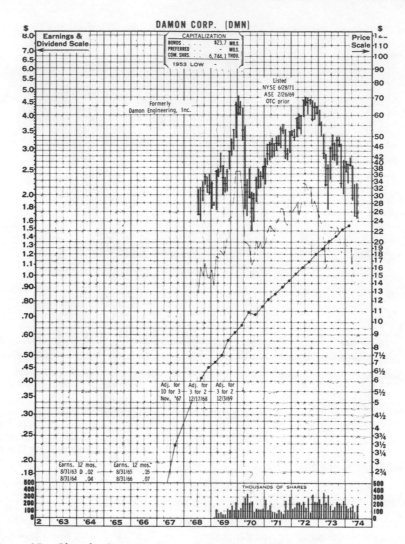

Figure 65. *Chart by Securities Research Company, 208 Newbury Street, Boston, Massachusetts.*

when many commentators are still bearishly disposed, properly weigh the odds that the favorable development will occur rather than an unfavorable one, and correctly interpret the technical signals that show movement is taking place. Not only are you exercising independent judgment, using objectivity and disassociating yourself from the hysteria of the moment, but you are performing the one function vital to making money in the stock market—forecasting the future. You do not make extraordinary profits in the stock market always following the crowd. Once it is obvious to everyone that a situation has strong earnings potential, most investors have already taken their positions and many may be ready to start nailing

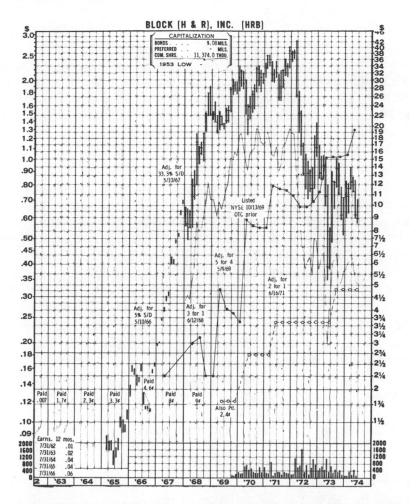

Figure 66. *Chart by Securities Research Company, 208 Newbury Street, Boston, Massachusetts.*

down profits. It is far more profitable to be able to analyze the economic, supply-and-demand, governmental, political, and social forces and anticipate a trend or development before the majority of investors. This is not always easy to do, of course. It does require some experience and a knowledge of the economy and industries, and also of the operation of the stock market. Technical tools have to be used to confirm your hypothesis and to help avoid buying too early. Putting all these tools together in arriving at your buying decision is an art, but one that can be very rewarding once learned.

Sometimes you may be able to anticipate the improvement in more than one trend that can tend to have a leverage effect on the earnings of a company. The spring of 1970 presented such an opportunity with regard to First Charter Financial, a California savings and loan holding company. Housing starts, one of the main earnings determinants of savings and loans, were at historically low levels. Investors were very bearish about the outlook for the housing industry at the time and the investor had to have a very good understanding of the situation in order to avoid being caught up in the pessimism. The low level of housing starts was due mainly to high interest rates and the relative unavailability of mortgage money. Anyone who understood the industry knew the odds were that the government had to expand credit and make mortgage money available eventually if there were going to be enough new housing units to meet the shelter needs of the American people. The high interest rates, also, had resulted in an outflow of funds from the savings and loan companies. Any move by the Federal Reserve to increase credit breaking out of the upper trendline or the successful test of the downside, could Lower interest rates would also be likely to help savings and loans improve the spreads between the interest they charge for mortgages and what they pay for funds. Thus, an improvement in interest rates in 1970 could have been forecast to produce a compound effect on the prices of savings and loans stocks. This is a kind of fundamental analysis which produces big profits in the stock market. In a situation like this you are in the enviable situation of having the odds on your side and anticipating trends rather than following them after they have had been underway for some time.

Once you have determined that First Charter Financial would be a good stock to buy, you next have to determine when to buy it. The general market made a rather climactic bottom in May of 1970 and you could have used the selling climax as a signal to buy. Playing the price action of the stock itself, i.e. the breaking out of the upper trendline or the successful test of the downside could have indicated a buying opportunity. (See Figure 67.) You would not have gotten in near the low (about 12) waiting for these confirmations, but you could have bought the stock around 15 and still have more than doubled your money in the next two years. In case you forgot that stocks do not grow to the sky, you would have been reminded of it by the decline in 1973. At the end of 1972, housing starts had recovered sharply and were running at high levels. Interest rates had also declined. Now both of the concepts for buying the stock were not longer valid; in fact, they could now be concepts for selling. Interest rates could rise again and housing starts slump, both of which actually did happen. At this point, the odds appeared to have shifted against the investor.

Issues Which May Give You the Most Trouble

It is very easy in the euphoria of the second stage to lose sight of the fact that all stocks do not have the same potential and that many should be sold at some point, even if they are acting well at the time. You have to almost constantly

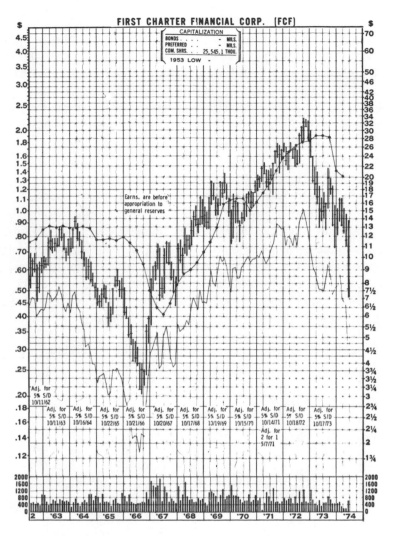

Figure 67. Chart by Securities Research Company, 208 Newbury Street, Boston, Massachusetts.

remind yourself that because a stock that is acting well does not necessarily indicate that everything is lovely with the company. The stock market and investors are notorious for the mistakes they make in bidding up the prices of stocks of companies that later turn out to be duds. Of course, some companies whose stocks are in demand do continue to do very well for years, but you cannot assume this happy outcome will always follow.

I have in mind two examples of stocks that could have made a lot of money for investors, or if they had bought at the wrong time, could have made them lose a large portion of their investment. Wyly (formerly University Computing) was a computer software company. The cost of software (computer programming) was actually growing faster than the value of the mainframe computers and the field looked like a bonanza to investors. Earnings of the company were rising sharply and investors were ecstatic. As can be seen in Figure 68, the stock shot up from a level of about 2 in 1964 to almost 200 in 1968. However, what investors were not aware of was that developing computer programs was expensive and the company was not charging off costs as they were incurred. Instead, it was deferring them with the intent of amortizing them once it sold the programs. As a result, writeoffs had to be taken and the stock fell from favor, while other stocks continued higher in 1972 after coming off their lows. Many investors bought the stock in 1970, undoubtedly thinking that it would bounce back to its former highs. Unfortunately, such was not the case. Rarely does a speculative stock return to its previous peak or price-earnings ratio after it has fallen from favor. Almost invariably conditions and profitability have changed radically so that the prospects of the company have been altered completely. Investors have to look at such stocks realistically. Even though they may be down sharply from their peaks (they should not have been so high in the first place), it is quite possible the investor

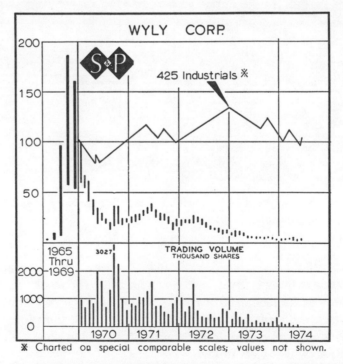

Figure 68. *Chart Courtesy of Standard & Poor's Corporatiion OTC Stock Reports, 345 Hudson Street, New York, New York 10014.*

would have a better chance in recouping some of his losses in another issue. Often, investors will stay with issues whose outlook is very uncertain just because they do not want to admit a loss or feel locked in. Sometimes, however, it is just better to clear out the deadwood and start over again, and try to avoid making the same mistakes. Wyly is now a diversified company, although much of its future prospects hinge on its success in establishing a national data communications network.

Another spectacular performer in the early 1960s was Mohawk Data Sciences. Mohawk is a computer peripheral equipment manufacturer. Just as with the software manufacturers, investors in the 1960s suddenly discovered that the sales of peripheral manufactures were growing at a rate faster than that of the computer industry as a whole. This stock, too, had an explosive rise from about 1 in 1965 to over 100 in 1968. Earnings kept rising sharply until 1969, however, when they were off sharply. The following year a deficit was experienced, primarily as a result of increased competition from IBM. The stock showed extreme weakness as it broke a major support level at 60 and declined almost as fast as it went up. Many investors were trapped when they bought at the 1970 bottom and did not get out fast enough when the ensuing rally collapsed. (See Figure 69.)

Situations Which May Be Disappointing in the Second Stage

By definition, the second stage of the market develops as investors become aware of the profit potential of stocks as the economic recovery unfolds. Thus, stocks of companies that can benefit from increases in productivity and possible price rises (assuming there are no government controls on prices) can be expected to do the best in the second stage. The main beneficiaries of the economic trends in this stage, as I have discussed, would tend to be the cyclical stocks and the quality growth situation. On the other hand, stocks which may be among the most disappointing are likely to be stocks which may find it difficult to increase productivity such as retail chains and utilities. Woolworth is a good example of how a conservative stock can run out of steam in the second stage. (See Figure 70.) The stock had good momentum coming off the 1970 market bottom, but early in 1971 profit-taking came in and there was little buying interest.

All stocks, even in the same industry, cannot be expected to participate to the same extent in the second stage. Normally, investors concentrate their buying in the better quality stocks in the early phase of a market or economic recovery when there is still a great deal of uncertainty. Since the quality stocks, which are associated with companies having the more dominant position in the economy and involving less risk, are available at reasonable prices, there is no urgency to reach for the more speculative secondary stocks. Although one cannot say there is no buying in secondary stocks concurrently with the buying of quality stocks, often

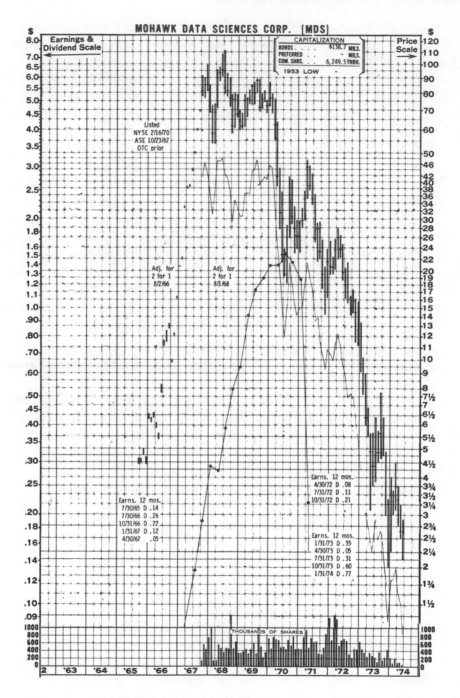

Figure 69. *Chart by Securities Research Company, 208 Newbury Street, Boston, Massachusetts.*

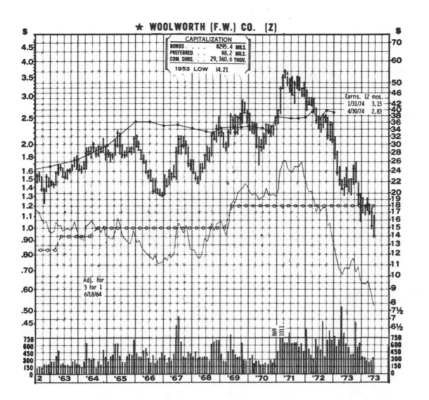

Figure 70. *Chart by Securities Research Company, 208 Newbury Street, Boston, Massachusetts.*

the focus on secondary stocks occurs when the quality stocks appear fully priced. This rotation of market interest to secondary stocks can be said to be more characteristic of Stage 3 than Stage 2, however. We can see in Commercial Solvents, a relatively small chemical producer (see Figure 71), the weak pattern that developed in the latter part of 1971 compared with one of the leading chemical stocks, Dow Chemicals (see Figure 72). Mead Corp., one of the smaller factors in the paper industry, did relatively poorly marketwise after 1971 (see Figure 73), compared with International Paper, the major company in the industry (see Figure 74).

Signs of a Second Stage Top

I listed quite a few characteristics of market tops in Chapter 2. However, it is not practical for investors to assimilate them all. Investors can do a very good job of catching market tops if they watch just a limited number of key technical

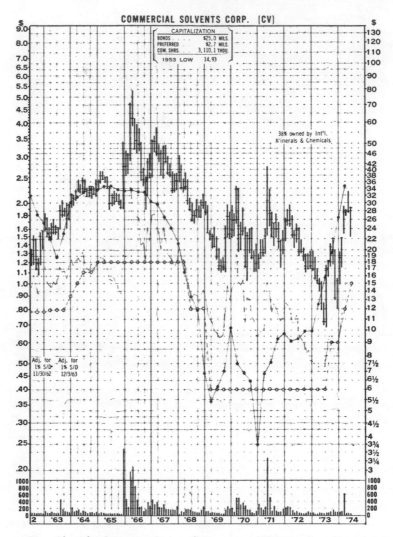

Figure 71. *Chart by Securities Research Company, 208 Newbury Street, Boston, Massachusetts.*

indicators, have a good understanding of economic trends, and are able to weave the two together in order to make a market judgment. The economic outlook is the major determination of stock prices, but there are several problems in using an assessment of the economic prospects by itself. First, the economy is subject to misinterpretation (witness the varying predictions of economists), and second, knowing the economic outlook still does not tell you how far ahead stocks are anticipating it. The technical tools I will describe admirably fill the gap and should help you to determine for timing purposes when the market is recognizing the fundamentals. There also has to be some cross-checking in order for you to

Figure 72.   Chart by Securities Research Company, 208 Newbury Street, Boston, Massachusetts.

correctly evaluate both the fundamental and technical, since both approaches can mislead you if you are not careful. Playing each against the other can help confirm or call into question your conclusions with regard to each approach.

The 1971 market top was particularly difficult to perceive since the economy was still robust and actually did not start to slow down appreciably until the latter part of 1973. Also, many cyclical stocks did not even reach their previous peaks. General Motors, for example, did not come near attaining the high it had reached in 1965. General Motors did give an indication that all was not right in 1971, however. Even though earnings were making good progress relative to the poor year of 1970, the stock was unable to make much headway. I remember thinking at the time that "this stock acts as if it were topping out, but how could that be when there is no indication that the economy is slowing down yet?" As it turned out, the technical indicator was telling the truth and my fundamental estimate of the situation was wrong. In my opinion, how stocks react to news is the best indicator available to the investor. If you have any hint that a stock may be anticipating peak earnings and the stock fails to respond to good earnings reports, you should consider selling. When the cyclical stocks of several industries are

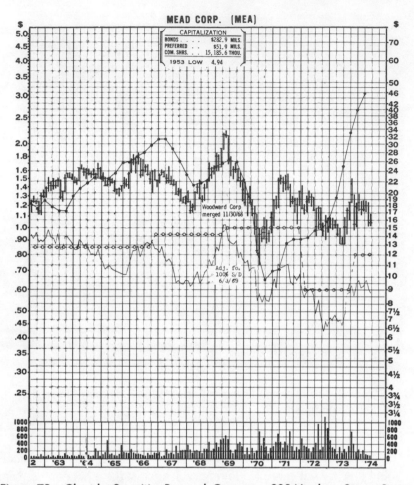

Figure 73. *Chart by Securities Research Company, 208 Newbury Street, Boston, Massachusetts.*

ignoring good earnings you should give serious thought to the possibility that the second stage is about over. As a practical matter you can do a very effective job of predicting broad tops (do not forget that tops may span several months and involve periodic rallies—even now highs) if it is obvious many of the cyclical stocks are not reacting to good news and it appears that investors are aware of all the possible good news in the foreseeable future.

Mistakes You Can Avoid in the Second Stage

One of the major mistakes investors can make in the second stage, or in any stage, is to assume all stocks will move together. Many in the same group or

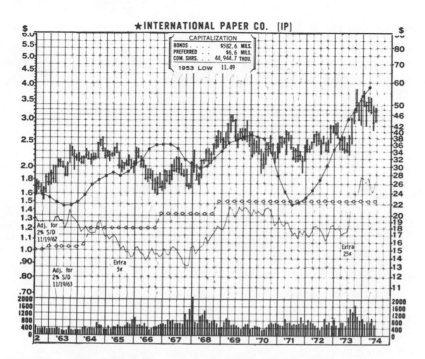

Figure 74. *Chart by Securities Research Company, 208 Newbury Street, Boston, Massachusetts.*

industry will move together, but there will be a few that do not and you might miss out on some substantial profits if you sell the superior stocks along with the mediocre. Try to determine if there is any particularly appealing concept behind each stock and let the market tell you if investors are recognizing it or not. Watch to see if the stock responds to favorable news, if it churns on high volume, or if it breaks important support levels. Do not let favorable news about a company or industry deter you from selling if the stock does not react to the news. Successful investors have that knack of realizing when a stock has discounted its favorable prospects and have disciplined themselves to sell when optimism is high. One of the axioms of the investment world is that market peaks are made on good news. Otherwise, how could investors get other investors to buy their stock at the top of a long market rise? As in Stage 1, you also have to be aware of concepts that have run their course. There is nothing more discouraging than trying to revive a "busted concept" or one in which investors have lost interest. On the surface, nothing seems to be going wrong at the moment, but foresighted investors may see trouble way down the trail. The only thing that is clearly obvious at the moment is that the stock keeps going lower.

It is quite possible, however, that a cyclical stock has taken on the characteristics of a growth situation because of the likelihood that its earnings improvement might extend far into the future. Such stocks can experience temporary weakness along with the rest of the market, but grudgingly so. It is best to stay with such stocks as long as the concept appears to remain intact. These concepts, too, can become shopworn and have to be watched, however.

7

The Techno-Fundamental Strategy
for the Third Stage of the Market Cycle

Signs of the Beginning of the Third Stage

The third stage of the Market Cycle also cannot be precisely delineated. It even may overlap with Stage 2 and not be distinct at all. It represents a portion of the stock market cycle in which the economy is operating at a high level, and it is difficult for aggregate corporate profits to show a sharp increase. In the 1953-1958 market cycle the third stage could be placed in the period from mid-1956 through mid-1957 (see Figure 1). In the 1958-1962 cycle the third stage is not really separate from the second stage. During the 1962-1966 cycle it again is not readily apparent. However, in the 1966-1970 cycle, the period from mid-1967 through 1968 can be considered Stage 3. The stock market spends more time in Stage 3, sometimes for periods of several years, than in any other stage.

Once stocks are in Stage 3, glowing economic news has already had its impact on the market. Cyclical stocks have had sharp moves and may be ready for profit-taking. However, once they experience declines, investors may note that the economic news continues to be good and, in some cases, bid the stocks back up again. Certainly, during the beginning of the third stage the leading economic indicators can be expected to be showing strength. The Federal Reserve Board index of production continues to rise, durable goods orders are higher, new car and other consumer durable goods sales are up, installment debt is increasing, corporate profits are doing well, and unemployment is declining. Retail sales in general are rising and housing starts are likely to be at relatively high levels. Capital spending appropriations by corporations usually will be showing strength and inventories increasing as businessmen become more optimistic about future sales. On balance, the stock market and the economy are entering a period of euphoria. The aura of optimism can be misleading, however, and the investor has to be on his guard more than ever in Stage 3.

Investment Strategy for the Third Stage

The third stage is characterized by some unique market patterns. A knowledge of these patterns can make this stage much more profitable for you. By and large, Stage 3 is a trading market. There is a time to buy stocks, even cyclical stocks, and a time to sell them. Selectivity can become accentuated in this stage. If you are in the wrong stocks you may think you are in a bear market, but if you are in the right stocks you can do exceedingly well. A rotation among groups and industries is another characteristic of the third stage. Investors tend to run stocks up until they are well-exploited and then they cast them aside for something newer and fresher. Rotation occurs in other stages, also, but the strategy appears to be more widespread in Stage 3.

New fads abound in this stage. Since the economy is now operating at a high level, the possibilities for sharp earnings gains among the bulk of the stocks is limited. Investors are, thus, eager to find some new industry or concept which holds promise of exceptional gains. It may not matter even if risks are great since investors are now in a state of mind in which they ignore risks and only look at potential. Witness the frantic rush for the computer leasing, nursing home, and franchise stocks in the late 1960s. Going back further (showing how stock market phemomena repeats itself), we saw investors chasing the bowling, boating, and transistor stocks. You can take advantage of all these market quirks in Stage 3 if you continually remind yourself that they exist, remain flexible and, above all, watch your technical indications and have the courage to sell when they weaken substantially after the stocks, and particularly speculative issues, have had a long market rise.

Somewhere in Stage 3 you might also run into the new issue craze. It might look insane to you, but you can take advantage of the frenzy while it lasts. Just remember that fads, fashions, and investment philosophies have a way of coming and going, and do not overstay the market. By using your fundamental and technical tools you can get a good idea of when the risks substantially exceed the potential—and when it happens that is the time to get out. Let someone else have the balance of the profits which must be considered exceedingly dangerous to realize at this point.

Low-priced speculations that investors would not be caught dead with in a bear market may come in for demand about the same time. Although the sustainability of earnings growth may be very questionable, investors are attracted by the increases in stock prices. Enjoy the ride while it lasts, but remember that these stocks are mostly trading vehicles and there is a time to part company with them, also. In the same category are the over-the-counter stocks, although many of them may not be speculative. The OTC industrials, nevertheless, tend to move as a group in weak stock markets, not so much from internal problems as from lack of market liquidity. When investor confidence is at a low point, buyers for over-the-counter stocks just seem to vanish.

Emerging Industries and Concepts Can Be Particularly Profitable

A good concept or new growth industry is appreciated in any market. The third stage is particularly propitious for new concepts, however, since investors are looking for something that other investors will recognize as a new capital gains vehicle and one in which all can cooperate in driving the price up. Since the concept is new, there has not been enough time, or even the opportunity, to reveal how vulnerable the concept might be. Still surrounded by a certain mystique because of its unproven nature, investors can make practically any claim for their new discovery. Occasionally, some of these speculations work out very well (IBM, Xerox, and Polaroid were speculations at one time); however, the odds are heavily against you that you have found an enduring investment. Many more new concepts, industries, and products falter than achieve success.

At the writing of this book, a stock in one emerging industry, with its favorable prospects reinforced by a currently popular concept, appeared to have substantial capital gains potential. In mid-October of 1973 one of the financial advisory services had discussed the stock, Occidental Petroleum, stating that the company had an interesting turn-around potential based on the likelihood that it had overcome the worst of its difficulties of the past two years and could be on its way to worthwhile earnings improvement. The stock had built about a five-month base (see Figure 75) and the computerized short term market strength had turned positive three weeks earlier. Adding to the potential of the stock was a coal mining subsidiary and a new process the company had developed for extracting oil from shale rock with an underground process. The stock, which I recommended at 11¼ on October 16, initially acted very well, but then the Arab oil embargo hit the stock market and Occidental went down with most other stocks. In January, a nationally syndicated newspaper columnist discussed the company's extraction process for shale oil. He pointed out how competitive the cost was with existing petroleum prices, and stated that considering how huge the reserves of oil shale were in the western United States, this process could solve the fuel shortage. Investors were well-tuned-in to the fuel shortage by this time and it was not difficult to attract attention to a stock of a company that might have the answer to the fuel shortage. The intriguing part of this story is that I do not yet know how it will turn out, but the situation has most of the ingredients you should look for in a capital gains situation—a concept, favorable stock action, and a reasonable value. The only favorable elements missing were that it could not yet be said that the worst of the economic news was behind the economy, or that the general market

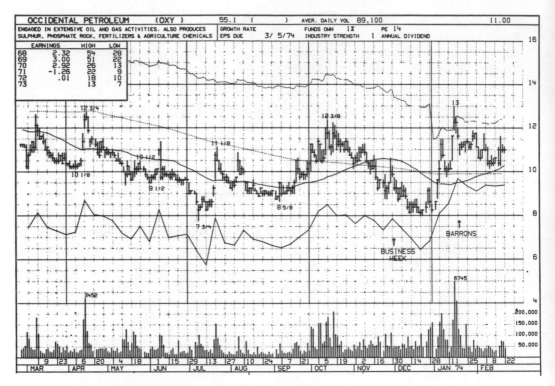

Figure 75. *Chart Courtesy of DAILY GRAPHS, P.O. Box 24933, Los Angeles, California 90024.*

had seen its low and was in an uptrend. Also, investor confidence had by no means returned yet. Nevertheless, the general market had already had a major decline over a period of months, it had been exposed to much unfavorable news and to many dire predictions of things to come, and bearishness was widespread. The odds were certainly now in favor of the investor. The lifting of the Arab oil embargo really held the key to the short term outlook for the market, but longer term it seemed likely that the oil embargo would be lifted and the economy would continue to expand. However, only time will tell how well the recommendation will work out. At this point, the stock must be considered a trading vehicle (earnings from the oil shale process could be years away, if they develop at all) but it is possible that in time it could take on investment characteristics.

This Investor Capitalized on His Fine Sense of Timing

The third stage can be particularly profitable for astute traders. Sophisticated investors are continually looking for ideas which are becoming popular. As the

technical strength improves in individual issues, they take their positions. However, once a stock has had a long rise and investors are enthusiastic about it, the
traders are usually ready to nail down their profits. Stocks do not go straight up
without intermediate corrections, and traders try to anticipate when a concept has
run its course and the speculators have pretty much gotten their mileage from the
stock. Traders, also, keep an eye on the general market. Since most stocks will
tend to fluctuate with sharp moves in the popular market averages, anticipating
moves in the market can help them catch swings in individual stocks. In Stage 3,
shifts in economic news tend to have a greater impact on the market than in the
other stages since the economy at this point does not hold promise for either great
gains or losses. When economic news has been favorable for some time and the
market no longer reacts to it, the probabilities are that the next news might be less
favorable and the market could sell off. Conversely, once unfavorable news has
had its impact on the market and stocks resist selling off further, the likelihood is
that the next news might be more optimistic and the market could rally.

There are not many investors who have the fine sense of timing to be able to
take advantage of the fluctuations in the general market or in individual stocks.
The overwhelming influence of the market action at both peaks and bottoms tends
to mislead most investors. It requires experience, training, and discipline to go
against the market at such times. One investor seems to have mastered the art of
sensing the right time to buy and sell stocks to maximize profits. Dr. Charles
R. has an investment strategy of buying stocks with strong possibilities when they
are low and selling them when they are high. He deliberately buys when investors
are bearish and sells when they are bullish. Many investors profess to follow this
strategy, but Dr. R. actually works at it. The semiconductor stocks were among
the better acting groups of August of 1973, although there was still widespread
concern about the general market. Demand for semiconductors was up sharply
and earnings forecasts were very optimistic. Technically, the stocks had built
good chart bases, relative strength was improving, and the long term strength
(six-month price comparisons) turned positive. The short term strength (price
action over a period of one month) also turned positive. Dr. R. bought Fairchild
Camera and Instrument at 51, National Semiconductor at 43, and Sprague Electric
at 15⅜ in August (see Figures 76, 77, and 78). In October, when the stocks had
had sharp short term rises and investors were becoming very enthusiastic about
them, Dr. R. sold Fairchild at 88 in October 1973, up more than 50 percent;
National Semiconductor at 94, up over 100 percent; and Sprague at 31⅞, up over
100 percent. He sold National Semiconductor short at the same time. Dr. R.'s
sense of timing was very good. The odds were in his favor that a correction would
set in before too long. The economy was expected to slow in the months ahead
and the semiconductor industry has been known for price weakness in periods of
slow demand. Dr. R. also had a fortuitous assist from rumors that a shortage was

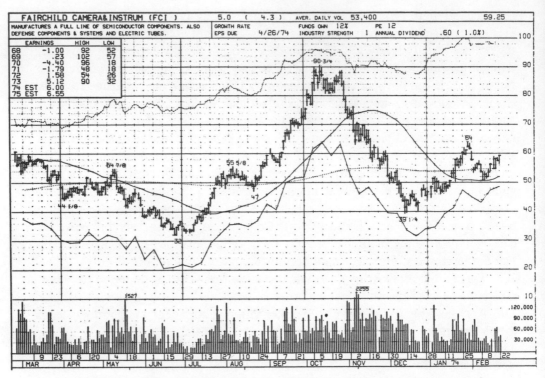

Figure 76. *Chart Courtesy of DAILY GRAPHS, P.O. Box 24933, Los Angeles, California 90024.*

developing in silicon used in making semiconductors. It does often happen that when all the good news concerning an industry or company is known that problems can arise that few investors see coming. Dr. R., of course, not only sold the shares he bought, but he went one step further and sold short. I want to point out that there is a vast gap between taking profits when you think a stock is fully priced or overbought technically (all the news is out and most investors have bought their stock and may be looking for a signal to take profits), and having the confidence that a stock is going down and can be sold short. Selling short is a strategy that can help you to meet your goal of tripling your money in the stock market but it is an extremely difficult operation (regardless of how easy it may appear), as I will discuss in Chapter 10.

The Importance of Low-Priced Speculations in the Third Stage

Inexperienced investors often think only in terms of price-earnings ratios and earnings trends. These factors are very important in the investment analysis of

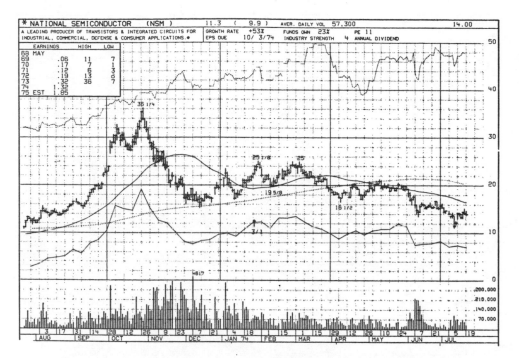

Figure 77. Chart Courtesy of DAILY GRAPHS, P.O. Box 24933, Los Angeles, California 90024.

common stocks, but they do not include one very critical consideration —psychology. Investors are very much influenced by the action of other investors, and stocks and groups become fads, just as ideas and social practices can become fashionable. When stocks or groups are moving higher they attract additional buying just because they are moving. Nobody loves a winner more than investors. They are always looking for profit opportunities. After the third stage has been underway for some time, many of the profit opportunities will have dried up (except, perhaps, for relatively unpredictable emerging industry stocks), and investors will tend to look toward the more speculative, low-priced issues. These stocks are usually the greatest casualties during periods of market weakness, but as investor confidence picks up as the third stage progresses, investors become less concerned with the risks involved in speculative, low-priced stocks and instead think of them only as behind-the-market capital gains opportunities. The earnings prospects to not have to change appreciably, just the attitude of investors. However, often the earnings outlook does change, although usually the new improvement in income is of a nonrecurring type and not sustainable. Investors, nevertheless, frequently talk themselves into believing that the earnings gains will last forever.

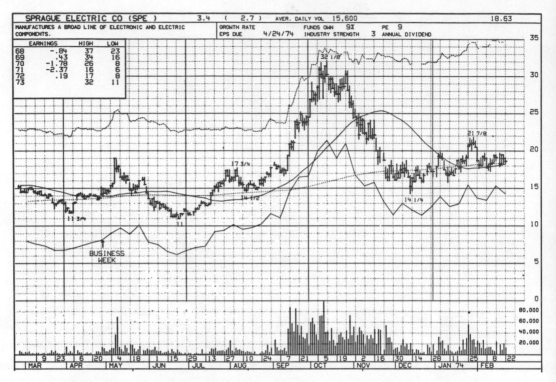

Figure 78. *Chart Courtesy of DAILY GRAPHS, P.O. Box 24933, Los Angeles, California 90024.*

The decade of the 1960s revealed some excellent examples of the widespread popularity of low-priced speculative stocks. Two industries came into prominence that provided substantial capital gains opportunities for investors, the space and the commercial aircraft manufacturing industries (later investors came to combine the two as the aerospace industry). The fantastic growth of the space industry from practically nothing made this industry particularly appealing to investors. The rapid increase in space-spending probably would have been enough to attract investors, but the favorable atmosphere for low-price speculations made the market atmosphere just right for these stocks. (I have seen investors ignore stocks with just as much potential when the investment climate was pessimistic.) As the speculative fever spread, any small company associated with the space industry was in demand. The commercial aircraft industry went through the same phase of sharply-rising demand and speculative excitement when it started converting to jet airliners. Here, also, the stocks of practically every large and small supplier of the industry ran up on frenzied buying by investors. While these stocks were running, it seemed almost impossible that they would ever weaken again, but the inexorable stock market cycle eventually claimed them as its victims. One of the leaders among the space stocks was Thiokol. In the early 1950s, before the solid-fueled missile became a reality, Thiokol was a relatively obscure company that had developed a curious but not exciting rubber-like compound. When the United States needed a solid-fueled missile to provide a deterrent against the Russian ICBM threat, Thiokol had the chemical know-how to develop the solid rocket fuels that powered the Minuteman Intercontinental Missile. The stock had a spectacular move as the ICBM solid rocket program got underway. In 1956 Thiokol rose from below 4 to almost 60 in less than three years. In 1959 the major percentage gains in the ICBM program had taken place, and the "ball game was over." (See Figure 79.)

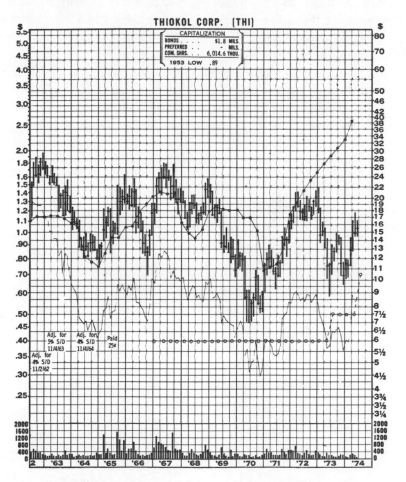

Figure 79. Chart by Securities Research Company, 208 Newbury Street, Boston, Massachusetts.

Thiokol is still heavily committed to producing solid rocket fuels for U.S. defense, but in recent years has emphasized diversification, particularly into synthetic fibers and aerosol devices. Another small space company, Aerojet-General (now a wholly-owned subsidiary of General Tire) was a major manufacturer of liquid-fueled rocket engines. This company participated in the liquid-fueled ICBM program. The combination of a speculative market atmosphere and a brand-new industry also produced dramatic results for the stock. (No chart available.)

The mundane aircraft industry was not without its excitement when the new jet airliners started rolling off the production lines. Investors were enamoured with practically all companies involved in any aspects of the manufacture of jet airlines, from the toilets to the landing gear. Monogram Industries, which made sanitary systems for the airlines, went from practically 1 in 1963 to 80 in 1967. (See Figure 80.) Pneumo Dynamics, a manufacturer of landing gear, rose from about 8 in 1965 to over 35 in 1969. (See Figure 81.)

Investors had an opportunity to make some fabulous profits in the four stocks I have just mentioned, but you can notice that there was a time when the stocks had to be sold or most of the profits would have been lost.

You have to be careful with new products and new industries. Investors tend

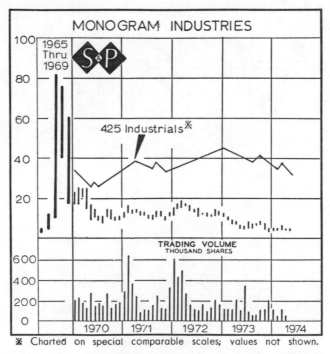

Figure 80. *Chart Courtesy of Standard and Poor's Corporation OTC Stock Reports, 345 Hudson Street, New York, New York 10014.*

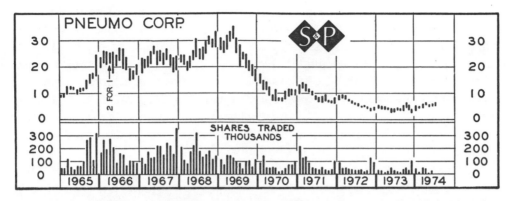

Figure 81. *Chart Courtesy of Standard and Poor's Corporation OTC Stock Reports, 345 Hudson Street, New York, New York 10014.*

to run the prices up beyond reasonable valuations and then, once everyone is aware of the bright prospects of the individual situation and the price-earnings ratio has expanded sharply, or the bulk of the earnings gains has taken place, the novelty of the concept wears off and investors tend to try and realize their gains before others start selling. What makes it difficult to pinpoint just when the selling will start coming in is that no one can be sure what will trigger it, and often there is no clear sign that earnings are deteriorating or that problems are developing. It may be just that investors think things are so good that they cannot get much better and that the risk exceeds the potential.

The Importance of Over-the-Counter Issues

It is not possible to generalize about all over-the-counters stocks. They can vary from the most speculative, unseasoned issues to the highest quality equities available to investors. Many well-known life insurance companies and commercial banks are traded in the over-the-counter market, for example. The bulk of the stocks traded over-the-counter, however, are small companies relative to those listed on the national exchanges. In some cases, they have excellent records, are very sound financially, and are solidly established in their industries. Others, however, may involve a high degree of financial risk, earnings records may be erratic, or their future may hinge on the success of one or two main projects. Not only should investors be cognizant of the wide variation in financial risk among over-the-counter stocks, but they also should be conscious of the unique market risks and potential associated with over-the-counter stocks, particularly the industrials. During periods when investor confidence is low, the over-the-counter industrials are usually the first to suffer from a lack of liquidity. Investors often just back away from the group regardless of how good the fundamentals are, and other investors, desiring to sell, just do not find many bidders. Sale of large blocks of stock may require substantial price concessions. Conversely, when investor confidence is high, as it usually is during the latter part of the third stage, investors often believe that over-the-counter stocks offer some of the best values in the market. The demand for these stocks then may impinge on a limited supply of stock and some dramatic gains may be seen. Lack of liquidity in this market, thus, can operate in both directions. The fundamentals of an over-the-counter stock cannot be ignored, however, since they can reinforce and accentuate the swings in market price due to lack of market liquidity.

Buckbee-Mears is a good example of how an over-the-counter stock is influenced by general market conditions and swings in investor confidence, plus its own earnings performance. In 1970 Buckbee-Mears was essentially a manufacturer of aperture masks for color television tubes. In early 1970 the general market was selling off and the earnings of Buckbee was also on a decline. The stock dropped from 15 to 5. (See Figure 82. Prices are before adjustments for a three-for-two stock split in 1973). The market rallied in the latter part of 1970 and the earnings outlook for the company in 1971 was improving considerably. The stock moved from 5 to a high of 20 in 1971. During the general market decline of 1971, the price of Buckbee was halved, even though earnings in 1971 were up sharply

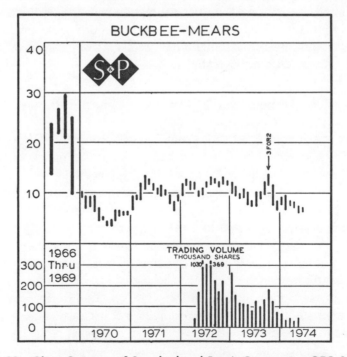

Figure 82.   *Chart Courtesy of Standard and Poor's Corporation OTC Stock Reports, 345 Hudson Street, New York, New York 10014.*

over 1970 and the expectations were for another good earnings gain in 1972. As confidence returned to the market in the latter part of 1971 and in 1972, Buckbee climbed from 10 to almost 20. Earnings showed another good increase in 1973, but that did not prevent the stock from slipping as the general market deteriorated again. Buckbee, which has now diversified into other fields such as optics and precision components parts for the electronic and computer markets, might have done better in the optimism of 1972 if it were in an emerging industry. Buckbee had been a spectacular performer when color television was in its early growth phase, but the investment magic of color television had worn off somewhat by 1972.

An example of an over-the-counter stock that continued rising sharply in 1972 was Data General Corporation. This company manufactures minicomputers for industrial, scientific, and educational applications. The minicomputer field was held in high regard by investors for its growth potential and the price of the stock paralleled the earnings growth in 1972. (See Figure 83.) Earnings growth can be accompanied by a price decline in a stock, however, if investors have a skeptical attitude. The earnings of American Music Stores registered sharp gains in 1972 and 1973, but the stock topped out early in 1972. Investors who were gauging the future performance of the stock on its expected earnings results would have been

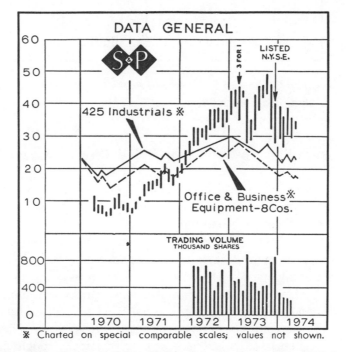

Figure 83. *Chart Courtesy of Standard and Poor's Corporation OTC Stock Reports, 345 Hudson Street, New York, New York 10014.*

caught flatfooted. It seems in this case that investors did not believe earnings growth would be sustainable. The earnings record had been erratic and they may have decided to take their profits when the company was doing well. (See Figure 84.)

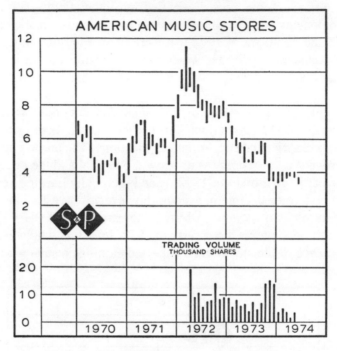

Figure 84. *Chart Courtesy of Standard and Poor's Corporation OTC Stock Reports, 345 Hudson Street, New York, New York 10014.*

New Issues Play an Important Role in Stock Market Profits

The new issues market is influenced by investment psychology probably more than any segment of the stock market. Since companies selling common stock for the first time are usually among the smaller, unseasoned companies, they find it very difficult to sell stock when the public is pessimistic about the market. However, often these new, relatively untested companies have the potential for sharp earnings gains if they have products or services in strong growth areas. During periods of investor optimism these stocks can come in for great investment demand as investors ignore the risks and concentrate on the potential. Thus, practically the same type of new issues that investors considered too risky to buy in an uncertain market climate may be enthusiastically sought after when the stock market environment has turned optimistic. The market for new issues is, perhaps, at its height in the latter part of the third stage after investor confidence has had ample opportunity to build up.

One of the most turbulent periods of new issue activity was in 1968. Investors were climbing over each other to get in on the original offerings. Some were able to double or triple their money within days. Some investors who bought in the secondary market were able to make substantial gains, also. Such companies as medical electronics, computer leasing, and computer peripheral equipment were among the ones in most demand. A small company called Bio-Dynamics was one of the participants in the medical electronics new issue boom. It is best known for its in-office blood testing system. In 1968 it rose from 32 to 74 (see Figure 85) even though earnings were lower in 1968 than in 1967. Earnings also declined in 1969 and the stock turned down. Earnings recovered in 1970 and continued up through 1973, but the stock stayed in a trading range through 1973.

Figure 85. Chart Courtesy of Standard and Poor's Corporation OTC Stock Reports, 345 Hudson Street, New York, New York 10014.

How to Use Conservative Issues in the Latter Part of the Third Stage

Toward the end of the third stage conservative stocks can provide a means of taking a defensive posture. At this point in the stock cycle, many cyclical, secondary, over-the-counter, and new issue stocks may have seen, or are nearing, their peaks. Investors expectation may already be reflected in the prices and price-earnings ratios of these stocks and risk may be approaching potential. Although there is no way of knowing what may trigger the end of Stage 3, sending the general market into a decline, these stocks now represent above-average risks. Once such stocks have been exposed to all the good news expected and their technical action is poor, investors should at least consider either going into cash or switching into conservative issues. If you miscalculate and the market has much farther to go, you can still participate in the market in conservative issues, but your risks would be much less. There is one word of caution. If sharply-rising interest rates are responsible for the decline in the general market, then conservative stocks may also do poorly. In addition, problems can arise in conservative stocks, and you cannot just ignore these problems, assuming that everything will work out smoothly. A high level of consumer debt, declining discretionary income, or a drop in real income, for example, could slow consumer spending and put pressure on retail store common stocks. Electric utilities can be hurt by depressed industries in their areas, high interest rates, rising construction costs, high fuel costs, or adverse regulatory decisions. In addition, defensive-type stocks can become overpriced and lose much of their defensive qualities.

Helping You Recognize the Signs of the End of the Third Stage

The length of time that the market spends in Stage 3 is probably the most unreliable indicator to use in trying to determine the end of the third stage. How long this stage continues depends on the performance of both the stock market and the economy. How quickly speculative excesses and over-valuation develop in the market will have an important bearing on when investors will decide common stocks have become too risky. Some characteristics of the approaching end might be an upsurge in demand for over-the-counter stocks. It also might take the form of a rapidly advancing new issues market. More likely, both phenomena may be occurring simultaneously. The signs to watch for in the economy of an approaching end of the third stage are more complex and can vary considerably from cycle to cycle. The economy itself may become overheated, rising at too rapid a rate and borrowing demand from the future. This type of economic "blowoff" has occurred in the past but is less likely in the foreseeable future. The limitations in the availability of energy and of many raw materials used in manufacturing processes may act as a constraint on future economic excesses. The American economy has always been influenced by fluctuations in demand. We may now be at the point in time in which limited supply may be the main influence on economic growth. Inflation can even be increased by the rising prices caused by shortages. An increasing rate of inflation and higher interest rates could well mark the approach end of the third stage. The government might even arrive at the decision that it is less dangerous in the long run to cut government spending and to reduce the growth rate of the money supply and risk a short term recession, then it is to allow a high rate of inflation to continue and take a chance on an eventual depression. There are, of course, factors on the demand side that could slow down the economy. Private debt could reach the level where individuals were inclined to try to reduce their debt load and to avoid taking on any more debt. Under these conditions consumer durable goods spending would decline. If interest rates were rising (perhaps mainly because of inflationary expectations), the housing industry would likely be adversly affected. Depending on the amount of excess industrial capacity, if any, capital spending could go into a slump, also. Inventories, one of the more volatile sectors of the economy, could come in from some liquidation. Of course, once these factors on the demand side become evident, the stock market would probably already be in a decline and well into the fourth stage.

Mistakes You Can Avoid in the Third Stage

Probably the biggest mistake investors make, not only with regard to the third stage, but concerning all stages of the market, is to fail to recognize that the stage of the stock market can have an important influence on what particular stocks or groups of stocks perform the best. Putting it another way, it is not always the intrinsic value of stocks that determine how well they do, but the attitude of investors plays a significant role, and the attitude of investors can change significantly with the market stage. If you understand this basic fact, you will find it easier to accept the principle that you may have to buy certain stocks which you ordinarily might not buy if you want to achieve the best possible performance, and you may have to sell when it goes against your instincts if you want to avoid losing a large part of your gains.

Since the third stage represents that portion of the stock market in which the substantial gains in the economy and the market have already taken place, investors tend to rotate from one group to another and from exploited stocks to unexploited stocks to enhance their profits. Thus, if you experience a worthwhile gain in a stock, you can assume that other investors also have large profits and may start getting restless. About the time you start feeling complacent, the traders might begin nailing down their profits, and much of the paper profits you had will disappear. Of course, how high such stocks run and whether any setback is temporary or not will depend on the fundamentals and the earnings potential of the particular situation. A mistake that investors often make is to immediately reinvest the proceeds from the sale of the exploited stock into a stock considered to be undervalued. It frequently happens that once your stock has had a substantial move, the entire market may be overbought and ready for a reaction. It may require patience, since it sometimes takes weeks for a distribution pattern to form prior to a significant correction, but it may be worth your while to wait for a correction before reinvesting the proceeds. You have to consider all the aspects of the economy and the market, as I have discussed in previous chapters, to avoid mistaking the beginning of a major market decline for a temporary correction.

Toward the end of the third stage it is easy to get carried away by the bullish action of secondary and over-the-counter stocks. They may look cheap on earnings even though they have had sharp rises, but remember that historically they may have sold at much lower price-earnings ratios and could well return to these former valuations in times of market pessimism. They are apt to be among the poorest performers when the general market finally does turn down. Also, many of these stocks are basically trading vehicles (as one senior analyst put it, you take them out for the evening but don't take them home to Mother) and can lose their support quickly once traders feel that they have gotten their mileage out of them.

We have in Connecticut General Mortgage and Realty, a mortgage investment trust, a good example of how investors look far ahead. At the beginning of 1973 the economy was doing well and the mortgage investment trusts, as a group, were showing sharply-rising earnings. One would think that Connecticut General Mortgage would have been a good buy then. As it turned out (see Figure 86) the stock trended lower throughout 1973 even though the earnings trend was up. Apparently what happened was that interest rates started rising and investors were fearful that the spreads between what the trusts pay for money and what they charge borrowers would narrow. Some trusts actually were squeezed as the year

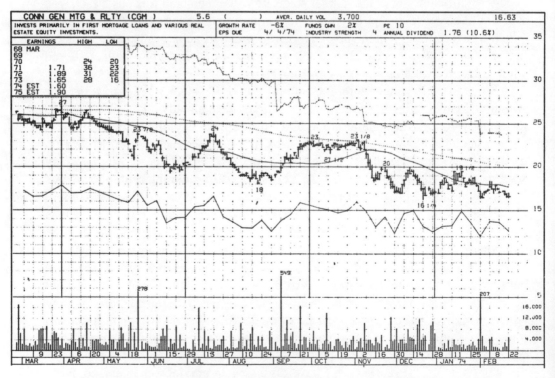

Figure 86. Chart Courtesy of DAILY GRAPHS, P.O. Box 24933, Los Angeles, California 90024.

unfolded. There were other worries, also. A great many new trusts were being started and overcapacity could develop. On top of these concerns the economy had enjoyed a long expansion and might start slowing down. None of these possibilities was a certainty, but investors who had good profits evidentally decided not to wait to find out. The technical violation of the 24 level in May confirmed that investors were taking these possibilities seriously. The outlook for such stocks was uncertain and earnings growth was not considered sustainable. Traders like to sell when the news is good and everything looks rosy, particularly when they can look down the road and see problems developing eventually.

Cyclical stocks are, also, sometimes very tempting near the end of Stage 3. Earnings are running at high levels and they may look very cheap. It is easy to overlook the fact that earnings may have increased sharply already and that earnings could be on a plateau for several years, or worse, they could decline back to former levels in the next economic downturn. Current yields, also, may be at historically low levels. In some cases, of course, dividends may be increased, but more often they will not.

Selling stocks when problems are not obvious is not an easy thing to do (as well as avoiding selling them too early is not easy), but the combination of technical and fundamental tools can give you a fighting chance to achieve the proper timing.

8

How You Can Apply Techno-Fundamental Strategies to Turn the Difficulties of the Fourth Stage to Your Advantage

The Signs of the Beginning of the Fourth Stage

It cannot be emphasized too much that all stocks do not turn down at once as the stock market enters the fourth stage. Cyclical stocks, in particular, may see their peaks many months before the popular averages turn down. The cyclical stocks may not decline sharply immediately, but they can spend several months in distribution patterns without making new highs. This sluggish action of the cyclical stocks is one of the first warning signals of the beginning of the fourth stage. If the new issues market has been active, a leveling off and decline in some of these recent favorites could be another warning signal. Not too far behind the topping out of cyclical and new issue stocks would be a reduced interest in secondary and over-the-counter stocks. Experienced investors are well-aware that the markets for these stocks are the most illiquid during market declines and that they can have some of the sharpest falls regardless of the fundamentals. One of the indicators of a deterioration in the secondary issues is a divergence between the advance-decline line and the popular market averages. Most of the stocks represented by the advance-decline line are secondary issues, and when this indicator does not make a new high along with the popular averages, or makes a new low when the popular averages do not, it is one of the first hints that the investors are starting to worry about secondary stocks.

Investors are usually very reluctant to accept the possibility of a general market decline. In Stage 3 of the stock market they have become so conditioned to prosperous times and easily-made stock market profits that they literally cannot envision a time when the economy may not be doing well or when the stock market may be declining.

The first reaction of investors to a market decline as the fourth stage begins is that the market drop is only a temporary correction. So far, business has not shown any signs of weakness. It is only the most astute who can realize that economic excesses carry in them the seeds of future weakness. A sharp rise in consumer spending can lead to an economic slowdown later. Consumer spending accounts for two-thirds of the Gross National Product. An unusually high level of automobile sales and retail sales in general are good indications of unsustainable consumer spending, as well as a sharp rise in consumer installment debt. A sharp drop in the individual savings rate can be expected to occur near the end of a business expansion. A low savings rate not only reflects the confidence that is characteristic of a strong economy, but also results in lower liquid savings to pay for consumer goods in the future. Other sections of the economy, such as capital spending and housing, can hit unsustainable levels of activity, but these sectors lead to recession only infrequently. Very high inventory accumulation may lead to inventory liquidation. In the past, inventory accumulation in the steel industry prior to strike deadlines has resulted in subsequent liquidation of inventories and a drag on the expansion of the economy. General inventory liquidation in the past, also, has been one of the prime causes of recessions. Of course, on an historical basis the years or decades of spending and inflationary excesses have to be paid for by an extended period of difficult economic times.

The actions of the Federal Reserve Board also can have a substantial impact on the stock market. If the rate of growth of the nation's money supply jumps sharply or has been running at unsustainable rates, it is likely that a reduction in the growth rate is in the cards. A sharp cut in the growth rate could result in a slowing down of the economy, but even if the economy does not go into a recession the stock market can be adversely affected.

Another warning signal of the fourth stage is the building up of inflationary pressures and rising interest rates. Increased commodities futures prices, expanding federal deficits, and scheduled labor negotiations in major industries could all lead to higher inflationary pressures. Shortages can, also, have an inflationary impact on the economy, but there is little monetary policy can do to alleviate shortages over the short run. If the Federal Reserve is moving to tighten monetary policy and restrict inflation, the first indications might be seen in a decline in the net free reserves of member banks. Other indications of tighter money is an increase in the Federal funds rate, prime rate of commercial banks, the Federal Reserve discount rate, or in the required reserves of member banks. All of these indications can be very helpful in suggesting when the fourth stage might be beginning. One of the most convincing indicators, however, is a lack of market response to continued good corporate profits and favorable economic news. If the market should then sell off, rally, and then decline again to lower levels on sharply higher volume, the chances are that Stage 4 is underway.

A Strategy to Make Money in the Fourth Stage

The fourth stage of the stock market is marked by investor pessimism and utter lack of confidence. This stage is the most discouraging and trying for investors of any of the stages, although it need not be. Most investors lose money in the fourth stage, unless they recognize the dangers and withdraw to the sidelines. Many who do get out of the market initially, however, often try to get back in long before the end of the decline has been seen, and when they are caught in another selling wave they are apt to sell at a loss. The most astute investors may be aware that they are in a substantial market decline, but they think they can be nimble enough to get in, make a profit, and get out before the decline resumes again. These investors, also, usually find that bear market rallies can end with a suddenness that they did not anticipate, and that they are lucky if they are able to get out quickly enough just to break even.

Bear markets are a frustrating experience for investors in several ways. For the investor who has been active in the stock market, sitting out a market decline for what might amount to a period of many months can be maddening. All his investment instincts rebel against this strategy. Nevertheless, if you have the discipline to follow this strategy it has much to recommend it. Simply, just stay in cash or short term debt instruments until you have solid evidence (both fundamental and technical) that the bottom of the market has been seen or is very close. However, this approach is one of conserving capital, and not a way to increase your capital. If you want to achieve your goal of tripling your money you cannot have your money sitting idle for months (except for the interest return, of course). You have to keep it working. There are ways in which you can pursue a strategy of action in a bear market and still have the odds on your side. One way, of course, is to sell short. Before you go this route, it is important that you have already seen much of the technical and fundamental characteristics of the beginning of the fourth stage. You cannot successfully sell short unless you have the greatest confidence you are in a major decline or you are sure the fundamentals of individual issues are deteriorating badly. Even then, the short side will test your mettle as no other market operation can. You may find that you do not have the nerves for this strategy. These is another investment strategy, however, which can enable you to act positively in a bear market. This strategy is to buy gold stocks.

Buying gold stocks is not without its pitfalls, also. There are many traders in them and they can be quite volatile. They are influenced by international and domestic monetary and economic crises and the fluctuations in the free market price of gold. They also frequently move in the opposite direction of the general stock market. It is usually wise to sell gold stocks once a crisis has deepened, because any resolution of the crisis can result in traders taking their profits. On a long term basis, gold stocks have much to recommend them. As long as governments indulge in massive deficit spending and inflate the money supply to pay for their expenditures, gold will remain in style. It is the only medium of exchange that people throughout history have believed in consistently. Paper money can become worthless when mismanaged by governments, which are under intense political pressure to be extravagant, but gold tends to remain faithful as a store of value. Until governments can show that they have the will to control inflation, gold stocks will be in demand, even though there may be periods of tranquility when investors look elsewhere for capital appreciation. The investor that I mentioned in the previous chapter regarding his ability to make money in trading markets, used a buy-and-hold strategy with a gold stock and has seen his investment increased dramatically. He bought a company which invests primarily in South African gold stocks, ASA Limited, at about 7 (adjusted for splits) on February 18, 1964. He still holds the stock after about a seven-fold gain. (See Figure 87.) Gold stocks can not always be counted on to go counter to the general market as you can see in Figure 87 (no general rule in the stock market is inviolate). ASA declined along with the general market in 1969 and rallied in 1970. The stock had a sharp rise prior to 1969 and traders may have taken their profits. In 1973, however, the gold stocks got back on track as inflation increased rapidly, the dollar weakened, and the free market price of gold soared.

This Normally Risky Strategy May Be the Most Conservative Way to Make Money in the Fourth Stage

I briefly referred to short selling in the previous paragraph as one of the major strategies you can use in taking advantage of the adverse market conditions in Stage 4. Short selling is one of the strategies which can enable you to act positively to enhance your capital investment in any market. The subject will be discussed more thoroughly in Chapter 10, but short selling is particularly relevant to the fourth stage when it is so difficult to make money on the long side. The common mistake investors make is to sell short after practically all the bad news one can think of has been predicted, the market has had a substantial decline, and investors are universally bearish. These conditions, of course, are characteristic of a market bottom, or near-bottom. If you go short near a bear market bottom you can lose money faster than you ever dreamed possible. A somewhat similar mistake made is to sell on extreme weakness during a decline just before a technical rally is apt to occur. It is much better to sell short after the rally appears to have run its course and when the next major move could be down. You can see

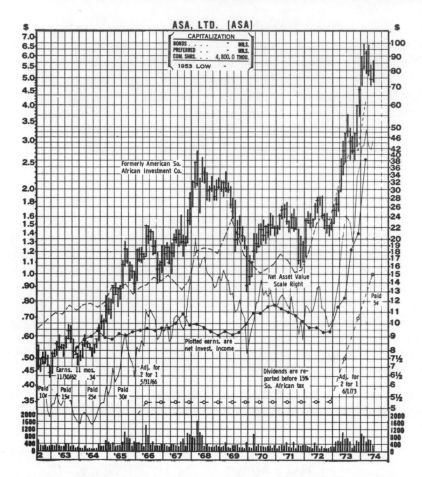

Figure 87.   Chart by Securities Research Company, 208 Newbury Street, Boston, Massachusetts.

in Figure 88 how many technical rallies there were during part of the 1973-1974 decline. Each one of them would have given you heart failure if you had gone short just before the rally (the rallies were essentially short-covering rallies). The first sharp move of a stock after you sell short is, thus, very important. If you sell short at the wrong time and the stock immediately goes against you, consternation reigns. You immediately assume you made a mistake. What compounds the problem is that the likely short-sell candidates are usually high price-earnings ratio stocks which could have ingredients for sharp earnings gains, and you will worry that something favorable is happening you did not count on.

There is no sure formula for easing the anxiety of selling short. That is why you have to be emotionally stable enough to withstand the gnawing uncertainties of selling short. If your plan is well calculated, however, you should be able to go

Dow Jones Industrial Averages

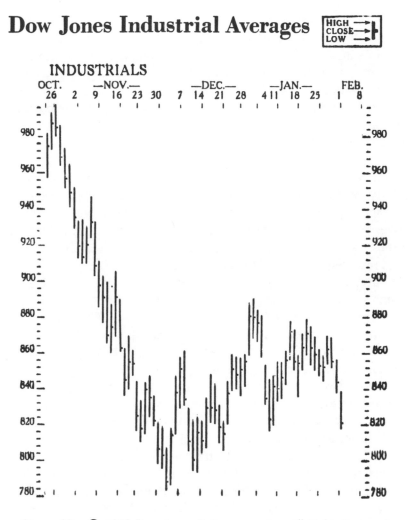

Figure 88. © 1973 Dow Jones & Company, Inc. All Rights Reserved.

through the ordeal without too much strain. Although stocks go down in other stages of the stock market, selling short is such a difficult operation (it often looks deceptively easy) that it is usually best to confine it to markets in which it is hard to make a profit on the long side. Thus, you should have fundamental and technical confirmation that the market is in its fourth stage. In staying with the fourth stage you also have the major market trend going with you. It is very helpful to have good reason to believe that the fundamentals of the stock you are selling short are deteriorating. If you can be confident that a concept has run its course or will turn unfavorable, you can overcome the panic that usually grips an investor when the stock he is short has a technical rally. The other major requirement for selling short is some technical deterioration which will show that investors are skeptical of the stock. Breaking down from a head and shoulder chart pattern, violating support levels, or just not responding to favorable news, such as good earnings, are signs that the stock is weak. Once you have your short position you can stay with it until you start seeing indications, mentioned at the beginning of this section, that the bottom might be near. At this point the odds are shifting against you. You may still get a few more points, but your risks have increased substantially since you want to cover your shorts while the general market is still weak. Some chart patterns may still look bearish, and you may think the market has a long way to go on the downside. However, do not allow chart patterns, particularly head and shoulder formations, which are often treacherous, to cloud your common sense. You should also ask yourself when you are starting to feel you might be close to the bottom, what could happen to turn the market around. Sometimes there is one major problem the market is worrying about, and if it should be resolved the market might rally sharply.

One investor was very successful in selling Tropicana short. He watched the stock climb sharply in 1970 and 1971. It was, in fact, one of the darlings of investors. However, the exceptional earnings performance was well-known and the price-earnings ratio had expanded substantially. The stock was certainly ripe for a reaction. (See Figure 89). The general market decline in early 1973 triggered the selling of Tropicana. At the time, also, the high price-earnings ratio of such stocks were being questioned by investors and institutions were being criticized for buying high price-earnings ratio stocks. The stage appeared to be set for a successful short. All we needed was technical confirmation, which was not long in coming. The stock in early 1973 broke an important support level at 42. The next rally back toward the support level is when the investor sold the stock short. On the way down the general market had some sharp rallies, but he was convinced from the international monetary problems, increasing inflation and rising interest rates that the market had a long way to go yet, and he did not cover his short position. However, when the stock was experiencing substantial weakness and went practically straight from 30 to almost 20 he covered on the weakness. The stock had another weak spell that took it to 16 and then it rallied back to 30. He did not sell short at the top or cover at the bottom, but he did make a good profit and he kept the odds on his side. He sold short when both the fundamental and technical considerations were in his favor, and he covered when bearishness was becoming widespread and it was dangerous to be short.

There is a way of avoiding the inevitable anxieties of selling short. You can purchase ''put'' options, i.e., an option to be able to sell a stock at a fixed price. If you believe a stock is going lower you purchase a put for a certain period of time, say 60 or 90 days, and you are entitled to sell the stock at the price which existed when you bought the put, regardless of how low it goes during the contract period. If the stock goes up instead of down, you do not have to exercise your put.

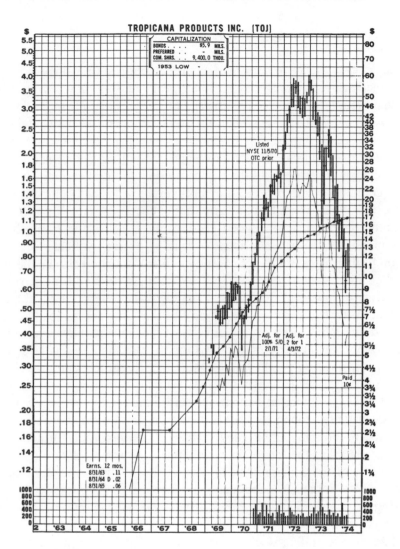

Figure 89. *Chart by Securities Research Company, 208 Newbury Street, Boston, Massachusetts.*

The fee involved in purchasing the put represents a fixed cost, but it is the maximum you can lose. Certain options are now traded on the Chicago Board Options Exchange and you can trade the options themselves without even buying the associated common stock. The opposite of a "put" option is a "call" option, which entitles you to buy a stock at the price existing when the agreement was made. There are also other sophisticated techniques such as "straddles," involving both a put and a call, which can enable you to make money if the stock fluctuates sharply in either direction.

What You Can Expect of Cyclical Stocks

Cyclical stocks, as I have noted earlier, are among the first stocks to top out in the stock market cycle. Some may see their peaks in Stage 2 when the market has begun to discount the expected earnings gains of the economic recovery that is to follow. Other cyclical stocks which investors may be associating with new growth sectors of the economy (such as nuclear power generation equipment or farm equipment) may continue higher into Stage 3. Cyclical stocks which topped out in Stage 2 when investors sold them because they thought earnings were at a peak, could continue lower in Stage 4 as unfavorable earnings comparisons are actually reported. You cannot be confident that cyclical stocks will not go lower in an economic downturn until a good portion of the economic slump has occurred. If you believe the worst is about over and you see cyclical stocks resist selling off on further reporting of poor earnings, there is a good chance the stocks have seen their lows. The "new concept" cyclical stocks could, also, run into trouble in Stage 4. Investors may have some second thoughts about them and remember that even with their new lease on life that they are basically cyclical stocks. More to the point, perhaps, the novelty of the concept may have worn off and investors who bought early may be willing to take their profits. Deere, for example, was still showing good earnings gains, but its earnings progress did not keep it from selling off in 1973. (See Figure 90.)

Cyclical stocks will tend to bottom out before the popular market averages. Since they are usually among the stocks that turn down first, they tend to be among the first to bottom out. If they happen to be favorably influenced by considerations other than the economic cycle alone, they may well turn up considerably in advance of the economic cycle. American Smelting and Refining, for example, turned up in the 1973 decline. (See Figure 91.) Investors were apparently thinking of the company in terms of its interests in natural resources, including silver, which provided a hedge against inflation. Nevertheless, investors are not adverse to selling stocks which have an attractive concept if all of a sudden they are brought back to current reality by an unexpected drop in earnings. Thus, you cannot just ignore near term earnings and expect the concept to conquer all.

What You Should Know About Over-the-Counter Stocks in the Fourth Stage

The over-the-counter market reflects the confidence of investors more faithfully than any other segment of the market. Toward the end of the third stage investors are imbued with confidence and the over-the-counter stocks are among

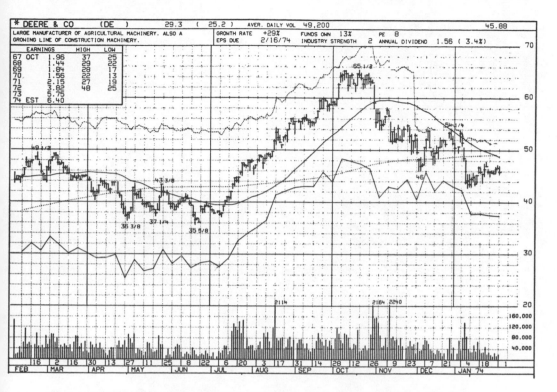

Figure 90. Chart Courtesy of DAILY GRAPHS, P.O. Box 24933, Los Angeles,
California 90024.

the best performers in the market. Conversely, in the fourth stage when investors'
confidence is low, or under extreme conditions investors may even be de-
moralized, there is little investment demand for the bulk of the over-the-counter
stocks. Price-earnings ratios are helpful in gauging the potential left in a stock or
the risk involved, but nowhere can it be seen more clearly how investors ignore
price-earnings ratios when emotions are running high than in the over-the-counter
sector. In periods of market ebullience price-earnings ratios can expand sharply.
Not only are earnings likely to be rising at such a time, but investors are willing to
interpret events very optimistically and assume that the upward trend will continue indefinitely. The financial press tends to emphasize the favorable side of the
news and to play down the unfavorable developments. When the market is
steeped in pessimism, favorable developments are largely ignored as being only
temporary, and the unfavorable news is emphasized. Under these conditions it is
often surprising how low price-earnings ratios can go. Sometimes the low price-
earnings ratios are justified because earnings do eventually deteriorate. One problem can lead to another, and difficulties can develop that no one can anticipate. If

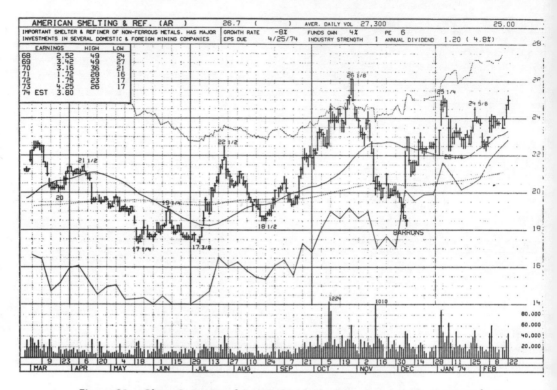

Figure 91. *Chart Courtesy of DAILY GRAPHS, P.O. Box 24933, Los Angeles, California 90024.*

an over-the-counter stock belongs to a propular group in an optimistic market, the expansion in the price-earnings ratio is accentuated, just as the contraction of the price-earnings is exaggerated in a pessismistic market if the popular group falls out of vogue. Unfortunately, some investors think these latter stocks will return to their former popularity and believe that they are getting a bargain. But the stocks rarely recapture their former popularity or command anything like the previous high price-earnings ratios. These price-earnings ratios included a great deal of optimistic psychology and when this psychology is pulled out, a substantial part of the price-earnings ratio is lost. The fact that the stock, or price-earnings ratio, declined, in itself, was damaging to investor psychology.

The wine group was one of the more popular groups prior to the 1973 market decline, and Taylor Wine was one of the leading publicly-owned companies. The price-earnings expanded substantially as the price rose sharply in 1972 when investors noticed that Americans were developing a taste for wine. (See Figure 92.) However, in 1973 the growth in wine consumption slowed, and Taylor Wine actually posted an unfavorable earnings comparison. The passing of the popular-

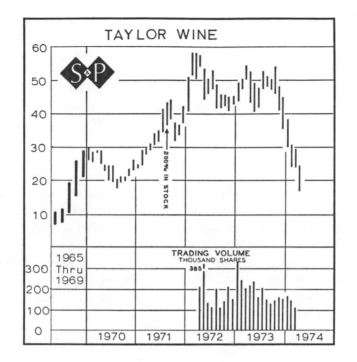

Figure 92. *Chart Courtesy of Standard & Poor's Corporation OTC Stock Reports, 345 Hudson Street, New York, New Yokr 10014.*

ity of the wine group, the decline in the general market, and the lower earnings at Taylor Wine chopped the price-earnings ratio, which was 44 in February, 1973, in half.

How to Deal in Speculative Stocks

Speculative stocks can be expected to behave much like over-the-counter stocks in the fourth stage. The only difference may be that since speculative stocks by definition are dependent upon future events and earnings are relatively unpredictable, if events turn out poorly the stocks can have precipitous declines. On the other hand if events turn out well, the market probably would not recognize the favorable developments in view of the skepticism concerning individual company's prospects in Stage 4. Many companies actually try to defer earnings to latter periods in this stage inasmuch as the market tends to ignore improvements at this time. By and large, speculative stocks should be sold late in Stage 3 or early in Stage 4. They can be bought at the bottom of Stage 4 although the better quality stocks can be expected to do the best until investors confidence returns.

Fidelity Mortgage Investors is a good case study of a speculative stock which came under severe selling in the 1973 decline. The mortgage investment trusts have to be considered speculative because many invest primarily in construction loans which carry above-average risk. The trusts had been under pressure for some months even though many had excellent records, brief as they were, and earnings trends were still up. Interest rates had been rising and it was likely that high interest rates would result in narrowing spreads between what money cost them and what they could loan it for. Also, one of the leading mortgage investment had announced that earnings were leveling off and the news triggered general selling in the group. (Often, when a leading company in a group sells off suddenly it is a warning signal that should nto be ignored.) The unexpected fuel shortage, also, aggravated the current inflationary pressures, which together with raw material shortages were hurting the building industry. Fidelity Mortgage reported that some of its loans were in default and interest was not being accrued. The stock lost over 50 percent of its value in about two weeks. (See Figure 93.)

Unitrode, a manufacturer of semiconductors, was another casualty of the 1973 decline. (See Figure 94.) In this case, earnings of the company were continuing upward at the time, but fears of investors caused them to ignore earnings.

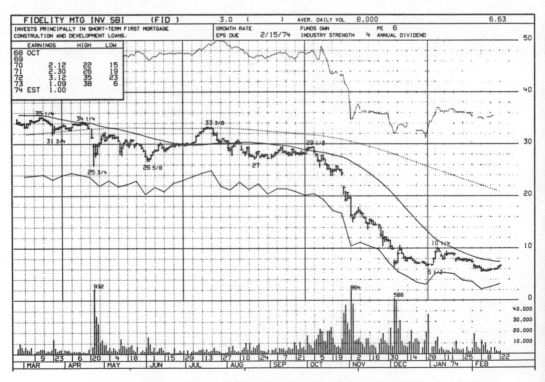

Figure 93. *Chart Courtesy of DAILY GRAPHS, P.O. Box 24933, Los Angeles, California 90024.*

Figure 94. *Chart Courtesy of DAILY GRAPHS, P.O. Box 24933, Los Angeles, California 90024.*

Unitrode was one of the smaller factors in an industry which is highly competitive. There were worries about a possible shortage of silicon and price-cutting if the economy slowed sufficiently and overcapacity developed. Even though none of these problems so far had actually occurred, and there was no way of being sure they would develop, the stock sold off anyway. The market climate in a major decline is one of pessimism and questioning, and investors assume good earnings are only temporary and that the next report may be unfavorable.

Developing a Profitable Attitude
Toward Conservative Stocks

As I have already mentioned, conservative stocks also can have some significant declines in a bear market (although perhaps not as sharp as may be experienced by over-the-counter and speculative stocks), especially if rising interest rates are one of the prime causes of the bear market. Since conservative stocks tend to be interest-rate sensitive, they cannot help but be influenced by changes in the interest-rate environment. If the market decline were more a result of a slack in demand (less likely to happen in the future because of developing raw material shortages), interest rates might even go lower, and, in this instance, conservative stock could do relatively well. In either case, conservative stocks would probably outperform most over-the-counter and speculative stocks.

Conservative stocks can play a particularly important role after a substantial market decline. Investors may be worried about the possibility of a recession and the chances of some volatile stocks selling off again. If the economy were, in fact, slowing down, interest rates also might be declining (particularly short term rates which are more directly affected by current business activity) and the yields on short term paper would be less attractive relative to the yields of common stocks. Instead of putting their funds in money market securities temporarily, investors might consider putting the funds in common stocks and possibly getting some appreciation. American Telephone and Telegraph is one of the favorite havens for funds at such times. Its market performance during the 1973 decline can be seen in Figure 95. Convertible stocks which provide good yields, also, might be in

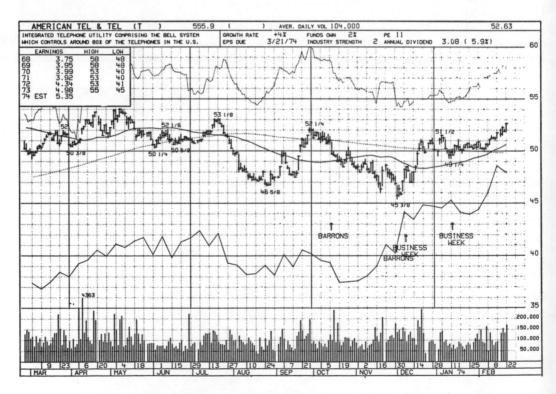

Figure 95. *Chart Courtesy of DAILY GRAPHS, P.O. Box 24933, Los Angeles, California 90024.*

demand in this period. The current return would provide some downside support in a still uncertain market, but also give you a chance to participate in a market rally if it should occur.

Quality Growth Stocks in the Fourth Stage

Quality growth stocks are stocks of companies that have dominant positions in strong growth industries as a result of outstanding proprietary products or exceptional marketing skills, have excellent management, and substantial financial resources. These companies had such fine records of consistent earnings growth, both in good times and bad, that investors were willing to pay substantial premiums for the stocks in terms of price-earnings ratios over what they were willing to pay for stocks of companies with less predictable growth. In some cases, the earnings would have to continue at the high growth rates for ten years or more before the price-earnings ratios at current prices were as low as the price-earnings ratios of the popular stock averages. The stocks were avidly bought by the institutions, which tended to hold them rather than sell them and, thus, provided market support. Many an investor has been badly burned trying to sell these stocks short too soon near market tops, and also at bottoms of market declines because they looked so over-priced. Even in major market declines, the quality growth stocks were among the last groups to turn down.

It was not until the 1973 market decline that a questioning of the high price-earnings ratios of the quality growth stocks and of the large concentration of the funds of many portfolios in these stocks was first observed. Here and there the earnings growth rate of some of the quality growth stocks was slipping, and occasionally there would be an almost unheard of lower earnings report. The buying of the quality growth stock as a group was a concept as much as any other concept. The idea was that only one decision had to be made and that was to buy. No one had to worry about selling. However, once investors began questioning the concept the handwriting was on the wall. The selling that developed in some of the stocks was particularly severe since institutions held such large quantities of them and when the selling began there were few buyers. Simplicity Pattern had a particularly severe decline when earnings faltered. (See Figure 96.) Avon Products predicted a slowing of its rate, and this prospect coupled with some skeptical articles in leading financial publications brought selling into that stock. (See Figure 97.) The earnings of some companies, such as IBM, held up well, but these stocks, too, were not immune to the selling of the concept and the general market pessimism. (See Figure 98.)

The quality growth stocks did not decline without plenty of technical signs that could have alerted investors to the dangers. Simplicity Pattern, for example, received a sell from a computerized market program in the beginning of October

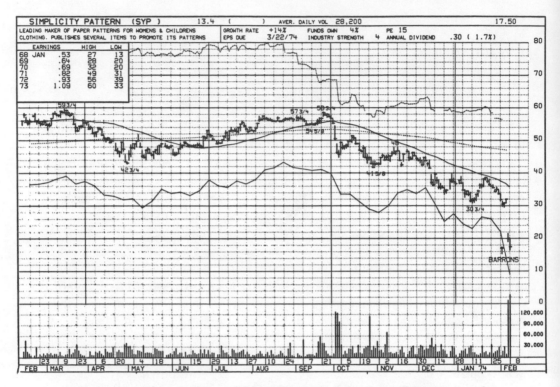

Figure 96. Chart Courtesy of DAILY GRAPHS, P.O. Box 24933, Los Angeles, California 90024.

1973 when the stock declined below a six-month distribution pattern. On the short-term chart (see Figure 96), the stock failed to make a new high at the end of September and dropped below an ascending channel. It, also, penetrated the 200-day moving average line on the downside and the line itself was turning down. The clincher was the violation of the support level of April. At the time, it was also apparent that investors were reappraising the high price-earnings ratio growth stocks since many were showing signs of technical weakness. When the technical indications started revealing that investors were recognizing the new attitude toward quality growth stocks, the prudent move was to sell and wait until the dust settled before assessing their new prospects. It is not likely that investors are abandoning quality growth stocks. They may turn to other concepts, such as natural resource stocks as inflation hedges, but the quality growth stocks as a group are basically sound investment vehicles. It is just that in the future, having once been burned, investors may be more careful of what they pay for growth stocks and price-earnings ratios may be more realistic. The fuel shortage may well mark the beginning of a new era for the American economy, from a cheap-energy

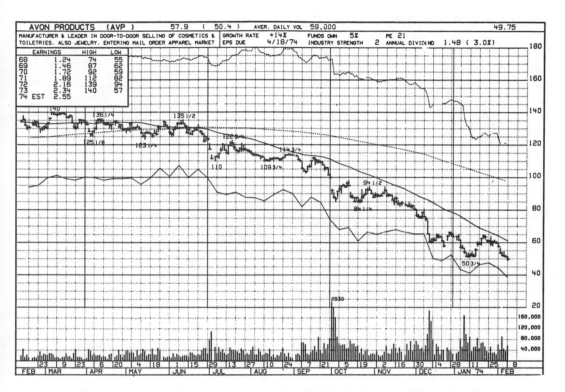

Figure 97. *Chart Courtesy of DAILY GRAPHS, P.O. Box 24933, Los Angeles, California 90024.*

economy to a high cost-energy economy, and during the adjustment phase the economic growth rate could slow and investors become more conservative with regard to price-earnings ratios and current returns from common stocks.

Knowing These Signs of the Bottom of the Fourth Stage Could Be Very Profitable for You

There is one general rule concerning both the economy and the stock market that is very realistic. When there is practically unanimity that the trend will continue in one direction, that is about the time the trend will change. Applying this axiom to the stock market fourth stage, when just about all investors are convinced that the bear market is going substantially lower, is when you should start questioning this forecast. This market indicator, of course, is very rough and applying it profitably is not a simple matter. The application requires good judgment, objectivity, patience, and emotional discipline. From the very beginning of

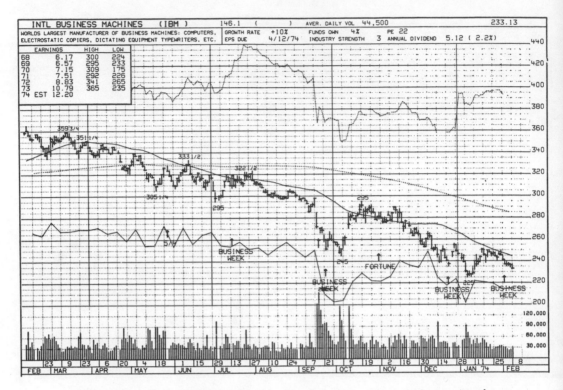

Figure 98. *Chart Courtesy of DAILY GRAPHS, P.O. Box 24933, Los Angeles, California 90024.*

Stage 4 it is difficult to accept that the stock market may be in for a prolonged decline. Thus, you have to be able to disassociate yourself from your emotions early in the game if you want to turn the treacherous pitfalls of Stage 4 into profit-making opportunities. You have to realistically and objectively assess the potential left in the economy and in the stock market. If the economy and various industries are operating near capacity, it is obvious there is not much room for improvement. Have the popular market averages, also, had a long rise? If so, the market must already have anticipated a big jump in profits. It is difficult to accept this intellectual conclusion because many stocks may be acting very well and it goes against all your instincts to sell them. Of course, our technical tools can tell us when such stocks are starting to break down and you can still get out with some good gains. The word of caution here, though, is not to ignore the technical warning signals once the risks appear greater than the potential. Cyclical stocks, in particular, and some speculative stocks, also, should be sold when they look the cheapest because that is when the earnings are doing the best. The next major move in earnings may be down, and the stock prices will go with them.

Assuming you were able to recognize the signs of the beginning of Stage 4 and had the strength of character to become liquid, you are in position to use the positive-action techniques discussed earlier in this chapter to substantially increase your investment funds. On the way down you will have many difficult moments. Every major decline is characterized by false rallies which are largely technical in nature, i.e., there is no change in fundamentals to justify them. You can see in Figure 99 that in the decline in 1973 there were quite a few short rallies even though the major trend was down. These rallies are primarily short covering rallies. In September-October a longer rally took place when the prime rate was raised to 10 percent and investors thought the last major increase in interest rates was behind the market and the trend in interest rates would be done thereafter. The rally collapsed in October when the Arabs instituted the oil boycott. The market rallied again in January when margin requirement were lowered to 50 percent from 65 percent.

You should always ask yourself when these rallies take place if there is any fundamental reason why the market should all of a sudden turn around. You should also remember that major declines do not turn and go straight up. There invariably is a period of consolidation when investors try to determine whether the bottom was for real or not. The bottom can be very irregular as nervous investors take profits after very little rally. After the market has declined for some months, investors have been exposed to a great deal of unfavorable news, financial advisory services are largely bearish, and investor confidence is at a very low level, the conditions are ripe for an approaching bottom of the market. Under such conditions you should consider covering your short positions and start looking for buying opportunities. At this point you may see various stocks moving horizontally and perhaps even some breaking out of bases of several months duration. Perhaps computerized market programs may start flashing buy signs for some individual stocks that are breaking out of six-months bases. These signs are very encouraging, but they do not preclude the stocks turning down again if there is a reverse in the economy or a situation which has an adverse influence on the market. You cannot really be confident that these indicators can be believed until you are sure that the worst is behind the market, whether it is the economy or any other special condition which is worrying the market.

By and large, if the economy is far from showing any gains, any improvement in other factors may only have a temporary influence on the stock market which, even if it does rally on certain favorable news, is apt to fall back and consolidate until the worst of the economic news has been absorbed. At this point in the market you have to start weighing the risk involved against the potential. What disasters could still befall the market, or, on the other hand, what are the possibilities of the market experiencing a good rally? If the potential problems appear to outweight the possible benefits it is best to wait for more confirmation of a bottom. Making certain the danger of a disaster is past is the best way to play it safe. I also have found that when a bottom has been seen the popular market

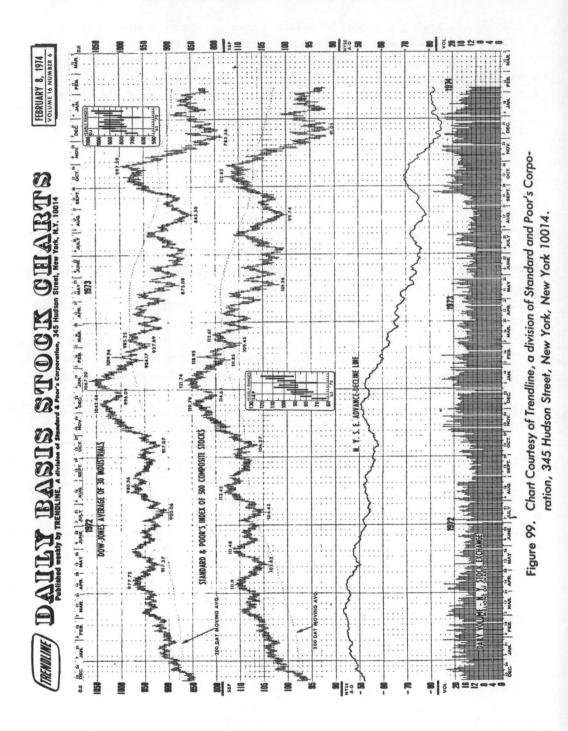

Figure 99.   Chart Courtesy of Trendline, a division of Standard and Poor's Corporation, 345 Hudson Street, New York, New York 10014.

averages have done a thorough job of testing it (often producing an inverted head and shoulders pattern—see Figure 3), the economic visibility has improved considerably and you have a very comfortable feeling that the worst is behind you and the next development will be for the better. This latter approach may not get you in at the bottom, but it will help you avoid being trapped halfway down the decline. Early in 1974, the risks involved in getting back into the market before the Arabs eased the oil boycott appeared to outweight the advantages of trying to anticipate the easing of the boycott. Even with the easing of the boycott, a continuation of the high price of oil would put a strain on the economy and require some time not only for this country, but for the entire Free World, to adjust to the sharply higher cost of energy. Thus, even if the market were to rally, it would likely fall back until investors got a better idea of just how the economy would be able to adjust to the new conditions.

Serious Mistakes You Can Avoid in the Fourth Stage

The first mistake you can make in the fourth stage is to assume every decline is about the same. Instead, you should try to analyze what conditions are different or changing and what the implications might be. Once the decline has run its course, perhaps a new investment strategy is needed. The stocks that were in demand before the decline may not be the same ones in demand the next time around. For example, in the post war period raw materials were cheap and the best strategy was to buy the processing companies. Subsequent to 1973 and the energy crisis, it looked as if raw materials might be in short supply and be in a rising price trend. Then it would be costly for the processors to buy them and stocks of the raw material companies might be the better investment. Actually, the entire investment environment might change. When energy was cheap and plentiful, there was a certain devil-may-care attitude on the part of investors and consumers alike. Now, with a shortage of energy, perhaps investors will be a little more conservative in what they expect in the way of growth and in what they are willing to pay for it. Once the market does bottom out and then turn up, stocks that embody the old stories tend to rally, also. But they may not be the stocks that will continue to lead the market. Investors who have been holding these stocks may take the opportunity to sell them to switch into the new stories.

Another major mistake that is too easily made in the fourth stage is to dump all your stocks after the market has had a long decline and investors are very bearish. You may be selling just before the market bottoms out. It is entirely possible, of course, that the market may spend some time going sideways at the bottom and some individual stocks can still have substantial selloffs even if the popular averages have leveled off. If an entire group is weak, in particular, and your stock in the group has not turned down yet, it might be better not to take a chance and to sell. If an entire group has not participated in the downturn, you have to be very cautious. The probabilities are that eventually it will join the rest of the market. What particular news will cause the group to finally turn down may not be obvious, but usually something comes along. If you do not see any great improvement in the fundamentals for the foreseeable future or investors' attitudes toward a group appear to have changed from the worse, you might as well sell because the chances are that you can employ the funds more profitably elsewhere when the market finally turns around. One mistake investors make that prevents them from making money in the stock market is that they refuse to sell stocks that are out of favor and appear to have little chance of returning to favor, simply because the stocks have declined too far and they do not want to take the loss. What they do not realize is that the loss is there whether they take it or not and the question they should be asking themselves is whether their funds will do better in the future in those common stocks or in other stocks.

One of the more common mistakes in a decline is buying too soon. Many investors have become aware that the best values exist in a pessimistic market environment after a major market decline. What they are not as aware of, however, is that you do not buy stocks just because they have gone down substantially. They also have to have reasonable prospects of becoming attractive to investors again before too long. Some stocks should have never been as high as they went in the first place, and once they start down, the bubble has burst and the ball game is over. Such stocks may look cheap, but maybe their problems were only the beginning. In 1973, many mortgage investment trusts looked very cheap with current yields of 14 and 15 percent on the last twelve-month payments. Some of them, however, had to cut payments sharply when builders in trouble defaulted on their loans and the trusts no longer accrued the interest from these loans and, in some cases, had to increase loss reserves which were insufficient. One way of avoiding getting trapped is to wait until the economy appears to be back on an even keel again, or to wait until the problems of a company have a chance to show up, or earnings themselves start showing improvement. By and large, it is better to allow the market to be exposed to all the bad news rather than assume it has been discounted. If the market no longer reacts to continued bad news, and you have good reason to believe things are improving, you do, at least, have a reasonable basis for buying then.

The most horrendous mistake you can make in the fourth stage, of course, is to sell short right at the bottom. It is not difficult to do. Often the news is the most pessimistic, the market acting the worst, and bearishness the greatest at market bottoms. Thus, after a long decline if you are utterly convinced the market is going much lower, you should catch yourself and consider the possibilities that you may be selling short just before a rally. It can turn out that your candidates for selling short will be the best gainers in the ensuing rally. As I have already noted, there will be several false rallies during the fourth stage decline, some of which you can ride out if you are short. But, if you try to ride out a genuine rally from a major bear market bottom you are in for a rough ride. If there is any news that could change investors' attitudes about any important problem that may have been responsible for the decline, do not hesitate to cover your short positions. You can avoid getting into such a predicament if you look at all the adverse developments that have already occurred before you sell short and ask yourself what else could happen that could make the market go down farther. If you cannot think of any more plausible problems, you better not go short, but instead start thinking of looking for buying opportunities. Just as the odds shift against you when you buy after the market has had a long rise, so the odds are no longer in your favor when you sell short after the market has had a long decline.

9

Timing Your Purchases and Sales for Maximum Profits with Techno-Fundamental Tools

These Market Timing Tools Can Mean the Difference Between Success and Failure

I have already made frequent references to timing in your buying and selling. In this chapter I will attempt to "pull it all together." What amazes and confounds the average investor is that he may buy a stock which seems to be well-regarded by the investment community, yet immediately after purchase it turns down and over a period of time sustains a substantial loss. Conversely, investors may have held an inactive stock for months and finally sold it in exasperation, only to see it turn up sharply after the sale. Although there is no sure method of avoiding such mistakes in the stock market, employing techno-fundamental techniques can help you considerably in purchasing stocks that subsequently go up instead of down and selling stocks that afterwards go down instead of up.

The most common problem investors have in timing their stock transactions is trying to judge the major trend of the stock market. In any major market trend, whether an uptrend or downtrend, few stocks are able to go against the major trend of the popular averages. The trend of the popular averages has a marked impact on the psychology of investors and, to a large extent, reflects investor confidence in the future. If you take advantage of the major market trend, your chances of successfully investing in stocks are improved considerably. On the other hand, if you ignore the major trend or try to fight it, your chances of success are diminished sharply. It is not easy to know how long a major trend will last or when it will reverse, although there are indications, discussed in the next section, when the trend may be changing. Sometimes it takes patience before you have ample evidence that a new trend has been established, but it is usually well worth the wait to be confident the general market is on your side. There are usually indications when a trend may be exhausting itself, but until it has actually changed the indications are usually not very conclusive.

Within the major market trend there are always groups that are outperforming the market. These groups may reflect expected earnings improvement or new favorable attitudes on the part of the public. Occasionally, a concept or story will take hold of investors' imaginations and focus attention on a group. Earnings may or may not be expected to go up in the near future. Some investors are willing to accept concepts which hold promise for sustained long term earnings growth without prospects for immediate earnings gains. Some individual stocks can be expected to do better than others. Both fundamental and technical approaches can be used to indicate the stocks which might give superior performance. Stocks which appear to be undervalued in terms of earnings prospects, or have possibilities of sharp earnings increases, are most likely to be among the stronger stocks in the market. All that remains is how to know when investors are recognizing the potential. How stocks react to news, charts, and computerized market programs can provide some very good insight into how much investor interest there is in the stocks, when they may be ready to move, and the relative strength of the various issues. The foregoing tools are just as helpful in timing sales as well as purchases. Knowing when to sell is almost as important to your investment program as knowing when to buy.

One of the Most Important Factors in Successful Investing

If I were to select the most important factor in making money in the stock market (other than discovering the next IBM, Xerox, or Polaroid) I would say it is taking advantage of the major market trend, both uptrends and downtrends. Although it is practically impossible to isolate the influence of general market trends on individual stocks, many analysts believe the general market accounts for a significant portion of the moves of most stocks. Sharp moves in the popular stock averages tend to set the tone for the entire market. The Dow Jones Industrial Average and the Standard and Poor's 500 composite average are two of the leading popular stock averages which have the greatest impact on investor psychology and confidence. The Standard and Poor's composite average is, also, a leading economic indicator, and when it declines the weakness may well forecast a downturn in the economy. Thus, the leading averages not only have their own impact on the herdlike instincts of investors, but may also presage a decline in corporate earnings which cannot help but affect stock prices. The technical eventually has to follow the fundamental (economy), even though technical indicators often anticipate changes in the fundamentals.

Technically, trends are depicted on charts as channels. (See Figure 100.)

Dow Jones Industrial Averages

Figure 100. © 1973 Dow Jones & Company, Inc. All Rights Reserved.

Channels can be considered short term channels, as in Figure 100, or they can cover a period of months or even years. Of course, the longer term channels are much broader, and those that are used to encompass years of a market move may include entire bear markets and bull markets within the upper and lower trend lines. When a trend is just beginning it is not easy to discern just how steep the trend may be since channels which last several months or more contain short term or intermediate channels representing small declines or rallies within the main channel. The beginning channel, whether it is an ascending or decending channel, may just be too steep to be maintained, and eventually will become part of a main channel that will settle down to a degree of steepness which is sustainable for some time. To make the picture even more complicated, frequently there are parallel channels within the main channel. These inner channels are formed by tops of rallies and bottoms of declines which do not reach the trendlines of the outer channels. As you can see, attempting to determine what the major trend is strictly from charts is not as easily done at the time of formation as it is with the aid of hindsight once the channel's shape is well defined. Some backup from fundamentals is also very helpful and reassuring when you are trying to ascertain whether a trend is in the making. Certainly, the condition of the economy, whether the market is starting out from a low point or from a high point of economic activity, is an important consideration. From the point of view of the stocks themselves, whether the market is in a liquidated or undervalued condition or in an inflated and fully-valued situation is extremely pertinent to the direction of a trend and the distance it can be expected to go. The turning points of a major trend also can be detected more reliably with a combination of fundamental and technical indicators.

Fundamental and Technical Indicators of Major Trend Turns

It is easier to determine through the use of fundamental and technical tools when a major trend has turned than it is to determine when it is near its end. Even though you do not get out at the top, or in at the bottom, if you can catch the turns you can take advantage of most of the major move. Again, though, I have to reiterate that nothing is certain in the stock market and you can never say definitely a trend has changed until it has carried some distance in the opposite direction. Also, it will be hard to accept the change emotionally because you have become conditioned to expecting the trend to continue. There are indications when the trend may be running out, but there is no way of knowing how far the momentum will carry it until the end is seen. However, once both the technical and fundamental factors suggest the end of a trend, the odds are definitely in favor of the trend changing. Even if you have lingering doubts that an uptrend has run its course in spite of the fundamental and technical indications, it is probably better to sell on a precautionary basis. You can always reinstate your position, but you cannot always get out without a loss once a decline has begun (it is quite possible that even if the market has another rally, that the topping out process has begun).

There are many fundamental and technical indicators I could cite that are characteristic of turns in major trends. However, it would be impossible for the investor to assimilate them all. They can help confirm your conclusions about the economy and the stock market, but the main purpose they serve is to give you an overall impression of the economy and the market. This impression, however, can be gained more directly and, perhaps, just as accurately by observing the obvious manifestations of tops and bottoms of major trends. At the top of a major trend you can expect to see the economy doing well. In fact, the economy has probably been in an expansion phase for some time. The generally accepted fact that the economic outlook is bright is one requisite of a top since once practically all investors are optimistic about the economy, they all have had a chance to buy stocks if they were so inclined. You do not have to be a genius to be aware that the economy is humming away. All you have to do is visit the department stores and observe the crowds. You can read the newspapers and note how consumer installment debt is climbing, how well housing starts are doing, and how auto sales are going. When the economy is in this happy state, growing inflationary pressures are probably not far behind. Rising commodity futures will be one indication (assuming price controls are off). You may start seeing on television how food prices and other consumer prices are going up. If you read the *Wall Street Journal* or the financial pages of your favorite newspapers (both of which you should be reading if you are a serious investor), you should be able to note any increases in interest rates, particularly the prime rate of commercial banks, the Federal Reserve discount rate, bond yields, and commercial paper rates. When you see all, or many, of the foregoing signs, the fundamental background is suitable for the termination of the upward trend. From the technical viewpoint, there are also some signs which suggest the time is ripe. If the popular averages and many individual stocks have had long rises, the conditions are favorable for a change in trend. It does not matter whether stocks appear reasonably priced or not (earnings, of course, may be near peak levels for some companies), if investors have large profits they can be easily tempted to take their profits if they think the risks exceed the potential. There is usually a very bullish tone to the market when the end of a trend is approaching. The investment community has to be bullish; otherwise, how could the investors with large profits sell their stock? Volume is likely to be running at high levels, reflecting the enthusiasm and intense interest of investors in the market. Now that both the fundamental and technical backgrounds are suitable for the end of the upward trend, the only thing left is to watch for the technical indicators that tell you it may be occurring. A movement of one of the popular averages through the downside trendline of the ascending channel is an indication that the trend is changing direction (our fundamental and technical information suggests the change will be in the downward direction). We cannot, however, be entirely confident the trend will not be sideways until we see one of the popular averages make a pattern, as shown in Figure 101 (the Dow Jones Industrial Average). This is a head and shoulder-type pattern.

While the pattern is being traced, the stock action can be very confusing. There will be rallies which make you think the uptrend is resuming and then declines which convince you the market is going down, then another rally, etc. When the right shoulder fails to reach the previous peak and turns down, you can be more confident that the pattern is being completed (if the right shoulder topped out at the same level as the previous peak, it would become a double top, which is also bearish). However, until the average declines below a trendline connecting the two lows of the pattern (the neckline) you cannot assume that the trend has turned down. Many individual stocks will be developing the same type of pattern and it is possible some of these will break down before the popular averages. If you are holding any of these stocks, it may be well to sell them when they break down before waiting for the popular averages to turn down. In addition to the head and shoulder patterns, there may be other strong indications of the trend reversal. Stocks may fail to respond to good earnings reports, one of the more believable signs of the exhaustion of a rally, or occasionally, the very top of the market may be pinpointed by a "blowoff," a sharp rise of the popular averages on relatively high volume, then a decline with the closing near the low of the day. The rally, in some cases, may be explosive enough to have a "gap opening." Even after the penetration of the neckline, the market can still give you some moments of concern. The popular averages (and individual stocks) often pull back toward the neckline before declining in earnest.

Much the same indications are characteristic of the end of a major downtrend, only in reverse. A substantial deterioration can be expected to have been seen in the economy. The growth rate of the Gross National Product is likely to be sharply lower, and the Federal Reserve index of production should be declining. New orders for durable goods will have slipped. Unemployment will be edging up. Interest rates, particularly short term rates, are likely to be near their peak or declining. Commodity futures may also be dropping. Auto sales and sales of other consumer durable goods will be weakening. Some markets declines may have their own unique problems which may make investors afraid to buy stocks even if they do appear ridiculously cheap. In 1974, it was inflation, the acute fuel shortage, fears of horrendous balance of payment problems on the part of the oil consuming countries, and the possibilities of competitive devaluations and trade wars that made investors shy away from stocks. The United States economy is based on a huge amount of debt and someone usually points out what chaos would ensue if there were a massive liquidation of this debt. Many financial advisory services can become very articulate about the dangers lying in wait for the economy after a long market decline.

Technically, the best evidence that the trend is changing direction is the penetration of the upper trendline of the decending channel as the popular averages break out of their downtrends. Here, as in the case of the ascending channel, individual stocks may point the way by breaking out of their channels before the popular averages. You will, also, be able to detect a widespread bearishness and pessimism at the bottom of a trend; in fact, this pessimism can hardly be avoided and will have a depressing effect on the entire investment community. Hand in hand with the bearishness will go a certain amount of apathy and resignation. The overall market volume usually will be relatively low as a result. When you see this type of market climate you are likely not to be far from the bottom. A little more patience and you should finally see some type of market bottom chart pattern, as shown in Figure 100. This chart of the Dow Jones Industrial Average shows an inverted head and shoulder formation, one of the more reliable bottom formations. After the right shoulder has tested the downside and held, and the average has pushed above the previous peak, the odds are favorable that the bottom has been seen. If you're confident that the worst of the economic news is now behind the economy, you can assume with even greater assurance that the bottom is passed. Sometimes the very bottom of the decline will be marked by a "selling climax," in which the market sells off sharply on relatively high volume and closes near the high for the day. There does not have to be any particularly good

Dow Jones Industrial Averages

Figure 101. © 1973 Dow Jones & Company, Inc. All Rights Reserved.

economic news to make the market turn up. Investors have plenty of cash at this point and all they have to be confident of is that the next major news will not be any worse, and could even be better. Overall, just as investor confidence is high at the top of an uptrend, it is mighty low at the bottom of a downtrend.

How You Can Avoid Buying When You Should Be Selling, and Vice Versa

Most investors probably have had the experience of buying a stock just before it sold off sharply, even though it recovered to higher levels later. Similarly, many investors have undoubtedly sold a stock before a sharp rally even though it declined to lower levels later. There is no way to completely avoid these problems of improper timing, but a knowledge of some of the more common pitfalls can help you improve the percentage of your successes in timing your buying and selling. In particular, you should be cautious about buying a stock after it has had a long rise. After a stock has had a good upward move, unless there is obvious potential for much higher prices, traders tend to take their profits, causing a consolidation and possibly a decline. You may have to exercise patience for several weeks before the uptrend is resumed. Sometimes the stock will rally again almost immediately and you will think you have missed it, but usually you will get another chance. Missing a buying opportunity is one of the chances you take in not chasing stocks, but remember that there are always other buying opportunities. More often, after a long rise, a stock will form some type of continuation pattern which will give you time to take a position and also give you a little more confidence that the reaction is not going to be serious. In a like manner, after a stock has had a sharp decline there is apt to be a rally since many investors who bought at higher prices may want to average down (often a mistake because investors' attitude toward the stock may have changed permanently), or investors are looking for bargains (one of the big mistakes investors make is thinking they are getting a better buy if a stock is going down than if it is going up). If a technical rally does occur the stock will probably fall back eventually. Many traders will recognize the rally as primarily technical in nature and use it to get out of the stock. Before you should seriously consider buying a stock which has had a good decline you should wait for a solid base to be built (which may take six months or more) and either wait for the breakout on the upside or have good fundamental reasons to expect the next major move will be up. Too often investors want to buy a depressed stock in which the fundamentals have changed drastically and it is either going sideways or lower, but not up. Any time you are buying a stock because of certain developments you expect to happen, you should check the price action of the stock. If it has risen sharply prior to the favorable news and no particularly optimistic good news is expected later, it is likely that investors who bought in anticipation of the news will sell on the news release. Conversely, traders who sold short in anticipation of unfavorable news will tend to cover once a decline has taken place and the unfavorable news is out. Also, investors who are confident all the pessimistic news is out may well be buying once the news is known.

Stocks which may be in for more of a serious decline often have been climbing for some months, perhaps even independently of the general market trend. They usually have some story or concept which has focused attention on the stock. It is impossible to generalize concerning how long concepts will propel a stock. It depends on how valid they are, or how well earnings of the companies do, and on how much additional news of the same type is expected. But almost invariably, at some point the concept runs its course and investors tend to lose interest. There may be no more mystery about the outcome, no new news to bring in buying, or perhaps the stocks are amply priced even if everything goes exactly as anticipated. You can expect to find the concept fully believable and investors universally bullish at the top when a concept has about run its course. This fact leads to another check you can use when buying stocks. If investors seem to be very bullish you should ask yourself if you are, perhaps, buying when everyone knows the story, has already bought the stock, and may be ready to take profits. Although many investors believe something has to be going wrong with a company if a stock is selling off, frequently nothing is really amiss. It is just that all the news is known and investors are taking their profits and looking around for new stories.

The same reasoning can be used in selling stocks which investors have been avoiding because of a negative concept. When everyone is bearish and convinced that the stocks are going lower, you should consider the possibility that they may be near their lows. The situation is somewhat different with declining stocks than with rising stocks, however. Except for possible short covering, which depends to a large extent on the amount of trading interest in the stocks, there may not be much demand for the issues until there is some conviction that an improvement in fundamentals is not far away. They may not go much lower, but they may not go much higher, either. The probabilities, however, are that some type of rally will be experienced. If the stocks have spent some time in a sideways movement, the possibilities of a substantial rally are good if the fundamentals are not too poor. Before selling depressed stocks, you should give some thought to whether the groups or industries with which the stocks are related could receive renewed investor interest, or whether some development could occur in the companies themselves which could boost the stocks. If the situations look helpless from all angles, it may be best to sell and look for stocks that appear more promising and may be close to completing their base formations. The fact that a stock is depressed is not enough justification for continuing to hold it once the technical rally has taken place, investors are showing little interest in it, and there is nothing to indicate above-average potential. Your funds usually can do better in the stock of a company in which there is some investor interest and which has above-average potential.

How a Stock Can Tell You What It Will Do

Common stocks often can be very accommodating and practically tell you what they intend to do next. Of course, you have to be able to understand what they are saying. The language is both technical and fundamental. As the theme of this book has stressed, neither the technical nor the fundamental approach alone is the complete answer. They are complementary and only the combination of the two can do the job of forecasting satisfactorily. The technical is primarily short term oriented (although it may have long term implications) and the fundamental can indicate the long term potential. Subjecting the technical to fundamental screening can help you catch false technical signals (both approaches have their weaknesses and possibilities of misinterpretation). Probably the best indication of what a stock will do short term is given by its reaction to news. If a stock fails to react to good news, particularly news of a type it has reacted to favorably before, or to a good earnings report, it may have exhausted its near-term potential. Whether the technical indication has more serious implications depends on several considerations. If the stock has had a substantial upward move over a long period of time and the story is generally well-known, failure to respond to further good news could mean the stock may have peaked out for the foreseeable future. Another consideration is how good the fundamental outlook is. If there appears to be a possibility of substantial earnings gains, the lack of response to good news may result in just a temporary consolidation of the stock. Essentially, you have to weigh how much news is already in the stock and forecast how much optimistic news is ahead. (This method applies to the entire market as well as to individual stocks.) The foregoing reasoning can be reversed for stocks that may be bottoming out. They tend to ignore pessimistic news and poor earnings reports. In the case of stocks that may be bottoming out, you should refer to the fundamentals in trying to decide what the potential appreciation might be. A large technical base does suggest that the upward move may be sizeable, but unless you can find some reason for expecting an improvement in the fundamentals, the odds would be better if you found a situation in which both the technical and fundamental are favorable.

You also have to remember that the technical indicators sometimes have a mind of their own over the short term, but eventually they will tend to conform to the fundamentals and shape of the economy. There are times when the fundamentals are so uncertain, or the risks so great, that it is better to stay out of the market until the outlook is better defined. It may well be that firmness in the technical indicators presage improvement in the fundamentals, but the technical indicators are occasionally wrong when the fundamentals do not turn out as good as hoped.

How to Take a Broad View of the Market

The successful investor not only has to be on top of the current stock market, but he also keeps one eye on the broad trends. Price-earnings ratios are important as a gauge of the risks and potential, and the direction of the momentum of earnings is helpful as an indicator of the near-term outlook for a stock, but broader trends can override the implications of high or low price-earnings ratios and earnings trends. These broad trends can broadly be classified as cyclical and secular. The cyclical trends can include the various individual industry cycles, trends associated with the stock market stages (discussed earlier), and trends related to concepts which come and go. The secular trends are concerned with investor confidence which may be reflected in what investors are willing to pay for earnings (price-earnings ratios and their demand for current yields), shifts in investor interest from one major investment sector to another, and changes in investment philosophy.

Investor confidence can be affected by problems other than a downturn in the economic cycle. Uncontrolled inflation is probably the greatest threat to investor confidence at this writing. Fears of energy shortages, international monetary crises, competitive devaluations, and trade wars, all of which are interrelated, can also shake investor confidence. Increased government encroachment upon the private sector, including wage and price controls, tend to weaken investor confidence. When confidence is at a low level, investors are less sure of future earnings and are wary of high price-earnings ratios which are anticipating a continued high earnings growth rate for years into the future. The better quality stocks tend to be in more demand than speculative issues. Along these lines, technological stocks which are so dependent on vigorous economic progress may be less in demand than say, natural resource stocks. During periods of uncertainty, investors become more concerned with protecting their capital with high current returns and asset values. Since commodity prices usually climb during periods of inflation, natural resource stocks are particularly attractive to investors during such times.

Changes in investor philosophy develop slowly. The pendulum sometimes may swing too far in one direction, but it usually will swing back. After the Great Depression, investors were concerned with preserving their capital and were more interested in current yields than capital appreciation. Stocks were considered very risky in those days. In the post war period the love affair with growth stocks began. Early in the 1970 decade the growth-stock philosophy—growth at any price—may have run its course. The economy underwent a radical change from a low-cost to a high-cost energy economy. Investors appear to be thinking more conservatively, in tune with the changing times. Nevertheless, it is not likely the success of the growth stocks in the 1950s and 1960s will be forgotten. How these conflicting views will be reconciled remains to be seen. One of the more common shifts in investor interest occurs between the consumer and capital goods sectors. This shift takes place when activity has been running above the long term trend in either sector. Sometimes consumer spending for durable goods has been holding at high levels for several years and demand has been borrowed from the future. At the same time, industrial capacity additions may have been running behind consumer spending. Under these conditions, investor funds are likely to flow from the consumer durable goods sector into the capital goods sector. At other times, the situation may be reversed and the funds could flow in the opposite direction.

Taking Advantage of the Institutional Mind

The institutions represent the most concentrated buying (and selling) power in the stock market. It is very difficult to make money in the market buying individual stocks when the institutions are selling them. It is, of course, not easy to know just what the institutions are doing. If large blocks of a stock are being sold it is likely that institutions are doing the selling. Very sharp gains or drops in a stock also suggest that institutions are responsible for the heavy volume. Mutual funds are required to report their transactions and their holdings quarterly. The investor can tell from the current holdings how many shares are left that might be sold if a fund has been selling the stock. Insurance companies have long reported their holdings, but banks were only recently required to do so. Institutions tend to confine themselves to the stocks of companies with a relatively large number of shares of common stock outstanding so that they can buy and sell large blocks without disturbing the market too much. However, often they cannot prevent sharp price movements if several institutions try to buy or sell at the same time. Although some institutions may be buying or selling the same stocks that other institutions are buying or selling, there is a herdlike instinct among institutions just as there is among investors. Institutions are influenced by popular groups in the stock market, also. Since those that are subject to public scrutiny want to show stocks in their portfolios that are currently in the public eye, they are under pressure not to miss out on popular groups. In fact, they often make portfolio adjustments just before reporting periods in order to present the best possible appearance to the public. In the 1950s and 1960s the institutions were avid buyers of quality growth stocks, and these stocks showed some spectacular gains. In some cases, they owned significant percentages of the outstanding stock of these companies. In the early 1970s the institutions had some second thoughts about the high price-earnings ratios they were paying for quality growth stocks and many of these stocks had substantial declines from their selling. It does not take much imagination to see the advantages of being able to anticipate the buying and selling trends of the institutions. There is no way of being certain how long the buying or selling in specific groups will continue even if you think you are able to detect the beginning of it, but if you believe there is a good concept for the buying or selling, and particularly if you see some support for such concepts in the financial publications, you may be able to turn the buying and selling of institutions to your advantage. Such buying and selling, of course, is subject to the timing considerations discussed in this chapter and in Chapter 10.

Knowing the Proper Use of Charts and Computerized Market Programs

Charts are among the more controversial tools used in the investment world. If used improperly and if too much is expected from them, investors can get badly burned. There are "pure" technicians who say the investor is better off if he knows nothing about a stock and is guided strictly by the charts. I find this thesis hard to accept and consider this approach fraught with danger. In fact, it may be responsible for much of the controversy that surrounds charts. I believe the safer, more effective approach is to employ fundamentals to make the basic decision to buy or sell and to use the charts to tell you when the market is recognizing the fundamentals, i.e., for timing purposes. Using this latter approach, some stocks in which the favorable fundamentals might not be known would be missed, but this is better, in my opinion, than taking a chance on false technical signals. If you do not know the fundamentals at all, if the stock goes against you initially you would have no idea what to do. Charts can also be used to help confirm the fundamentals, or to call them into question. I believe that if the charts do not confirm the fundamentals, it is possible your information on the fundamentals was wrong and it would be better to pass the situation by for one in which both the fundamentals and charts appeared favorable. Charts show where stocks have been, and this knowledge in itself is very helpful. If the charts show a substantial move has taken place before some particular news is known, it may well be that the news has been discounted. Also, some chart formations have forecasting value in that, based on past performance, the probabilities are that some chart formations will provide certain moves. The length of the consolidation patterns indicate how much of a move might be expected when a breakout occurs either up or down (assuming the fundamentals can support such a move). The volume characteristics (volume is shown on bar charts) is important in trying to determine the validity of a breakout. Normally, a valid upside breakout is on higher relative volume. Breakouts on the downside may or may not involve substantially increased volume, although usually higher volume can be expected if investors are really concerned about the stock. No discussion on charts could be complete without mentioning the "random walk" theory, which holds that stock prices move in a random fashion and are not influenced by previous price moves. Anyone who looks at the symmetry of chart formations could hardly be expected to believe this theory. I will agree, however, that investors who follow the technical approach only can get whipsawed, but the proper use of the combination techno-fundamental approach should substantially cut down the frequencies of whipsaws.

The computer and computerized market programs have become important tools in technical analysis. Although computerized market programs are shrouded in much mystery and appear to be very complicated, essentially they provide the same information bar charts provide, only in figure form. The computer uses the same raw imput, stock prices, volume, and time, as do the charts. Charts and computerized market programs are complementary. The charts can provide a good picture of a stock's past history, including resistance levels, support levels, channels, and volume characteristics, but chart formations can easily be misinterpreted. Computerized market programs do not provide a visual picture of the stock's price action (although graphs can be made that can be extremely helpful for timing purposes as discussed in Chapter 10), but they can be more easily interpreted and can actually be programmed to give buy or sell signals. These computerized programs can enable you to keep on top of the entire market of listed stocks on a weekly basis, and can reveal all the breakouts, both on the upside or downside, that have occurred during the week. Most programs provide both the short term and long term appreciation of stocks. As with charts, the basic assumption is that trends once set in motion will continue, and that the stronger the momentum (price appreciation over a certain period of time) the longer the move. Some programs provide elaborate weighing of the price appreciation by volume and time, but I do not believe this weighing significantly changes the results. The relative strength among the stocks is also given by most computerized programs, as well as the volatility of stocks. The stocks with improving relative strength are expected to do better than those with declining relative strength. The computer can, also, provide price momentum and relative strength for entire industries. You can see that the computerized market program is a valuable tool. I will have to point out, however, that it does not have all the answers. Since it depends on trends to trigger signals, it usually will not get the investor in at the bottom or out at the top, but depending how long the bases and distribution patterns are, can catch the major part of price moves. At major tops and bottoms some false signals may be triggered, but fundamental screening should help eliminate many of them. The computerized program cannot predict how far moves will go. Again we have to employ fundamental analysis to complete the picture. It also cannot predict the unexpected, but neither can any other approach.

10

How Techno-Fundamental Trading in Common Stocks Can Produce Profits

How to Recognize the Risks in Trading

The term "trading" is a very general one and has to be further defined before we can discuss it intelligently. There is "day trading," a type of trading in which the trader buys and closes out a position all in the same day. This is probably the most difficult type of trading that can be done and requires a high degree of professional skill, if not a lot of luck. Outside of day trading, practically any length of time that does not stretch into several years could conceivably be called trading. Trading is, in fact, an attitude of mind to a large extent. When the investor buys, he already has in mind some objective, such as a specific development that might take place, a price-earnings ratio, a technical signal, a certain level of industry activity, general market conditions, the amount of price appreciation he will be satisfied with, etc., which he will use as a guide in making a decision to sell. Many traders will expect to stay with a stock at least six months so they can qualify for the capital gains tax, but they are, nevertheless, willing to take profits earlier if a stock runs up sharply and appears to be exhausting its near-term potential. In other cases, investors may stay with a situation for a year or more if the potential still warrants the commitments. After he has been in a dormant stock for several months, however, the investor has to ask himself if he could do better having his funds in another situation. In order to answer this question he has to draw on all his knowledge of techno-fundamental strategies. There is a big risk here that just about the time he (and all the other traders) gets discouraged and sells, the stock might be ready for an upward move. Considering the technical aspects, questions that should be asked include: Is the relative strength improving or deteriorating? Is the short term and long term momentum accelerating or decelerating (information learned from computerized market programs? Using charts: Are support levels being broken? Are trendlines being violated? Are bullish or bearish chart patterns being formed (more on this later in the chapter)? The possibility that the entire market may be turning down cannot be excluded. What stage of its cycle is the market (and the economy) likely to be in? Is the market (and the stock) responding to favorable economic news? Concerning the industry or group the stock is associated with, is it possible that the concept or its market popularity has run its course? Turning to the fundamentals, the first item worthy of note is the possibility that near-term earnings may be unfavorable. The outlook for the industry and the results of any similar companies that have already reported earnings can help in assessing the earnings situation. The company's earnings may have already seen their major gains. Competition may be developing, shortages may be a problem, or if the stock is interest-rate sensitive, interest rates may be on the verge of rising. After a thorough analysis of the technical and fundamental factors, you have to make your decision whether to sell or stay with your stock. Certainly, you cannot have your money tied up indefinitely in a below-average situation. Time is money in the investment world.

An even more perplexing situation is one in which the stock turns down immediately after purchase by the trader. You can help avoid this problem by being cautious about buying stocks that have had a sharp advance after a spate of good news. The same technical and fundamental questions have to be asked here as in the example just discussed, only the urgency is greater in this instance since the stock is already declining. If you cannot make a decision to hold or sell on the technical and fundamental factors, you should then fall back on the 10 percent rule. If a stock drops more than 10 percent after purchase, sell and cut your losses. Too often traders will not cut their losses and find themselves no longer traders, but long term investors. By and large, traders can do better by switching out of unusually weak stocks and into relatively strong stocks.

Another mistake traders make is to sell too soon. In the heat of the chase it is easy to forget that stocks can be expected to encounter profit-taking periodically during a long rise. As long as no important support levels are broken, the reactions can be considered primarily technical. The main burden, however, falls on the fundamental approach to determine how much potential the stock might possess. While a top is being made, or after it is passed, there are usually ample technical indications. If you have some patience, the technical indications usually will tell you when it is time to sell. The tendency of many traders to take profits too soon points up the difficulty that the very nature of trading creates. Traders are under pressure to make money quickly and they have little patience waiting for situations to work out. There is a fine line between being too patient and too impatient. Much of the pressure can be removed if you take less of a short term attitude toward stocks. I call a more relaxed trading attitude, ''conservative trading.'' In this type of trading approach, the idea is to take at least a six-month view. In this frame of mind you can watch market action less emotionally and more objectively, and wait for definite technical signals before acting. However, if the stock works out more quickly than expected, you can always take your profits early. If, after six months, the stock still has substantial potential you can hold off selling.

Probably the biggest risk of all is overstaying the general market, i.e. failing to recognize that the uptrend has ended. If the general market has entered a distribution phase where irregular rather than sustainable moves are characteristic of the market, you have to be very nimble to make money trading. If it suddenly dawns on you that your stocks have not been doing well lately you should consider taking to the sidelines until the trend becomes better defined again. At such times patience and discipline can really pay off. You should only be in the market when the odds are in your favor. If you have no idea of what the trend is you can save a lot of money by staying out of the market. Certainly, if you are convinced that the trend has turned down you should consider selling short rather than buying long. (Buying precious metal stocks is another alternative.) Short selling involves some unique risks (some of which have already been discussed).

How to Profit from Options

The buying and selling of options (security options as opposed to commodity options) is a stock market operation used primarily by traders. It is short term in nature and the risks and rewards have to be weighed carefully for the trader to be successful. A "call" option entitles you to buy a stock at a certain price during a specified period of time, usually six months and ten days, but sometimes a little as 30 days or as much as two years. A "put" option entitles you to sell a stock at a certain price during a specified period. In order to obtain the privilege to buy or sell a stock at a certain price, you must pay a fee called a premium, which is a sunk cost whether you exercise your option or not. There is also an option called a straddle, which is merely a combination of a call and a put. Properly used, straddles can increase your success ratio considerably. Another way of making money in the option market is to write options, i.e., provide the stock on which the calls are written and to promise to buy the stock on which puts are written.

The best way to show how options work (for the option buyer rather than the option writer) is to take an example of the actual price performance of a stock, such as Amerada Hess. In selecting stocks, it is best to select volatile stocks (the computerized market program can assist you here). It is particularly important when buying straddles to stay with stocks that are likely to have sharp fluctuations. In figure 102 you can see that Amerada Hess has had very sharp moves, making it an ideal stock for the option buyer.

In attempting to time your purchase, you can use either a computerized

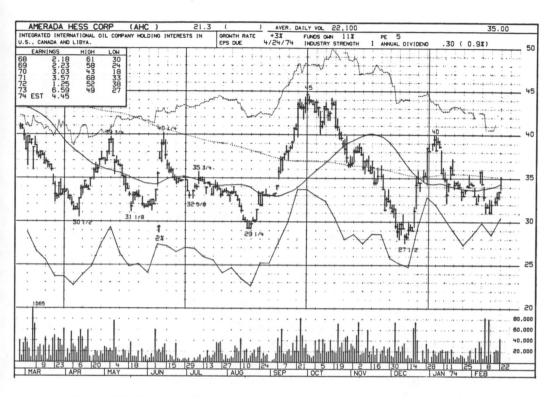

Figure 102. *Chart Courtesy of DAILY GRAPHS, P.O. Box 24933, Los Angeles, California 90024.*

market program (assuming a printout is available) or charts. In early September, 1973, the short term strength of Amerada turned positive, giving a short term buy signal. On the bar chart, the stock broke out from a short term base on a gap opening. Both these signals would justify buying a call option. Assuming the "striking price" is 36 (price at which the stock can be bought if a call or sold if a put), if you exercised your option and finally sold the stock at 42, you would have made 6 points, a gain of over 16 percent on the purchase price in less than a month. (The net profits would be less after deducting the cost of the option, the New York Stock Exchange Commissions, and taxes.) If the stock did not rise after you purchased the option, you would merely let it lapse. Thus, you cannot lose more than the cost of the option. Another thing to keep in mind is that the bulk of your funds are not tied up while you are waiting for the stock to move as they would have been in the outright purchase of the stock.

Buying a put follows the same procedure, only in reverse. You watch for a signal from the computer or charts, indicating that the next short term move may be down. The short term strength turning negative or the stock breaking below the support level of 40 would indicate the point at which to buy a put. Assuming the striking price was 39 and you eventually purchased the stock in the open market at a price of 31, you would have made more than 20 percent on your investment (also, excluding the cost of the option, NYSE commissions, and taxes). Buying puts allows you to make money in down markets, but avoids much of the anxiety associated with selling short since your maximum loss is limited to the cost of the option. The market action of Amerada Hess was perfect for buying straddles. With a straddle it does not matter which direction the stock moves, as long as it does move. It is possible to take advantage of the swings in the prices of common stocks with a relatively small investment compared with the actual buying or selling the stocks, by trading the options themselves. The Chicago Board Options Exchange provides a market for specific options where you can trade the options without ever buying or selling the underlying common stock. These options have the same basic characteristics as short term warrants.

Other Trading Strategies That Can Work

Some trading strategies can become quite complex and are best left to the professionals who have the time and, perhaps, the up-to-date knowledge of situations which can give them an edge. It does seem that the simpler the trading strategy, the easier it is for the investor to understand it and the more likely he will be successful. Trading does involve risk, and the shorter the time horizon of the trader, the greater the risk involved since he is not allowing time for values to be built up in the stock. There are some arbitrage situations which virtually assure the trader a profit, but they are rare. Usually, when the average investor stumbles on an arbitrage situation which appears to offer a sure profit there is a catch somewhere. The usual arbitrage situation involves the acquisition of one company by another and the terms of the agreement in principle call for the exchange of the acquiring company's common stock for the stock of the company to be acquired. Once the merger proposal is known, the stock of the company to be acquired often has a sharp rise, but it may still be undervalued in terms of the stock the acquiring company is offering in the proposed exchange. The reason for this undervaluation is usually that there is always a possibility that the merger may fall through. If large companies are involved, the Justice Department may object for anti-trust reasons. If regulated companies are involved, the regulatory agency may not approve. The merger may hinge on a favorable tax ruling from the Internal Revenue Service. There are many other reasons, some involving personnel and accounting practices, why mergers may not be consummated. Depending on the likelihood of the merger going through, the stock of the company being acquired will tend to reach an equilibrium point where the risk if the merger does not go through equals the profit-potential if it does go through. If the merger fails to go through, the stock of the company to be acquired usually sells off. Of course, if you are confident this stock deserves to be higher in its own right, then your downside risk is reduced. Also, frequently another company may compete for the hand of the candidate for acquisition, offering even more generous terms. In trying to take advantage of the gap between the market price of the stock of the acquisition candidate and its value in terms of the acquiring company's stock, you can, of course, just buy the stock of the former company. However, even if the merger is completed it is possible the stock of the acquiring company may decline and you will lose your profit. A safer procedure is to sell short the stock of the acquiring company and buy sufficient stock of the company to be acquired to cover the stock you sold short. Using this method you have your profit locked in and your own risk is that the merger may not be completed. If you already own the stock of an acquisition candidate, if it should run up close to the value of the stock of the acquiring company being offered in exchange, you should consider the desirability of selling in the open market on the possibility that the merger may not go through and the stock would decline.

Another trading strategy that can be very profitable is buying warrants. I mentioned warrants in the preceding section, but they deserve more space. Like the options on the Chicago Board Options Exchange, warrants can provide substantial leverage, both on the upside and on the downside. The leverage factor is related to the disparity between the price of the warrant and the price of the underlying common stock. A warrant represents a call on the underlying common stock. Warrants generally sell at a premium over the mathematical difference between the stock price and the lower exercise price. This premium primarily reflects investor interest in the stock, its growth potential, and the time left until the warrant expires. (Longer term warrants often sell at about half the exercise price if the stock is selling near the exercise price.) Sometimes the premium on the warrant is so large that it may be better to buy the common rather than buy the warrant. Occasionally, the price of the common stock has to appreciate several times before the warrant's percentage appreciation when the premium disappears at expiration is equal to the common stock's percentage appreciation. If it does not seem probable that the common will appreciate this much before the warrant expires, the common would be considered the better buy. Warrants can usually work out well anytime the underlying common has a sharp use, but perhaps the best time to purchase warrants is when the general market is coming off a major bottom.

Staying with a Good Story and Popularity Is One Key to Trading Success

As a trader you have to get straight in your mind what your goals are and what they are not from the very outset. They definitely are not to find the stock with the lowest price-earnings ratio, the highest current yield, or the highest asset value per dollar of stock price. Such situations may well work out in time, but you do not know when the market will start recognizing them. Your main goal as a trader is to maximize your return on capital. There are two objectives in maximizing your return: 1) achieving the greatest profits possible in 2) the shortest period of time. There is no way to be positive of accomplishing either objective, but the probabilities of achieving both are increased immeasurably if you confine your selections to stocks which have a good story and investor popularity. It matters little whether you have the greatest situation in the world if no one else is interested in it. On the other hand, even if a story turns out to have been based on false assumptions, if there is a great deal of investor interest in it the results can still be very pleasant. As a trader you want a stock to move higher soon after you buy it. The technical approach can indicate when a stock may be ready to move (chart breakouts, computer buy signals, response to favorable news, etc.) but unless you can see popularity building up, the move may be aborted or short-lived. Popularity does not develop in a vacuum. There has to be a story or concept to provide a basis for popularity. A new story is also highly desireable. Part of the secret of the attractiveness of a story is that no one can be absolutely sure of the potential of the stock since it is a new story. Once a story is known and the potential revealed to the investing public, the second time around it does not intrigue investors as much as it did the first time. A new story also benefits from the fact that there are not a lot of disgruntled investors who did not get out in time after the initial story was discounted by the market. The initiative lies with the buyer when investors become aware of a story for the first time. Of course, as the stock rises, more and more of the early purchasers will be taking trading profits. After a certain point in the rise, a new factor, short covering, comes into play which can boost the stock farther. It can sometimes take months before the short covering runs its course.

The popularity of a stock can be recognized in many ways. As I already noted, having a stock tied to a story or a concept alerts you to the possibility it can become popular. The mere fact a stock is moving higher suggests that investors are getting interested, and if it is going up faster than the popular averages or when the general market is going down, the signs are particularly propitious. Increasing volume also is very helpful in recognizing growing popularity. Of course, the news media, which is such a shaper of opinion in this age, should take notice of the popularity of the story or concept. Once the general public is fully aware of the popularity of the story, the short term risk is beginning to approach the potential. Traders often like to take profits when a story becomes popular. If the concept is viable, they will wait for weakness and then reinstate their positions. Occasionally, the story and the market action of a stock will give the appearance of a stock riding on a crest of popularity, but the situation may be basically poor and investors will use the strength to get out. You should always think realistically. Ask yourself this question: Is it likely the project will really work out and earnings will have a good gain? Most stories and concepts will eventually run their course and investors will tire of this particular game. After the story is well-known and a stock has had a long rise, if it starts breaking down technically do not fight it. Just sell and look for another interesting situation. Even though earnings continue upward, the charisma is over and the stock is not likely to recapture its old glory. It will have rallies now and then, but investors who failed to get clear in the first decline will be taking advantage of the rallies to sell. Eventually, if earnings do continue to increase, the stock will work higher, but the earnings may command a relatively modest price-earnings ratio. The common mistake with such stocks, sometimes called "fallen angels," is to think you have a bargain when they sell off and to get yourself locked into a deteriorating situation. The possibility of buying into this type of stock half-way down is one reason that it is usually not advisable to average down.

Watching How Stocks Act in the Market
Can Help You Select Winners

There is no better way of sizing up the short term potential, or lack of it, than watching how a stock acts in the market. Its response to news and to the influence of the general market is telling it as it is. We have three main ways of monitoring the behavior of a stock: 1) watching its daily price action, 2) getting a dynamic picture of the stock's past behavior from a computerized market program, and 3) seeing the static picture of a stock's performance on a bar chart. All three of these methods are used in trading in selecting stocks for purchase. Each has its own particular benefits as a trading tool. Watching how a stock reacts to earnings reports, internal developments, economic news, or the general market trend can be very valuable in helping you decide how much the stock has already anticipated or discounted news. Watching a stock act with regard to a strong movement of the popular averages is especially meaningful. If a stock can rise when the market is generally weak it means that there must be some buying taking place that has very strong convictions. Conversely, if a stock sells off in a market uptrend it suggests that selling is occurring under the mask of the general market strength. You can watch the price behavior of stocks with the aid of quotation machines, or you can even keep informed from the market prices in the newspaper. You should be careful not to be too quick to jump to a conclusion, however. It usually takes more than one day's action to give investors a chance to make a reasoned response to any development.

Although the best way to evaluate a stock's behavior is to personally observe its action in the market, it is not physically possible to watch all the stocks in which you might be interested. The next best thing is to have a computerized analysis of each stock's performance. Even the computer cannot always throw light on what the prospects of a stock are, but the computerized market program is especially helpful at major trend changes. Once a trend is underway the computer can only indicate that the trend is intact and whether or not it is weakening. It cannot predict how far the trend will carry. It can indicate that a trend may be shifting direction from changes in the short, long term and relative strengths of the stock. An indication that the trend may be turning up for a stock may be given when the short and long term strength turns positive and the relative strength improves. The short term strength in itself usually does not suggest a change in the long term trend of a stock, but at major tops and bottoms the short term strength may lead the way. The bar charts, in their way, also reveal much the same information. Penetration of the short and long term descending channels on the upside may indicate the beginning of a change in trend. Usually a base is formed before a major uptrend begins. This base-building process sometimes takes several months. Breakouts often coincide with the buy signals of the computerized market program. Breakdowns from chart distribution patterns also may occur about the same time a sell signal is given by the computer. Bases and distributions patterns that are developing on the charts can often indicate when a computer buy or sell signal will be given.

You can see in Skyline's market action a good example of how a computerized market program and a bar chart can help you time your selection of a stock for capital gains (after you have decided that long term prospects are good). (See Figure 103.) Skyline had already reported lower earnings and the stock had experienced a substantial decline from a peak of 74 in 1972. The industry, nevertheless, was believed to fill a vital economic need. The first hint of a technical improvement in the stock was seen when the computerized market program short term strength turned up at the end of December 1973 at about 12. Ordinarily, the movements of the short term strength index have short term connotations, but at major bottoms and tops the short term strength may anticipate a change in direction of the long term strength. The trader could have bought on this signal, but if he wanted more confirmation he could have waited for some testing of the downside on the charts, a penetration of a trendline drawn along the top of the descending channel extending back to July, or the completion of the base about the end of February. The breakout from the base at about 16½ would have been another signal to buy. The move about the 200 day moving average line would have provided additional confirmation. The base, itself, is fairly wide, suggesting that the eventual move could be sizeable (appeared to be supported by the fundamentals).

A similar procedure, only in reverse, can be used to time the selling of stocks. Just as fundamentals are used in assessing the potential of a situation, fundamentals are employed in determining the risks involved in a stock. In the case of Disney (see Figure 104), the risk in early 1973 appeared to far outweigh the potential, even though on some days the stock acted very well. The sharp jump in earnings from Florida Disney World was already in the stock and it was very richly priced compared with other stocks in the industry, even though the

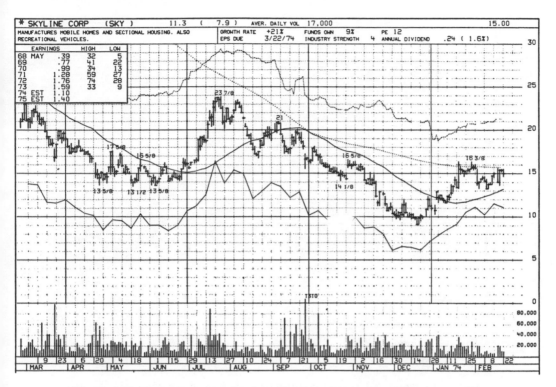

Figure 103. *Chart Courtesy of DAILY GRAPHS, P.O. Box 24933, Los Angeles, California 90024.*

company, without a doubt, was the oustanding one in the industry. The question was: When would the market recognize the over-valuation? The computer gave an unequivocal sell signal near the end of April 1973 at 87. Since the stock had a long rise over an extended period of time, this sell signal was particularly signific- ant. Even though weakness was developing in the stock, it did not go down immediately. It had some short term rallies (anyone who went short on the computer sell signal would have had some anxious moments) and did not break the major support level at 83-85 until early June. After a decline it rallied back and many sellers probably thought they had made a mistake. The July peak was below the previous high and the stock started trending down again. In October, it finally sold off decisively when the Arab oil boycott was announced and the threat of a fuel shortage became very real.

Traders can also find the computerized market programs and bar charts very useful in making short term trades. When stocks are in both rising and declining trends they tend to form "continuation" patterns which represent periods of profit-taking or short covering. These formations often take the shape of a flag, pennant, triangle, or inverted head and shoulder formation. They usually only last

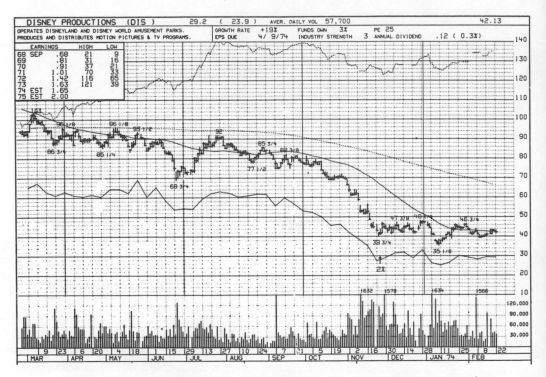

Figure 104. *Chart Courtesy of DAILY GRAPHS, P.O. Box 24933, Los Angeles, California 90024.*

three or four weeks and the volume tends to decline while they are being formed. The breakout from the formation usually is in the direction of the original trend. You can catch these breakouts both from computer signals and from the penetration of the upper trendline of the chart formation. When the computer short term strength turns positive, you have a short term buy signal. You have to know something about the stock, however, in trying to determine how far or how fast a move will carry. The more volatile stocks will probably provide the fastest moves (short covering may be a factor here) and stocks with the greatest potential and which are in the most popular groups currently will probably have the largest upward moves. Aside from the technical indicators, you also have to keep in mind any news or event that may be responsible for a stock's rise. Once the story is well-known or the event has already occurred, traders who bought early may decide to take their profits. National Semiconductor (see Figure 105) is an example of a stock that is a good trading vehicle. It is volatile and in a strong growth industry. In mid-1973 industry sales were increasing strongly and product prices were firm. The stock broke out of a base in early July and in about two weeks went into a continuation pattern. In this case, the continuation pattern did not last long enough to trigger a short term computer sell signal and, thus, there was no

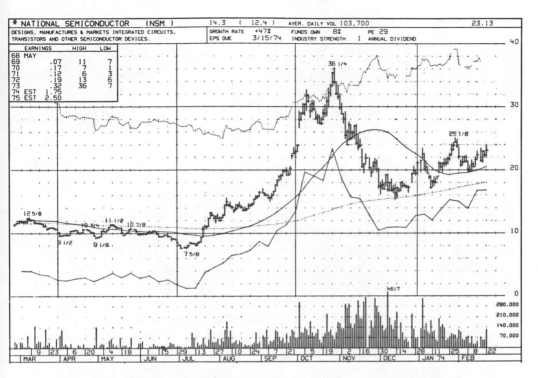

| * NATIONAL SEMICONDUCTOR (NSM) | 14.3 (12.4) | AVER. DAILY VOL 103,700 | | 23.13 |

DESIGNS, MANUFACTURES & MARKETS INTEGRATED CIRCUITS, TRANSISTORS AND OTHER SEMICONDUCTOR DEVICES.

GROWTH RATE +47%   FUNDS OWN 8%   PE 29
EPS DUE 3/15/74   INDUSTRY STRENGTH 1   ANNUAL DIVIDEND

EARNINGS	HIGH	LOW
68 MAY		
69	.07	11	7
70	.17	7	1
71	.12	6	3
72	.19	13	6
73	.32	36	7
74 EST	1.75	
75 EST	2.50	

Figure 105. *Chart Courtesy of DAILY GRAPHS, P.O. Box 24933, Los Angeles, California 90024.*

buy signal given when the uptrend was resumed. The breakout from the chart pattern at about 15 would have been an adequate buy signal, however. It is also a good practice to use stop-sell orders below the support level just in case the continuation pattern turns out to be a reversal pattern. At the top of the rally another continuation pattern was formed. The stock rallied out of this one, but the rally was aborted and the stock declined. When it violated the support level at 27, you would have been amply warned something was amiss. It so happened that rumors of a shortage of silicon in the semiconductor industry brought in a great deal of selling. Later on, fears of an electric power shortage and production disruptions depressed the stock further. It often happens that when a stock starts down, unexpected problems develop that were very difficult to foresee when all was going well.

A Good Trader Has to Be Able to Anticipate News

The successful trader cannot depend on acting on past news that is known to everyone. Once the news has been widely disseminated, there are no surprises left and those who intend to have generally made their buy-sell decisions. The trader has to be able to do far more than just react to events. He has to develop the difficult art of predicting how much of an impact these events will have on stocks and on which stocks. Furthermore, he has to make a judgment on whether the impact will be a passing thing or have a long term effect, and whether or not it will change the fundamentals of stocks. At this writing, traders are trying to make up their minds about the seriousness of the fuel shortage. Is it just limited to the shortfall of crude resulting from the Arab oil embargo, or are there other consider- ations, such as insufficient domestic refining capacity which could prolong the shortage? Is a shortage of gasoline or high gasoline prices going to change the life style of Americans? How much will governments interfere with industry? These questions are very pertinent regarding whether to buy stocks that are depressed because of the oil embargo. Once the stocks had fully reflected the problems stemming from the embargo, the likelihood that the embargo would eventually be lifted could put the odds heavily in favor of a trader taking a position in these stocks if their problems would disappear with the embargo. However, if the problems are more fundamental than just a result of the oil embargo, you would have to be alert to take profits early if the stocks run up on a lifting of the embargo, rather than assume you could wait for an extended rally. What can complicate forecasting even more is that it is not what actually happens that is important, but what investors think is happening. To keep straight what you believe to be the facts and what the market considers them to be requires a constant monitoring of the technical indicators. For example, the favorable news of a lifting of the oil embargo may not change the fundamentals of some stocks at all and any rally may only be a temporary interruption of a downtrend in these stocks. A weakening of the relative strength or the breaking of support levels would be indications that the latter situation was true. Often an event will be a one-shot affair, like the major Russian wheat purchase. Stocks of farm machin- ery, fertilizer, seed, railroad and barge companies all rallied on the news. In this case, it was not as much a matter of whether fundamental changes were taking place or not, as when the buying on the news had run its course and it was best to sell.

It is not easy to develop the ability to anticipate the news. Broad experience on the part of the investor is very helpful. Being constantly alert and keeping a questioning frame of mind are the best safeguards against being trapped into buying or selling at the wrong time. Any time a stock has a large upward move, ask yourself what news is already in the stock and what more can be expected to maintain the rally? What can happen in the future to this industry or group that would change investors' attitudes? Any unusual technical weakness should cause you to question your fundamentals. Technical weakness will often develop before any fundamental problems are widely known, and you sometimes have to sell on possibilities that might explain the technical weakness rather than on facts. The instinct is not to sell when a stock has weakened considerably (most investors would generally think that weakness would scare people into selling) because investors are afraid they have already missed the selling opportunity. Technical weakness may also mean that the concept has just run its course. Investors are willing to take their profits, and there is no new story to bring in new buying. It can never be determined with certainty that a stock is only consolidating and will turn back up. However, if weakness seems more than just a technical correction (breaking major trendlines, violating important support levels, relative strength slipping badly, failing to respond to good news, etc.) it is a good procedure to sell on a precautionary basis. Problems can develop that cannot be anticipated and one problem sometimes leads to another. The trader who retreats with his profits is in position to fight the battle another day. Of course, it goes without saying that you have to constantly try to anticipate national and international news that might affect the market, as well as news on individual industries and companies. Broad economic news will often override industry and company news. Thus, to be successful as a trader you have to have your finger on the pulse of national and international political, economic, military, monetary, and social developments. In short, you have to be a man of many talents. Once you have mastered the art of trading, however, it is a most satisfying accomplishment, as well as financially rewarding.

What You Should Know About Selling Short

Selling short is an essential tool you must utilize if you wish to maximize your profit in the stock market. There are times when the market is in a broad downtrend and it is just too difficult to make money on the long side. Put options, of course, is one very good alternative to selling short, and for many individuals who do not want to undergo the emotional strain of selling short, this is the preferred method. There are other individuals, however, who welcome a challenge and who are emotionally stable (and financially able) to engage in perhaps the most difficult operation in the stock market, selling short. Selling short is simply selling a stock which you do not own, but have to borrow from someone else (and while you are short, the stock's the real owner, rather than you, is entitled to the dividends). Thus, when you sell short at a certain price, you want the stock to go down so you can buy the stock at a lower price than when you sold it and you can give back the stock you borrowed. Some investors may feel that selling short is unethical or is expressing lack of confidence in the country. Selling short a stock which you regard as overpriced is just as moral as buying a stock you regard as underpriced. There are no implications regarding the outlook for the country in either case. Both operations help stocks return to their intrinsic values, although short covering can have some disruptive short term effects, as you will see later.

Selling short is never easy. When it appears to be too easy you may be in for trouble. The best time to sell short is after a long rise in the stock when investor psychology is still bullish. The worst time to go short (and the time to cover your short position) is after the market has had a long decline and the news is pessimistic. However, investors are bearish then and more inclined to sell short (and less inclined to cover). Thus, you can see, selling short requires much discipline and a fine sense of timing if you are to be successful. There is probably no way of taking the anxiety out of the short selling operation. The fact is that, theoretically, there is no limit to how much money you can lose selling short. On the long side, on the other hand, the stock cannot go below zero and you can only lose your investment. Stocks which have such a high short interest that there may be, in effect, a short squeeze (there may not be enough readily available stock in the open market so that traders with short positions can buy stock to cover their positions without paying exorbitant prices) move in response to supply-demand forces and practically disregard fundamentals. Also, the more volatile stocks are the most popular candidates for selling short, and they usually have ingredients which could result in sharply-increased earnings. Short sellers in these stocks can never be sure whether it is short covering which is driving the stock up or a big improvement in the earnings outlook. Selling short without a careful weighing of the risks involved can be very costly. You should first ask yourself what could happen that might turn the stock around (or the general market, for that matter). Natural resource stocks, for example, can be nerve-racking if sold short since you can never be sure what the companies will discover next. It is highly desirable that the stock is not only richly-priced in relation to its industry or group, but that the fundamentals are deteriorating, the industry or group is losing investor favor, and the stock is breaking down technically. Your timing has to be exquisite. If the stock rallies the day after you have sold short, it is difficult to know what to do. Is it a temporary rally, or have you been completely wrong on your fundamentals? It is also better to go short near the end of a rally rather than during extreme weakness. It is not always easy to know when a rally is ending, but if the other requirements for selling short are met, the rallies should not carry too far and you can usually determine when they are running out of steam. All kinds of things can be going wrong with a company, but until investors take notice of it you can have a long wait. What is very desirable is to see the stock failing to respond to good news. You then have some solid evidence that the stock should not jump sharply on more good news. Of course, there is always the possibility that some exceedingly favorable event might occur which would give the stock another boost. You should also be aware when you are in stocks which may have a high short interest and which can react dramatically to optimistic news about the company or even to a general market rally. Just watching the stock's performance, how it moves with the general market, can give you a good idea of its short-interest position. Stocks with a high short interest tend to rally more sharply than the general market, but during market declines they might decline less since traders with short positions may be so happy to get out of the situation that they cover on general market weakness. High short interests, which indicate a great deal of bearish sentiment on the part of many sophisticated investors, are a bearish indicator longer term, but for the shorter term they can be bullish since they indicate potential buying power. If anything favorable develops, the shorts tend to panic and cover. It is only when all the news is pessimistic that the short may resist covering.

Whether or not you have considered all the pertinent factors before selling short is a matter of judgment. You really will not know until after you have sold short if your judgment has been good. If you have not properly evaluated the situation you can be in for a wild ride. I know of one trader who sold Bausch and Lomb short in early 1971 at about 54. By all logical reasoning, this should have been a good short. The stock had already had a very sharp rise and was selling at a hefty price-earnings ratio. Bausch and Lomb had an exciting product, a contact lens made of plastic that would conform to the shape of the eye and also absorb moisture, that had excited investors. There was still some unanswered questions, however, and the company was not making money from the product yet. After the trader sold short, the stock sold off and he was very happy. However, the second day it rallied and he got a little edgy. The third day it went up again and he was getting desperate. As you can see from Figure 106, this trader had a most excruciating experience as the stock continued to climb to almost 100. Every time it started to decline, panic-stricken shorts would cover and tend to support the price of the stock. Other traders would sell short and when the stock rallied they would panic and cover, also. The trader was convinced the stock would come down eventually, but it seemed to be defying gravity. Near the top, to his consternation, the investor from whom he borrowed the stock wanted it back, apparently to sell because of the high price, and he had to cover. However, he did go short again, and as you can see from the chart, the stock turned down and he managed to break even. On the way up there was some unfavorable reports about the company which caused some temporary declines, but traders selling short on this news invariably panicked when the stock moved higher and covered their short positions. On the way down, shorts apparently were more confident of their ground and did not cover so readily. All in all, this episode was a classic example of selling a stock short at the wrong time. If the trader had waited until the stock stopped reacting bullishly to news and for it to violate an important support level he would have avoided much of his travail.

The Recommended Procedure to Limit Your Risk and Improve Your Profits in Selling Short

There are always some stocks going up and some going down in practically any market. However, just as you should not attempt to fight the odds against you in trying to select stocks that will go up in a general market decline, you should not try to sell short in a bull market. In every bull market there will be reactions,

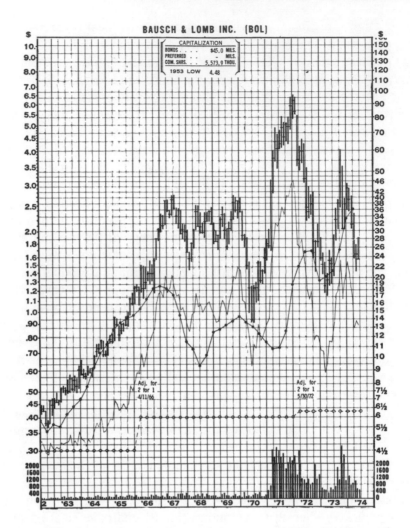

Figure 106. *Chart by Securities Research Company, 208 Newbury Street, Boston, Massachusetts.*

but you have to be very nimble to take advantage of them. Most traders lose money trying to do it. You can find industries and groups which may be turning down even though the general market is still going up, but it requires an extra measure of conviction to go short in these isolated situations in the face of a bullish market environment. Selling short is difficult enough under the most favorable circumstances, and as long as you can make money on the long side there is really no reason to subject yourself to the extra problems of selling short in a general market uptrend. There are stock markets which appear to be trendless. These probably are the most difficult markets of any to make money in, either on the short or long side. In the trendless markets, your conviction about the individual stock or industry can be the deciding factor. If you believe you have a good story which will focus investor interest on a stock which appears undervalued, you can buy it for capital appreciation. If you think a stock is amply priced and the fundamentals are deteriorating or the concept is losing its popularity, you can sell short. Although, it is something of an uncomfortable position to be in since you do not know whether you want to be optimistic or pessimistic overall, and you may be both long and short stocks at the same time.

Even though a major market downtrend is the most desirable environment for short selling, if you follow proper procedures you can limit your risk and improve your profit opportunities in any market. I believe that following the guidelines listed here will help you immeasurably in achieving success in selling short.

1. The stock should be amply priced with regard to its prospects. It is not economically justifiable to sell short stocks which are considered reasonably priced. In addition, unless you are convinced a stock is amply priced and could have a substantial decline, you can have some very anxious moments on the short side during periods when the stock or general market is rallying.

2. Fundamentals should be deteriorating or the concept losing its popularity. Stocks that have good fundamentals can decline, but it is difficult to know what to do when they rally. Conversely, stocks with deteriorating fundamentals can rally temporarily, but poor fundamentals are an added insurance policy.

3. The industry or group should, also, be deteriorating or running out of popularity. The fact that the industry or group is doing poorly substantially increases the likelihood that your short position will work out. Not only is more attention drawn to the stocks in the industry or group, but most stocks will not go against the industry or group.

4. The stock should be breaking down technically. Even if the fundamentals are deteriorating, until the market recognizes this fact, selling short can still be dangerous. If the stock does not go down immediately you will find it difficult to maintain your short position. It is best not to anticipate market deterioration, but to wait for a technical signal, such as a breaking of a major support level.

5. Sell short on rallies rather than on extreme weakness. This may sound like contradictory advice, but it often happens that traders sell short just before a technical rally takes place. It is much better to sell when a rally may be ending (even stocks which are breaking down have technical rallies), and the next move is likely to be down.

6. Put in buy-stop orders when you sell short. The buy-stop order can be put in at 10 percent above the market or just above the next resistance level, whichever is lower. If the stock has more than a 10 percent upward move or penetrates a resistance level, you may have miscalculated and it is best you take your loss. The danger of quickly losing 10 percent of your money is one reason why you want to take as many precautions as you can that the stock goes down after you sell short. If you cannot afford to lose 10 percent of your money, you probably should not be in this game.

7. Knowing when to cover your short position is not a simple matter. It may depend on how short a view you take of your short-selling operation. In any major decline there will usually be periods of consolidation or even rallies. You may not want to wait these out. They also can be nerve-racking when you are short. How far a stock may decline will depend on how richly priced it is and what problems the company is encountering. Often additional problems develop on the way down. The general rule is that when you believe all the unfavorable news is in the stock and it is experiencing extreme weakness, you should cover. An eye should be kept on any major support levels in the area. It would be better to cover above the support level. The general market also has to be watched since market rallies are often responsible for panic short covering which can send high short-interest stocks soaring. Just as with individual stocks, you should cover when the general market has had a long decline, the worst of the news is believed to be behind it, it does not respond to unfavorable news and investors are extremely bearish.

Simplicity Pattern and Ponderosa System represent two of the more common types of short-selling situations. The computerized market program flashed a sell on Simplicity in late April 1973 at 45. (See Figure 107.) The sell signal did not appear to be a false signal. Simplicity was richly priced on its earnings, the growth record was outstanding, but the stock had had a long rise, the price-earnings had expanded sharply over the years, and the situation was well-known. The dress pattern business hardly was as economically justified as, say, the computer industry. Nevertheless, Simplicity refused to go down at this time. It started a rally for about five months. Anyone who sold short on the computer signal would have had a very difficult five months. The problem here, apparently, was that the stock was highly regarded as a growth issue and there was not enough evidence of fundamental deterioration to shake out loyal holders of the stock. In October, the stock dropped below the ascending channel and broke below its 200 day moving average line. In retrospect, this would have been the better point to sell the stock short. The imposition of the Arab oil embargo then cast a pall over the entire market, and then as the stock declined the company management

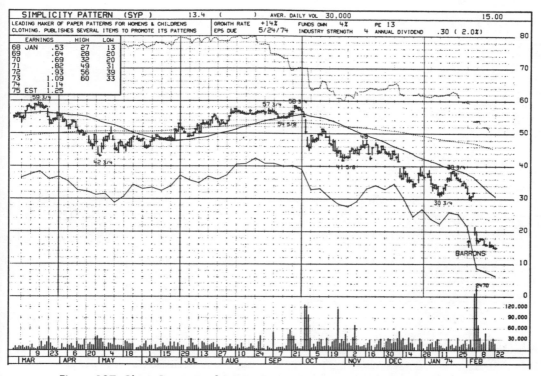

Figure 107. *Chart Courtesy of DAILY GRAPHS, P.O. Box 24933, Los Angeles, California 90024.*

announced that earnings growth was slowing, giving additional impetus to the decline.

Ponderosa System received a computer sell signal in early November 1973 at 45. (See Figure 108.) The stock was already in a steep decline. In this case, the bar chart gave an earlier sell indication when the stock broke below the ascending channel and violated a support level at about 73. (The bar charts and the computer will often give sell indications at about the same time, but if a stock drops sharply the computer usually will not give a sell signal until it is well down from the top.) The computer short term strength would also have given a good indication of when to sell. It would have turned negative substantially before the computer sell signal was given. Whereas the earnings growth rate of Simplicity was slowing, the earnings growth rate of Ponderosa did not show any evidence of being impaired. However, the fuel shortage was reducing traveling by automobile and investors were afraid the sales and earnings of Ponderosa would be adversely affected. Whether earnings are influenced or not remains to be seen, but it is not always what actually happens that is important as what the investors think will happen.

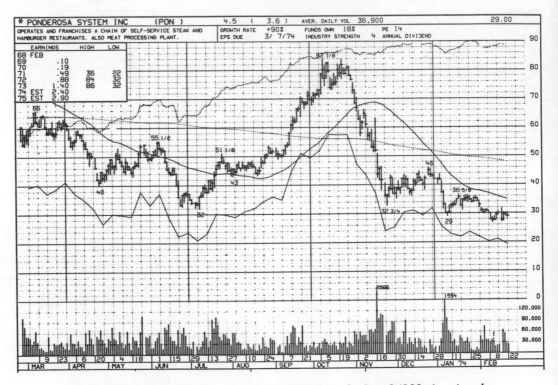

EARNINGS	HIGH	LOW
68 FEB		
69	.10	
70	.19	
71	.49	36	22
72	.88	84	32
73	1.40	86	32
74 EST	2.40	
75 EST	2.90	

Figure 108. *Chart Courtesy of DAILY GRAPHS, P.O. Box 24933, Los Angeles, California 90024.*

Selling Certain Stocks Short Which Can Be Rewarding and Less Nerve-Racking

Most short sellers tend to be very short-term oriented. They also rely primarily on selling short the volatile, high short interest stocks. The combination of these two approaches puts a great deal of pressure on the trader. If he does not achieve results quickly, he feels he is failing. The risks, even using buy-stop orders properly, are great. You cannot take too many 10 percent losses on your investments before it begins to hurt. (Also, you may not always be able to cover at the stop-buy price.) There is a way to reduce the tension and the risks involved in selling short, and that is to sell short the more conservative, less volatile stocks such as cyclical issues. I call it conservative short-selling. These stocks are not considered trading vehicles and usually do not have high short interests. When selling these stocks short you can take a more relaxed view. Cyclical stocks, of course, should only be considered as candidates for short selling after there has been a good cyclical spurt in earnings, industry sales are running near the peak levels expected to be seen in the foreseeable future, and current stock yields are

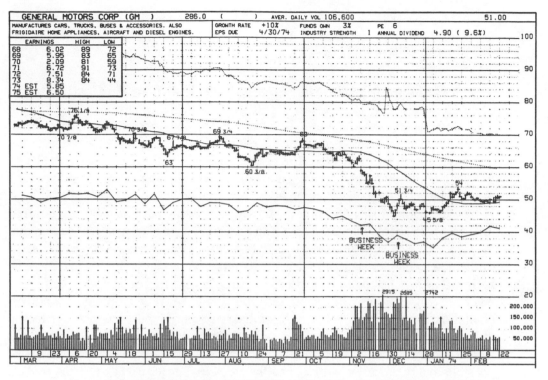

Figure 109. *Chart Courtesy of DAILY GRAPHS, P.O. Box 24933, Los Angeles, California 90024.*

near cyclical lows. Under these conditions, it is not likely that cyclical stocks will see a sharp jump in earnings. It is best to take a longer view when selling conservative stocks short, but sometimes you can be pleasantly surprised. The automobile industry is a typical cyclical industry and the stocks have wide price swings over the cycle of several years.

The computerized market program gave a sell signal on General Motors in early March 1973 at 74. (See Figure 109.) The stock continued in a general downtrend for the remainder of the year. Auto sales were running at a very high rate at the beginning of 1973 and earnings in 1973 were at record levels. In December 1973 the stock appeared to be leveling off. From a fundamental viewpoint, the fuel shortage sharply reduced auto sales, particularly sales of large cars, in the fourth quarter of 1973. The stock market, itself, had been declining for almost a year under the weight of a multiplicity of difficulties. Because of the complex problems facing the Free World, not the least of which were the financial and energy problems brought on by the use of oil as a weapon by the Arabs, economists are more divided than usual on the economic outlook. Nevertheless, in view of the technical indications of a bottoming process for General Motors and the amount of unfavorable news the stock and the general market have been exposed to, covering the General Motors short at the end of 1973 or the beginning of 1974 would have made sense.

Common Mistakes in Selling Short That Can Be Costly

Quite a few mistakes you can make in selling short have already been mentioned, but at the risk of being repetitious I will discuss a few of the more common or costly mistakes in selling short. The uninitiated (i.e., those who have not yet been badly burned selling short) often look at some of the "outrageous" price-earnings among the glamour stocks and think that selling these stocks short is like "shooting fish in a barrel." I have already noted that there are several criteria which should be met to give you a fighting chance to make money on the short side. A richly-priced stock is only one of the criteria and, perhaps, the least of them. The problem is that high price-earnings ratios can go higher and there is no law that says that overpriced stocks have to go down. The general rule is that when a stock is an obvious short sell you should be very suspicious. Another common mistake is selling stocks short that have a high short interest. Difficulty in borrowing stock in order to sell short is a good indication of a stock that might have a dangerously high short interest. When a stock has a high short interest, it is possible that the investor who loaned the stock may want it back and the broker may be unable to replace it with other borrowed stock, thus necessitating your covering the short position in order to return the borrowed stock. The short covering may have to be done at an inopportune time, perhaps at a loss. High short interest stocks can have very sharp rallies on any favorable news regarding either the company or the general market, which can be very nerve-racking to all but the most experienced trader. Perhaps the most common mistake of all is the tendency of traders to sell stocks short after the individual stocks or the general market has had a major decline. It is true that many stocks can go lower even after a substantial decline, but the risks do become greater and the major part of the decline may have already been seen. Certainly, after a great deal of unfavorable news, a long decline over a period of many months, and demonstrated ability to resist declining on further pessimistic news, the risk of selling short exceeds the possibilities of reward.

A Summation

I have discussed many investment principles and strategies in this book with the objective of helping you protect your capital and make money in the stock market. I would now like to conclude this book with a summation of the investment strategies which could help you triple your money in the stock market. They are embodied in the following guideline:

1. Do not fight the market. Follow the major trend and stay with stocks that are acting well technically.

2. Favor stocks which have a concept or a new story that can focus investor attention on them and bring in buying.

3. Look for undervalued stocks (relatively low price-earnings ratio, good current yield, price near net asset value) which have good earning potential, a strong financial condition, and possibilities of becoming popular.

4. Be willing to take your profits when it appears the concept has run its course, the novelty has worn off, popularity is running out, or the stock is breaking down technically.

5. Be willing to cut your losses if your assumptions are proven wrong (once a company starts encountering difficulties, problems can start multiplying and the stock could have a prolonged decline). Beware of buying stocks which have had sharp declines unless they have had a long period of consolidation and prospects are improving. Do not buy stocks just because they appear cheap—have a reason for buying them.

6. Keep a careful watch on inflationary pressures. Large federal deficits and excessive expansion of the money supply are danger signals. A slowing of the growth rate of the money-supply and a reduction in federal spending after a long rise in interest rates may indicate a buying opportunity. Coordinate with technical indicators.

Index

243